Learner

Please return
on or before

# Educational Interpreting

# Educational Interpreting

## How It Can Succeed

Elizabeth A. Winston,
*Editor*

NORWICH CITY COLLEGE LIBRARY
Stock No. 213603
Class 371.912 WIN
Cat. SSA M Proc. 3WL

Gallaudet University Press
Washington, D.C.

Gallaudet University Press
Washington, D.C. 20002

http://gupress.gallaudet.edu

© 2004 by Gallaudet University

All rights reserved

Published in 2004

Printed in the United States of America

Library of Congress Cataloging-in-Publication Data

Educational interpreting : how it can succeed / Elizabeth A. Winston, editor.
p. cm.
ISBN 1-56368-309-1 (alk. paper)
1. Interpreters for the deaf. 2. Teachers of the deaf. 3. Counseling in education of the deaf. 4. Deaf—Education. I. Winston, Elizabeth A.
HV2402.E38 2005
371.912—dc22 2004061964

∞ The paper used in this publication meets the minimum requirements of American National Standard for Information Sciences—Permanence of Paper for Printed Library Materials, ANSI Z39.48-1984.

# Contents

# Introduction

This book is a product of many long years of experience in, enlightenment about, frustration with, and hope for the education of deaf children. Several of the contributing authors began as interpreters in education. Most, like myself, have left the everyday work of educational interpreting in K–12 settings. But, some hope is clear, even for the despair felt by many. All the authors have continued to search for answers, information, and documentation to illuminate the ongoing problems with interpreted educations.

The lack of respect for interpreters in education, the disregard for language needs of deaf students, and the need to offer students schooling in their own districts at the expense of adequate services make up the rationale for this book. I first had the idea for this kind of book as an educational interpreter in 1982. At that time, I had neither the letters behind my name nor the experience and learning that those letters represent. Like most educational interpreters, I was used as a tool without regard to whether interpreting could work in providing an education. My input was not expected, and only through luck did I end up working with a teacher of the deaf (notice I do not say "for") who, although ignorant about interpreting (even after her deaf education graduate studies), was willing to learn. I did not have the credentials, just a gut feeling that the interpreting was not working. She agreed, and together we were able to affect some small change in a few classes. Those changes almost always resulted in finding more ways to avoid spewed interpreted information and promote direct, one-to-one communication.

That same gut feeling motivated me to spend the ensuing two decades researching, asking, observing, and discussing with others—and hoping that the need for this book would go away. Fortunately, in the twenty-plus years since I began, some improvements and changes have been made. Unfortunately, in the twenty-plus years that have passed, the need for research about interpreted education has not gone away. Too many students are still being abused in classrooms that fail to provide adequate access to language, to education, and to a "normal" least restricted environment. And too little research has been done to determine whether this practice of mainstreaming has any positive effects.

Some of the other authors in this volume also have been struggling with this concept, many for longer than I have. We have endeavored to present here the results of our experience and learning. This volume's authors also include fresher participants—some who have just begun experiencing interpreted educations and who have experienced it from the students' perspective. Their research brings new minds to the topic.

I have tried to bring together authors who have experience as interpreters or as students, who have had to sit day after day, watching the vacant, if not sleeping, faces of deaf students who do not have adequate language to understand direct communication let alone the more challenging interpreted language. We have seen the deaf child isolated daily in the larger world, befriended by few, and limited to participation and "friendship" with the few hearing students who learn the 500 vocabulary words so frequently taught in K–12 classrooms.

Some authors have brought their experience as educators of deaf children to their knowledge of interpreting. Others have brought their knowledge of language acquisition, cognition, and language use to the book. Some have brought their own experiences as receivers of interpreted educations. All have brought years of frustration with the disregard for the serious language issues raised by interpreted educations. And, all have brought years of research, experience, study, and learning—represented by the many letters after their names—to this attempt to illuminate the issues we have identified. Perhaps, the one-hundred-and-fifty-plus aggregate years of experience and learning will be noted by those who continue to abuse deaf children in the name of education.

Part 1 of this book, Deaf Students, focuses on the subject of our research—the deaf student. Four chapters focus on their perspectives, the language myths that surround them, the accessibility of language to them, and their resulting cognition. In chapter 1, the research of Brown Kurz and Caldwell Langer provides an insightful look at the reactions and thoughts of the primary recipient of interpreted educations—deaf students. This account of their impressions and experiences is a window into a world that few in authority have experienced and that even fewer consider when making decisions about providing interpreting without thought to learning outcomes. As part of their contribution, each author has added a final section describing her own experiences with interpreted educations—Brown Kurz from her experiences as a deaf student and Caldwell Langer from her experiences as a hearing student receiving an interpreted education in graduate school. These stories add to our understanding of not only the personal but also the thoughtfully considered effect of interpreted educations.

Chapter 2 focuses on one major issue of interpreted education—the need to have adequate language first before interpreting can be an effective tool for education. Monikowski presents a clear and cohesive discussion of the fundamental essential need for deaf children to have adequate first language skills in signing. Without these skills, watching the flapping hands of an interpreter is pointless. She also addresses the second language skills of the interpreters working in K–12 settings, highlighting the often poor skills they have. Finally, she addresses the misplaced expectation of schools, parents, and educators who believe that deaf students will miraculously acquire language by watching those flapping hands. We as adults would not subject ourselves to this kind of expectation, but we are willing to pretend that it is acceptable for children. The one aspect of language addressed neither in this chapter nor, in fact, by anyone (except in whispered conversations among interpreting educators) is the native English language skills of these interpreters. We pretend that interpreters can interpret into their L2 (American Sign Language) when they often lack adequate English skills. Anecdotal accounts of some interpreters reveal that they cannot recognize the difference between active and passive utterances, for example, the difference between *Mary told the story* (to someone) and *Mary was told the story* (by someone). Unfortunately, no research yet informs this critical issue.

Stack, in chapter 3, presents an analysis of the effects of English signing, the type of signing that is often required in schools and is usually better known by most educational interpreters. In this chapter, she asks whether or not children exposed to English signing systems actually acquire competence in English and argues that the answers lie in the disconnect between the grammar of SEE II and its phonological realization, a disconnect that does not exist in natural languages. Although SEE II is a remarkably easy system for native English speakers to learn, it does not guarantee its efficacy as a target language for small children; in fact, the research suggests the opposite. And although it is quickly learned, its lack of prosody makes it difficult to produce and comprehend sentences in SEE II, rendering it ineffective for real-time interpreting. After examining the role of prosody in language acquisition and surveying research into language acquisition by children exposed to SEE II, Stack presents the case of a deaf child, "Jamie," and her mostly unsuccessful efforts to develop language with exposure only to SEE II.

The fourth chapter, contributed by Schick, expands the discussion beyond the basic realms of language and discusses the interplay of language and cognition, investigating the interaction and reliance of learning and language for deaf children. Schick discusses the fact that language is essential for communication as being a widely understood concept. But language also serves another essential function in child development. It helps organize and stimulate cognitive development in children.

This chapter explores aspects of the interaction between language and cognition in development and the implications for learning by means of an educational interpreter. First, the development of Theory of Mind in deaf children is a major benchmark in cognitive development, but evidence indicates that some deaf children achieve this benchmark later than their hearing peers. Second, interactions with peers and with friendships positively affect cognitive development. Third, argumentation between children may positively affect reasoning and discourse skills. Fourth, for all children, learning is maximized when it is in the context of rich, scaffolded interactions that consider the cognitive understanding of the child. This chapter explores the question of whether such an important requirement for learning is achievable through the use of an educational interpreter.

Part 2 of this book, Interpreting and Interpreters, raises questions about the pivotal point of access for interpreted education—the interpreting. The authors question the support and training that interpreters have in and from the school systems, the qualifications that many interpreters bring to an interpreted education, and the accessibility of everyday classrooms for deaf students placed in these environments.

In chapter 5, Caldwell Langer explores an Internet discussion list for educational interpreters and its discourse about three current issues in educational interpreting. This discussion is informed by three similar issues in educational anthropology. The chapter begins with a discussion of the three critical issues: identity-role formation for educational interpreters in schools today, communication breakdown between teachers and interpreters, and control of bodies and spaces in classroom settings. Information and insights were gleaned from 19 interviews with members of the discussion list and from the archives for the group, which included more than four years of postings. The chapter closes with a discussion of the discussion list itself—the purposes it serves, why it is needed for this particular group of professionals, and advantages and disadvantages to meeting online.

Jones, in chapter 6, explores the demographics, interpreting competencies, as well as roles and responsibilities of sign language interpreters working in K–12 public schools in the United States. Competencies for this group are compared with competencies generally recognized by the field as necessary for sign language interpreters to produce equivalent target messages. The discussion raises serious questions and concerns that those working in regular "inclusive" education and special education should be addressing when considering not only qualifications of this important support service provider but also appropriate placement decisions for deaf and hard of hearing students in their charge. In addition, it raises questions about the education and preparation that interpreters are receiving. Current practice in the field of K–12 educational interpreter education is primarily provided within two-year associate degree programs. The model is not producing practitioners who are able to meet the needs of deaf and hard of hearing students in the mainstream educational setting. To truly allow the possibility of any access to public school education, the institutions of higher education in the United States must make a paradigm shift. Without this shift, access for deaf and hard of hearing students is a myth. The expectations should be to achieve equal access, which can be done by setting standards for skills and knowledge at the state level.

Winston, in chapter 7, investigates the interaction of interpreting and the classroom environment to analyze whether and how an interpreted classroom can be made accessible through interpreting. To understand this complex interaction, one first needs to understand those constraints of interpreting that cannot be changed: the lag time and the nature of an interpreted message. With these factors firmly in mind, Winston describes the types of activities teachers use to present content information in hearing-oriented classrooms, to consider the implicit and explicit assumptions about English-language learning that are made in hearing classrooms, and to analyze the discourse patterns of teachers that have an effect on interpreting an education—analyses that can help to address the institutional audism described by Turner (2002, 2004).

Part 3 of the book, Improving Interpreted Education, includes some of the suggestions that might be applied in deaf education. These suggestions are not presented as panaceas that so many believe in, and they will not change some of the basic problems of interpreted educations. They can, however, make some difference in the awareness of the process of interpreted educations and can perhaps improve the access currently available. Standards for interpreters and assessment of interpreters are key issues addressed in this section. Another issue not addressed in this volume is the assessment of deaf students themselves. Although an essential part of the picture, this issue is not an arena for interpreters. Deaf educators must begin to take responsibility for this challenge.

In chapter 8, Metzger and Fleetwood address a problem as old as educational interpreting—that of defining and sandardizing what educational interpreting is. They raise serious concerns about what needs to be done and why it was not done before. They present a series of suggestions that, though clear and possible, are not yet fully available, even after years of educational interpreting. They recommend that the field of interpreting (a) identify the purpose for which the job exists, (b) define standards of practice that identify job boundaries, (c) identify that corpus of knowledge and skills necessary for an individual to practice, (d) develop programs and materials that teach the identified corpus of knowledge and skills, and (e) develop a formal testing mechanism.

Although some of this work has been done, much of it has been done by teachers of the deaf and researchers while excluding or ignoring the input and expertise of those who are in the classroom everyday—deaf students and interpreters. With the input of all involved and with collaboration among them, Metzger and Fleetwood suggest that educational interpreting could provide more than illusionary access to education.

In chapter 9, Taylor presents questions with respect to assessing and supervising interpreters. These questions include a discussion of what the interpreter's reality is when working in an educational setting; what factors need to be assessed and the reasons why interpreters need to undergo assessments; who educational interpreters are and where they come from; what elements of an effective assessment process are; why interpreters should have a written professional development plan; why external evaluators are required to assess interpreters' skills; and how supervision of interpreters is unique and why it is necessary.

Schick and Williams present a discussion in chapter 10 about one approach that is being implemented in some school systems. As they point out, educational interpreting is an emerging profession. Despite the fact that federal oversight monitors the qualifications of teachers and paraeducators, still no requirements are in place for interpreters who work in the public schools (except that they must be qualified, without specifying how to determine this standard). Because of this lack of requirements, many states have adopted their own standards. One tool that is frequently used to specify minimum performance standards is the Educational Interpreter Performance Assessment, or EIPA, a tool designed to evaluate the voice-to-sign and sign-to-voice interpreting skills for interpreters who work in public schools. Chapter 10 describes the model of assessment used with the EIPA, which incorporates stimulus videotapes of actual classroom teaching and deaf children. Although the EIPA does measure some aspects of performance, the chapter explores how the EIPA fits into a broader concept of assessment, including what other aspects of interpreter performance should be evaluated. In addition, the chapter presents the many ways that states, school districts, and interpreter training programs are using the EIPA, ranging from professional development to mandatory certification. Finally, the chapter provides information to clarify the assessment results.

The authors of chapters 8–10 present a few of the possible suggestions for addressing the concerns of interpreted educations and focus primarily on the interpreter. This focus, though essential, should not lead readers to believe that the barriers can be removed by focusing solely on interpreters. Unless and until administrators, parents, teachers, students, and interpreters themselves recognize the inherent issues of access to education through mediation, especially when that mediation is based on assumptions that remain unproven, the focus on interpreting will make very little difference to the accessibility of interpreted educations. All involved must accept that substituting interpreting for teaching and interpreters for teachers does not provide education. Many believe that interpreters should do more teaching. This focus is misguided; if teaching is the answer, then teachers need to do it. Pretending that interpreting training and interpreters should address teaching issues instead of provide qualified, competent interpreters satisfies only one need: it provides cheap, unqualified "teachers" who can become the scapegoats when educators need to place blame for the illusionary access that deaf students currently experience.

Chapter 11, by Ramsey, is the closing chapter of the book. Ramsey's chapter is a reflection of her educational interpreting experiences that are interwoven with information and experience related to deaf education, learning, and language. Dr. Ramsey explores the goals of education for deaf children, questioning the developments that protect deaf children's rights to access at the expense of their ability to access. Too often, "instead of seeing interpreters as a means for providing equal access, interpreters are naively seen as the end in itself" (p. 207). She provides an insightful analysis of the system and of many assumptions about it, calling for all involved to question imposing interpreting in an education when it consequently outweighs the end of providing an education. She emphasizes the need to understand the sociolinguistic factors that affect the participation of deaf students in their courses. As a former educational interpreter who has joined her experience with research, her explanation of leaving educational interpreting is especially insightful: "The situations were so complex, and the stakes so high, that I could no longer tolerate the fragmentation and my inability to figure it out" (p. 207). Unfortunately, as we see throughout the volume, most involved, whether they are interpreters, teachers, administrators, or parents, also have not spent the time necessary to understand the complex situations and the resulting loss of stakes. The questions raised throughout the book return us again and again to two simple questions. Why does this practice of interpreted education continue with so little research and information, so few standards and requirements, and so little interest in the final outcomes of the practice? And, when will this research begin?

Elizabeth Winston,
Editor

Part 1

# Deaf Students

# Student Perspectives on Educational Interpreting: Twenty Deaf and Hard of Hearing Students Offer Insights and Suggestions

Kim Brown Kurz and Elizabeth Caldwell Langer

This chapter unveils the viewpoints and suggestions of twenty deaf and hard of hearing students with respect to learning by means of interpretation. First, students and their parents explain why they chose placements in mainstream settings with interpreters rather than in self-contained deaf classrooms or in schools for the deaf. Next, deaf students describe how interpreter skill levels affect them, how they view their interpreters' roles, and what social and academic challenges arise when learning through interpretation. The chapter also shares what deaf and hard of hearing students would like to say to interpreters, mainstream teachers, hearing peers, and interpreter coordinators to make education in the mainstream more comfortable and accessible for them. Finally, deaf and hard of hearing students and their parents offer helpful hints for effectively using interpreters in academic settings.

The coauthors of this chapter have come to this project from divergent backgrounds, but both have a great interest in, and personal experience with, learning through interpretation. Kim Brown Kurz is program facilitator of the Interpreter Training Program at Johnson County Community College. Brown Kurz received a bachelor's degree in social work and a master's degree in career counseling, both from the National Technical Institute for the Deaf at Rochester Institute of Technology. She recently received a doctoral degree from the University of Kansas. Before her current position, Ms. Brown Kurz worked as an educational specialist for the Gallaudet University Regional Center at Johnson County Community College. She has been a consumer of educational interpreting since fifth grade.

---

The authors would like to thank Brenda Schick, Sally Roberts, Betsy Winston, and Allison Sedey for their guidance and feedback on this chapter and for their ongoing support.

Elizabeth Caldwell Langer is a doctoral candidate at the University of Colorado at Boulder. Her areas of research revolve around linguistic input from teachers, parents, and interpreters to deaf and hard of hearing children. As a speech-language pathologist, Caldwell Langer worked with hearing, deaf, and hard of hearing students for eight years before returning to school for her doctoral degree. Although she is hearing, Caldwell Langer used educational interpreters in classes conducted in American Sign Language during her first two years of doctoral study. For more information about the backgrounds of these authors as they relate to educational interpreting, please see Appendices A and B accompanying this chapter.

## INTRODUCTION

Legislative acts in the 1970s and 1980s mandated that special education students be educated in the least restrictive environment. Since that time, for many deaf and hard of hearing students, this mandate has led to mainstreaming in regular education classrooms. Many administrators have interpreted the term *least restrictive environment* to mean that deaf and hard of hearing students need only the addition of an interpreter to achieve equal access to education. As this chapter demonstrates through the words of deaf and hard of hearing students learning through interpreters, the situation is far more complex than that.

In this chapter, deaf and hard of hearing students offer readers a taste of what it is like to access education through an interpreter. They start by explaining why they are in the mainstream setting rather than in a self-contained classroom or in a school for the deaf. They describe the roles their interpreters play and explain why certain learning environments and tools work well for them. They describe their interactions with hearing students and teachers. They evaluate how well they understand their interpreters, and they discuss various ways in which they modify their signing to be sure their interpreters understand them. Their wish lists for teachers, hearing students, interpreters, and interpreter coordinators suggest ways in which the students and professionals around them can help to make education more accessible and pleasant for them. Finally, they offer advice to students and parents who are new to educational interpreting. Of course, these students cannot possibly speak for all deaf and hard of hearing people. What they offer is a springboard for further discussion among interpreters, students, mainstream teachers, interpreter coordinators, parents, and administrative team members.

## METHOD

First, this section will introduce the pool of participants who volunteered to be included in this study. Second, it will describe the procedures used to recruit participants and to conduct, translate, and transcribe interviews with the participants.

### Participants

Twenty deaf and hard of hearing students and former students were interviewed in the preparation of this chapter. All currently use or have used signing educational interpreters at some point in their educational careers, and all had strong opinions and thoughtful insights about their experiences. Two were in elementary school, five were in middle school, six were in high school, three were in college, two were in graduate school, and two were college graduates now working. Thirteen of the subjects were female; seven were male. They came from a mix of states across the United States.

The group was heterogeneous, as groups of deaf and hard of hearing people tend to be. Twelve participants had hearing parents, seven had deaf parents, and one participant had one hearing parent and one deaf parent. Fourteen identified themselves as Deaf*, three identified themselves as hard of hearing, one said she considers herself to be both Deaf and hard of hearing, another said that identification depends on the social context, and one young student misidentified herself as hearing. Some participants came from families who sign fluently whereas others came from families who did not sign at all. Although most were proficient signers, a couple of the participants were not entirely fluent, requiring repetitions of some of the interview questions for full comprehension. Some of the participants were able to look back over years of interpreted experiences whereas others were currently involved in their very first mainstream classroom.

The participants' hearing losses ranged from mild to profound. Some are now part of the workforce; some are in graduate school; and some are children with hopes of becoming veterinarians, computer scientists, teachers, coaches, artists, actors, engineers, filmmakers, singers, lawyers, social workers, business people, and politicians. Some hope to go to Gallaudet University, some to the National Technical Institute for the Deaf at Rochester Institute of Technology, and some to nearby public or private universities.

These participants clearly indicated that their current and past educational situations are not, or were not, perfect. As these participants discuss their experiences in interpreted education, it becomes clear that a constellation of factors has to be properly aligned to achieve adequate access to education through an interpreter. Even if that alignment were achieved, these participants are quite aware that they still would not have equal access to education because of inherent alterations associated with the interpretation process. At the same time, for a common set of reasons, most of the participants perceive benefits to spending at least some time in the mainstream with an interpreter.

## Procedures

Older participants were recruited by use of online postings and by contacting university interpreter coordinators. Younger participants were recruited by means of notes sent home to children and their parents through teachers at their schools. The authors devised a set of open-ended questions and specific questions that covered demographic information; reasons for placement in the mainstream; and

---

*Following the convention proposed by Woodward (1972), in this chapter, *deaf* refers to the audiological condition of demonstrating a hearing loss and *Deaf* refers to identification with Deaf culture. When both deaf and Deaf people are included in a statement, for ease of readability, we have used the form *deaf*.

general, social, and academic aspects of the interpreting situation. Similar but simpler sets of questions were created for younger students.

All interviews were conducted by the coauthors of this chapter. One oral student was interviewed by Caldwell Langer in spoken English (see Appendix B pertaining to Caldwell Langer's background). Otherwise, all interviews were conducted in American Sign Language (ASL) by Brown Kurz, a Deaf person fluent in ASL, who used educational interpreters for most of her educational career (see Appendix A pertaining to Brown Kurz's background). Interviews ranged from thirty minutes to fifty-five minutes, depending on the age of the subject (older participants tended to give longer answers) and each subject's tendencies (some tended to be concise whereas others tended to offer more detailed, in-depth responses). All interviews were videotaped.

After all of the interviews were completed, the authors translated and transcribed all subject responses into English for the sake of readability in written form. Brown Kurz, fluent in both ASL and English, translated and transcribed half of the interviews from ASL to English. Caldwell Langer transcribed the remaining half of the interviews with the help of a certified interpreter, also a native user of ASL.

## REASONS FOR MAINSTREAM PLACEMENTS WITH INTERPRETERS

All of the subjects who were interviewed agreed that the ideal setting for them would be in a classroom with students and teachers who sign. However, for a variety of reasons, all of these participants were, or had been, in mainstream public education settings and had used educational interpreters at some point in their educational careers. For some, this use of interpreters was for certain years of school; for others, it was for certain parts of the day. Satisfaction with schools for the deaf and mainstream schools varied greatly by school and by individual. A few participants said they were unhappy in the mainstream setting and were there solely because of placement decisions they could not control. The great majority of the subjects in this study, however, indicated that they were now, or had been, in the mainstream or had decided to remain in the mainstream by personal choice. They said they were willing to sacrifice direct communication for a variety of academic and social advantages.

### Parents' Reasons for Initial Placement Decisions

Although a few participants made the decision on their own, the great majority of them were initially placed in mainstream settings by their parents. Some of the parents, hearing and deaf, told their stories about these tough decisions. It is clear from their stories that the decisions were not easy and were generally not made just once; parents often reevaluated their choices as their children progressed from one grade to the next. One deaf mother of a middle school hard of hearing student said that, even though her child is now in middle school, she is still always "experimenting with and testing" her daughter's placement. She emphasized that, for her, the definition of the "best placement" is constantly in flux as her daughter develops.

Parents, both hearing and deaf, discussed a wide array of reasons for having placed their children in mainstream settings with interpreters. Some parents listed practical reasons. In one case, the school for the deaf did not have a class for the grade a child was entering because of decreased enrollment. In other cases, the parents did not live near the school for the deaf and did not want their children to live away from home. For other parents, the reasons were academic. Some thought the mainstream schools offered more challenging classes, a greater selection of classes, and more extensive feedback on progress.

Other reasons were social. One mother discussed a variety of social reasons for placing her daughter in a mainstream setting:

> The positive side of my daughter attending a mainstream school is that she is exposed to many different kinds of kids with different backgrounds. Also, her behavior has improved dramatically. Part of the reason for that is that her class is much bigger. Sure, there are one or two kids with behavior problems. However, with sixteen kids, those behaviors don't disturb or interrupt the classroom activities. If kids with behavior problems were in a four- to five-student class at a deaf school, the whole class would be thrown off.

According to this mother, however, a negative side is that, now, her daughter is in the older grades of elementary school where "the kids play less and talk more," so her daughter is beginning to feel left out. Another social reason many parents mentioned for placing their children in the mainstream was the desire to expose their children to the hearing world.

Overall, parents said it took time for their children to learn to use interpreters effectively in the mainstream setting. They explained that their children were often overwhelmed or intimidated at first but, eventually, became more comfortable. In general, parents listed academic and practical reasons for the mainstream placements but wondered what education through interpreting meant for their children's social lives.

## Students' Views Concerning Educational Placement: Academic Issues

Students provided a variety of reasons for and against placement in self-contained classrooms, schools for the deaf, and mainstream settings with interpreters. Academic reasons for appreciating time in schools for the deaf or self-contained classrooms mainly centered on direct communication, easy participation, and an abundance of visually accessible learning tools. Academic reasons students mentioned for choosing the mainstream setting generally involved an increase in educational opportunities and a more challenging, rigorous learning environment. At mainstream schools, students said they found a litany of options: more elective classes, more internships, Advanced Placement classes, and honors classes. Students also explained that, in mainstream settings, they benefited from a greater number of academic resources, a more rapid academic pace, more feedback about their progress, a greater variety of perspectives from a larger student body, and a perception of higher academic expectations.

### *Faster Pace*

A deaf high school student with deaf parents said that the pace at the school for the deaf was too slow. "When I made the transfer to public school," he said, "I wasn't used to their rapid pace. If the school for the deaf could keep up with the mainstream pace, I would definitely stay at the school for the deaf." A middle school student who compared his self-contained classes with his mainstream classes echoed this view of the slower pace in self-contained classrooms. "I prefer the mainstream classes because the learning pace is often a lot faster than in the self-contained class. Self-contained classes are not challenging enough for me." One college student said friends at the school for the deaf gave her the impression that she should be thankful for her mainstream education. "I have friends who attend schools for the deaf, and they complain about how behind their education is compared to education at public schools."

### *A Greater Variety of Perspectives*

A college graduate pointed out that self-contained classes and classes at schools for the deaf are typically smaller and, consequently, students benefit from fewer perspectives. She said that she prefers to gain from the insights of a variety of different students from diverse backgrounds.

### *Perception of Higher Academic Expectations*

Four students interviewed for this study mentioned that they perceived higher levels of academic expectations at mainstream schools than in the schools for the deaf. For one college student, her experience volunteering at a school for the deaf made her happy with her choice to stay in mainstream education. "It seemed they had lower levels of language and lower expectations. So I think public school was better for me." As one high school student put it, "I didn't feel challenged at [a school for the deaf]. At public school, they require more pages for research papers, like ten, compared to two at the residential schools." A middle school student said, "Sometimes I feel like I learn more new things in a mainstream classroom than I would have if I had gone to a school for the deaf." A deaf high school student who has been in both settings said, "At mainstream schools, they are more strict. When a paper is due Tuesday at the deaf school, they will let you go past the due date, but at other schools, they won't."

### *More Feedback*

A high school student who had earlier attended a school for the deaf found that she got more feedback at the mainstream school. "In the English class at the school for the deaf, it was essays and journals. I wasn't learning anything. In mainstream classes, we do language units where you critique yourself and the teachers critique you. . . . They sit with you and give you feedback."

## Students' Views Concerning Educational Placement: Social Issues

From student perspectives, social reasons for preferring self-contained classrooms and schools for the deaf include getting to spend time with deaf friends, benefiting from direct communication with teachers and students, and receiving encouragement from teachers.

### *Greater Encouragement from Teachers*

As one high school student described it, "Residential school teachers are more encouraging. In the mainstream setting, the teachers can't sign, so there isn't the same connection."

### *Connections with Classmates*

A high school student said, "With my deaf classmates, we are able to discuss our ideas freely, and I really enjoy that." A college graduate remarked, "I can really see emotions through the signing of other deaf students."

Social reasons for wanting to be in the mainstream included a larger student body from which to choose friends and a perception of higher social expectations. Some students clarified that being the only mainstreamed student is markedly different from being one of a group of mainstreamed deaf and hard of hearing students. A high school student decided to leave the mainstream setting after most of his deaf classmates had left. Socializing with hearing students was generally easier for hard of hearing students than for deaf students. An elementary school student said, "Most of the time, I am comfortable, but sometimes I feel terrified of being the only deaf student there."

### *A Wider Pool of Potential Friends*

A deaf high school student said, "At the public school, I have more choices; I can be in different social groups. I don't like to be in just one group. I like to be in different groups." A hard of hearing middle school student said that she likes a mix of deaf and hearing friends, so a mainstream setting with a self-contained classroom works well for her.

### *Greater Independence*

A deaf high school student who had experience in both settings said she thought the staff members and services at the school for the deaf seemed overly solicitous. As she put it, "Sometimes, I have to say, 'Wait, I can do this on my own.'"

### *A Social Environment More Conducive to Learning*

A high school boy who was in a school for the deaf for the first eight years of his education said that he can pay attention better in a mainstream setting:

> When I was in seventh grade attending the school for the deaf, too many other students were fooling around, and they were not serious about learning. I wanted to learn. I felt like I was wasting my valuable time. I felt like the students at the school for the deaf don't respect their teachers, and I have no patience for that. . . . There are behavioral problems in the classes, and I want to learn. At the mainstream school, if a student misbehaves, the teacher will immediately send the student to the principal's office and not allow that student to interfere with the lesson plans at all.

> I feel teachers in my mainstream school have better control of their students and that the students pay attention more.

A middle school student said, "In the self-contained class, other deaf kids tend to bother me more than hearing kids do in my mainstream classes." A high school student talked about how being in the mainstream helps him stay disciplined: "In my mainstream classes, I am a serous student. I really have to pay attention. I can't afford to play around."

### *Showing Others That Deaf and Hard of Hearing Students Can Be Successful in the Mainstream Setting*

One hard of hearing college graduate who was mainstreamed starting in elementary school, said being in the mainstream partly meant proving to herself and others that she could do it: "It proves that the special education program is not always necessary for someone like me. I got through, and my test scores were very high. I even took some honors classes."

Clearly, all three placements—mainstream, self-contained classrooms, and schools for the deaf—involve pros and cons for these students, both academically and socially. Students in these settings may benefit from individualized, flexible, fluctuating placements that reflect the heterogeneity of those who are deaf and hard of hearing.

## Preparation for the Future

Many students see the mainstream setting as a training ground for learning to "survive" in the hearing world. Some thought this training prepared them for dealing with the majority culture after school years had passed. A college student looking back over her educational career said, "My experience working with interpreters during my kindergarten through high school years prepared me for college. I made the transition to college easily and felt well-prepared." A high school student talked about his mainstream education preparing him for future use of interpreters in work settings.

In contrast, another high school student in the mainstream on a full-time basis felt less sure that the mainstream had prepared her for her future. "I feel lost many times," she said. "The information is usually confusing to me. I get frustrated. I don't feel I can really plan for my future at this point." One college student who was mainstreamed for her entire education said that her concern is not fitting into the hearing world but being a part of the Deaf world:

> With certain people, I do feel a part of the Deaf community, but with the whole group, I am not sure. I don't know the culture as well. With my small group, yes, [I feel fine], but if I went to Gallaudet, I don't know how well I would be accepted.

One high school student who attended a school for the deaf for half of his day and a mainstream school for the other half said that this mix prepared him well for his future. "The mainstream school helped prepare me for the real world while the school for the deaf helped me prepare for a teaching job at a school for the deaf."

## The Compromise

In the end, most of the students saw pros and cons in both educational settings. Some try to gain the best of both worlds by first being in schools for the deaf for their early years and then in mainstream settings as they get older and subsequently want to learn more specialized information or broaden their academic horizons. Some try to compromise by spending parts of their day in the mainstream and the other parts in schools for the deaf or self-contained classrooms. Still others have decided to be with deaf friends for extracurricular, after-school activities and socializing but to try to gain what they can academically from the mainstream setting.

One deaf college graduate, looking back at her years in the mainstream setting, felt she had to sacrifice too much. Her above-average academic abilities had necessitated one-on-one instruction at the school for the deaf she attended in elementary school. Because of this situation, she was mainstreamed in middle school and high school. "If I could do it all over again," she said, "I would have stayed at the school for the deaf and continued with one-on-one instruction."

For one high school student, part-time in each setting works well: "I find it beneficial to attend both a school for the deaf and a mainstream school with interpreters. I have the best of both worlds." A college student sees the experience in terms of a cost-benefit analysis: "For many mainstreamed students, social life is a disadvantage," she said, "while education is a big plus. You have to sacrifice one thing for another."

A hard of hearing college student with oral skills, who was mainstreamed throughout her educational career, summed up the compromises as follows:

> Sometimes I do wish I had gone to a school for the deaf. I wish back then I had had the friendships and exposure I have now. I wish I had had a group I was totally comfortable with and felt like I finally understood everything. Sometimes, I am glad I was in a mainstream setting because there were more opportunities—like being able to speak and survive in the hearing world, being independent and not having to rely on an interpreter, meeting different people, and getting to play sports at the mainstream schools.

# STUDENT VIEWS OF ROLES AND RESPONSIBILITIES OF INTERPRETERS

At first glance, the role of the interpreter might seem as simple as one elementary school student's definition: "She signs for me." But, as with so many other areas of educational interpreting, interpreter roles are not clear cut. Many students see a predictable progression in interpreter roles as they advance through the grades. One high school student described his experience:

> In elementary school, [interpreters] are tutors and help you a lot. In middle school, they are more interpreters and help you only a little. In high school, they only help you if you really need it. I am now working on asking my teachers more than my interpreters if I have questions. I need to learn to rely on the teachers more in college, so this is good practice for that.

True to this suggested trend, younger students more often saw their interpreters as teaching assistants and tutors whereas older students generally said that they wanted their interpreters to draw the line at interpreting. One elementary school student explained how her interpreter serves as a teaching assistant. "If my teacher is too busy helping other kids," she said, "my interpreter will go and help hearing students to help out my teacher." A middle school student sees her interpreters as tutors, but only for English: "They explain what English words and sentences mean." By high school, many students feel strongly that interpreters should only interpret, not teach. Older students pointed out that interpreters are not trained to teach.

Besides tutors and teaching assistants, interpreters were also described as members of a support team, communication facilitators, and friends. But the issue of interpreter roles is clearly a controversial one. For instance, students disagreed about whether interpreters should befriend students. Some students felt clear boundaries should be drawn. Others felt it would be unnatural not to befriend the people with whom they interact every day. One college student said that she not only becomes friends with her interpreters but also even finds them to be great sources of entertainment during class. "I would have conversations and fun with them when the class was boring," she said. Other students felt this type of behavior was inappropriate.

## LEARNING THROUGH INTERPRETERS: GROUP DISCUSSIONS VERSUS LECTURES

Some of the responses from students about their preferences for lectures or group learning were entirely unrelated to the interpretation situation. For example, some students said that group situations offer them empowerment, hands-on experiences, and a greater variety of viewpoints. Others find lectures preferable because group activities can lead to frustration caused by inefficient use of time, transfer of misinformation, and behavioral issues. One college student saw both styles as beneficial, stating that she prefers group activities but also feels she needs lectures for "groundwork." A high school student agreed that a mix is helpful. "The teacher really knows things and can explain them well," she said, "but a group gives you good feedback. Maybe back and forth between the two is best."

Other responses with respect to preferences for lectures versus group discussions were clearly related to the interpreting situation. Again, student views did not reflect a consensus—some preferring lectures and others preferring group discussions. Of those who prefer lectures, some said that they find group discussions difficult to understand because it is impossible for interpreters to sign for all of the group members, especially as conversational turns overlap. Others prefer lectures because they find them easier to follow. Still others prefer lectures because, in groups, they have difficulty participating. As one graduate student put it, "Sometimes it can be really difficult to get in on the discussions when things are going quickly. It can be really difficult to connect with the group. Sometimes, I'm not even sure who is talking."

In addition, some students prefer group learning. The students in this subset unanimously prefer group activities because they, and their interpreters, feel more comfortable asking for clarification in a group setting. Students said that they and their interpreters find that interrupting the teacher for clarification is more difficult and embarrassing during lectures.

## LEARNING THROUGH INTERPRETERS: CLASS PARTICIPATION

Most students said that they participate less frequently in mainstream classes. The reasons they gave for this behavior were the processing time inherent to interpreting, concerns about clear communication, and self-consciousness. Processing time—the time delay between when something is initially said and when it is expressed by means of the interpreter—seemed to be the most prevalent concern. "Sometimes, when I try to raise my hand, and I want to give an answer," a middle school student said, "the hearing students beat me to it. It's hard for an interpreter to keep up so that I can also keep up with the hearing students." A graduate student said that, as a result of her frustrations with processing time, instead of participating during class, she just tries to talk with her teachers after class.

One hard of hearing college student said participation was difficult for her because she did not feel she could communicate clearly with her peers. "With interpreters [voicing for me], I didn't feel confident about their [vocabulary choices]," she said, "and with my voice, I had concerns about whether or not [the hearing students] could understand me." A high school student found herself feeling self-conscious using an atypical mode of communication during discussions. "Sometimes I feel embarrassed about making comments in my classes and having all of the hearing students' eyes on me," she said. A graduate student suggested that the blank looks on hearing students' faces might come from the fact that they are new to the interpreting process. "I think hearing students don't respond to my comments because they don't want to deal with the issue of going through a third party," she said. "It affects the group dynamics. So they back off."

## INTERPRETERS VERSUS NOTE-TAKERS

Most students reported benefiting greatly from both interpreters and note-takers. As one college student said, "The interpreter is important in class, and the notes are important later for review." One graduate student said he is in a position where he has to choose between the two. "My college refuses to provide more than one service for my doctoral classes," he said. "For example, I requested real-time captioning and interpreting. They told me I could only have one because of their budgetary restrictions. That needs to be changed."

Some students said they understand interpreters better than notes. One middle school student said, "Reading notes is more work for me. Sometimes terms that I am not familiar with appear on my notes while the interpreters can clarify and explain new terms right there on the spot." Other students, especially those who are hard of hearing and who reported working with unskilled interpreters, found notes to be more trustworthy and clear. A high school boy who communicates with both sign and voice said that, if he had to choose between the two, he would take the note-taker, saying, "I would pick the note-taker because I'm usually forgetful. Notes can help me later if I forget."

## INTERACTIONS WITH HEARING PEERS IN MAINSTREAM SETTINGS

Although a few students talked of having hearing friends at school, for most of the students, interactions with hearing students were limited. Deaf and hard of hearing students admitted that efforts were lacking on both sides. Younger, hard of hearing students seemed to have more interactions with hearing peers than older, deaf students. In early elementary school, where physical play dominates free time, deaf and hard of hearing students reported more interactions with hearing peers. But even at this early age, some degree of social isolation was evident. An elementary student said that her attempts to interact with hearing students are sometimes disappointing: "Most of the time, I do interact with hearing students. But sometimes, I feel left out."

In middle school and high school, where talk is more prevalent than physical play, deaf and hard of hearing students talked about social isolation. They reported going directly to class and leaving directly after class without making much effort to interact with hearing students. The types of conversations hearing peers started with deaf and hard of hearing students tended to involve their asking the same simple, predictable questions about signing or deafness. One middle school student noted that, even when he was with the hearing students at lunch, "we really didn't talk anyway." A college graduate looking back at her years in the mainstream said that she remembers talking with the interpreters rather than with the hearing students.

Deaf students reported sometimes wanting to interact with hearing students, but their interpreters were not there when needed for social situations. Students reported that interpreters tend to come in for, and interpret for, only official classroom business. Students were unclear about whether this tendency occurred because of school policy or because of teacher or interpreter choice.

## ROLE MODELS IN MAINSTREAM SETTINGS

Most mainstreamed deaf and hard of hearing students could easily name hearing teachers they see as role models. Indirect communication did not seem to be a barrier to student-teacher admiration. Their role models were picked for a wide range of reasons, including sharing a common heritage, showing an interest in deafness, learning to sign, motivating students, encouraging students to work hard, helping students with family issues, being "nice," having high expectations, challenging students, and showing that they care about their students. Students especially appreciated teachers who were interested in them because they were good students, not just because they were deaf.

Some participants also named their interpreters as role models. They were admired for their skills, demonstrations of respect for students, empathy, assistance on homework, and instruction about student responsibilities.

Students who spent parts of their days in settings where they had access to deaf adults also named copious deaf role models. Those who had never had access to deaf adults often expressed a desire to meet deaf role models. One college student explained that, although she has hearing role models, she imagines she would also greatly benefit from deaf ones:

> I think hearing teachers can be role models for me because that is what I grew up with. But I would also like to have Deaf role models just to show

that they have survived the obstacles that we have to go through in the hearing world. If they can do it, I can do it. I have always wanted that growing up. I wish I had an older sister or brother saying, "Keep going, keep fighting."

## COMPREHENSION OF INTERPRETERS

Participants were asked to answer the question, Thinking back across all interpreters and all interpreted classes, what percentage of the time do you believe you completely understand your interpreters? Elementary students were not asked this question because of their limited understanding of percentages. Table 1 shows the average percentages and ranges of percentages named by the students at each educational level.

Although the small number of subjects sampled does not allow for tests of statistical significance, an interesting trend did appear, which warrants further study. Namely, on average, older participants tended to feel they understood their interpreters less well or less often than did younger participants. The ranges of percentages named by the participants also suggest a trend toward greater variability in responses at high school and above. In middle school, the students all believe that they understood their interpreters at least 90 percent of the time. In high school and above, ranges started at 50 percent and spread up to 97.5 percent. Possible explanations include the following: that interpreters working with younger students are more highly skilled; that students become more discriminating about the interpreting process as they age; that interpretations suffer as academic content becomes more complex and specialized; or that students become more proficient language users as they age and, thus, take more serious note of miscommunications. Given that most participants in college, or with past college experience, talked about their college interpreters being more highly skilled than the interpreters they had worked with in earlier years, interpreter skill seems like the least likely explanation. More research is clearly needed to move beyond the realm of speculation on this topic.

Students also explained that the percentages they would pick would depend on a variety of factors. These included whether they based their answers on lectures or group situations, whether they counted times when their attention faded, whether they thought about substitute interpreters, and how much weight they put on times when they had lived in rural areas where skilled interpreters were

TABLE 1 Percentage of the Time That Students Judge They Understand Their Interpreters

| Educational Level | Number of Participants | Average | Range |
|---|---|---|---|
| Middle School | 4 | 94.5% | 90%–98% |
| High School | 5 | 80.5% | 50%–97.5% |
| College and Above | 6 | 72.9% | 50%–90% |
| **Totals** | **15** | **82.6%** | **50%–98%** |

hard to find. More specifically, a college student said that, although she understands the interpretation 90 percent of the time during lectures, in group situations, she estimated that she is confused or lost 50 percent of the time. A high school boy admitted that his attention plays a large part in this equation. If he is paying attention to the interpreter, his comprehension is about 99 percent, but when he is not, he believes his comprehension approximates 80 percent. (This student was not included in the above averages because the authors did not want to venture a guess at how often he was attending.) A high school student who had reported that she understands interpretations approximately 50 percent of the time said that this level of comprehension was because of unskilled substitute interpreters. One college student wanted to rate best and worst interpreters rather than give an average. She said that she could understand the best interpreter she has worked with approximately 95 percent of the time, and the worst interpreter, approximately 20 percent of the time.

If the interpreting situation was grim enough, students turned to writing, reading, and attempts at speechreading. For example, a high school student said that, sometimes, he writes his questions on a piece of paper and has the interpreter read it to the class. One graduate student went so far as to say, "It scares me sometimes that the interpreters will make me fail my classes and pull me down in my educational process."

## SIMPLIFICATION OR ALTERATION OF SIGNS FOR INTERPRETERS

The majority of the students said that, at various times, they needed to simplify, repeat, or alter their signs to make sure their interpreters understood them. Interpreters' difficulty reading fingerspelling was typically mentioned as an obstacle. Even a second grade student demonstrated awareness of the need to monitor the interpreter's sign comprehension abilities, saying, "Sometimes I repeat myself to make sure she understands me." A high school student talked about the ways in which he alters his signing: "I slow down my signing until the interpreter catches what I am trying to say." He continued, "Many times I have to sign more English-like in order for them to be able to understand my signs." Another high school student made this insightful, sad comment:

> Many times, I have to repeat what I am trying to say. Sometimes, the interpreter tries to guess what I am saying. I know this when the teacher's comment is irrelevant or doesn't make sense based on my comment. Often, I just give up and feel bad about it.

A college student discussed her frustrations about the same problem. "The biggest challenge is their signing skills. I have to simplify my signs for them to match their signing skill level." A middle school student agreed: "Sometimes, if the interpreter doesn't understand my signs, I have to fingerspell the words until they understand what I am trying to tell them."

One graduate student sees the process of matching her signing to the interpreter's receptive skill levels as an ongoing, dynamic process, saying, "If I'm talking with an interpreter and she seems to be having difficulty understanding me, I change the way I sign. Once the interpreter is comfortable, I will sign more naturally again." This approach sounds reasonable, but for some, making this kind of adjustment can be distracting and can add too much to the cognitive load. One high school student explained:

> Sometimes, I find that, if I have to sign slower for the interpreter, I make more signing errors. If I sign at my own pace, I find myself feeling a lot more natural.

Some participants feel that, when the interpreter makes mistakes in voicing for them, the results reflect poorly on them. As one college graduate put it, "I hate it when I say something and students think it is me that said something wrong while it is really the interpreter's error." Another college student finds this situation so frustrating that she avoids the interpreters and reduces class participation: "If interpreters don't have good skills, I tend to avoid them. I also tend to be more passive in that circumstance because I know they won't represent me well." A high school student expressed similar concerns:

> I find it annoying when the interpreter doesn't voice my messages correctly. Sometimes I wait to make comments until I know I've thought of something the interpreter can voice correctly.

Another high school student remembers a time when interpreter skills negatively affected a presentation she gave to her class:

> I had to present a paper on an artist. But the interpreter kept slowing me down as I was doing the presentation, and the kids were staring at me. I had to sign really slowly for the interpreter, and I would be done signing and the interpreter was still talking for a long time. I was embarrassed and frustrated.

A solution mentioned by many participants, which works when a student knows in advance that he or she will be presenting, is to practice with the interpreter before the presentation. Students reported that this technique seemed to help interpreters get used to their signs and styles. One graduate student said that she gives the interpreter her presentation notes beforehand so the interpreter can have a sense of what will be covered.

## WISH LIST FOR INTERPRETERS

What do you wish you could tell interpreters? This question elicited an intriguing array of responses. The following is a summary of what the participants said. Note that those interviewed generally had positive feelings toward their interpreters. At the same time, they had clearly done some serious thinking about the pros and cons of the interpreting situation. More important, they put serious thought into what they would say to interpreters if they were ever asked for suggestions about how to improve the interpreting situation. Because each situation and each participant is so unique, this list should not be seen as representative of what all students want in all situations, and it should not be seen as a criticism of interpreters. In some cases, it reflects an ideal that may not be attainable for various reasons. In some cases, student desires should be met by means of Individualized Education Plans. In other cases, what students want may seem contradictory, which is because this heterogeneous group did not unanimously agree on all the suggestions made. Most important, the list offers readers a chance to see the interpretation process through the eyes of deaf and hard of hearing students, and at the same time, it provides a springboard for conversations between interpreters and students.

***Interpret everything.*** Students across all age levels wanted their interpreters to interpret everything said from the moment they walked in the classroom door. Some interpreters apparently believe their job begins when the teacher starts to lecture. In contrast, students expressed their desires to know what the hearing students and teacher are talking about informally before and after class. "Their main responsibility," said a college student, "is to let me know all the information said in class. Whether it is important or not, if somebody says something, I want that." A graduate student said, "I want the gossip and the opportunity to network. If I don't get that, I feel left out."

Some interpreters waited for students to request access to discussions that occurred before the class officially began. A high school student said, "I wish the interpreter would always interpret side conversations instead of me asking her to interpret them for me. I want to know what the hearing students are saying." One high school student said that his interpreters watch for his "curious, what's-going-on-face" and then they interpret for him. One middle school student clarified that sometimes he just wants to be more aware of his surroundings: "Sometimes, I don't know when other students are talking, and I wish my interpreters would let me know." Some students felt inhibited about saying these things directly to their interpreters. A college student said, "Sometimes I would feel it just wasn't that important. It depended. Sometimes it wasn't worth it. I'd just let it go."

A college graduate noticed that the interpreters would often have side conversations with one another or with the students when they should have been interpreting. "That was distracting," she said, "and then later I would have to explain to them what was going on." A high school student found that interpreters were sometimes stubborn about their decisions about when to interpret:

> My work was done, and the students in the mainstream class were chatting and the interpreter just sat there—so I missed the side conversations. I wanted to know what the students were talking about, but the interpreter wouldn't interpret it.

Then the student thought a minute and added, "Sometimes the interpreters interpret *my* side conversations, and I don't like it. But I guess that is fair."

***Do not let your personal style interfere with my education.*** At times, students found that interpreters' style or dress interfered with their learning. What interpreters wear becomes the background for students watching them all day long. One college student remembered interpreters wearing bright, neon colors and polka dots. It was very difficult for her to read the signing all day against such busy backgrounds. Many students suggested attire contrastive to the background, although too stark a contrast had a numbing effect on one college student. "I hate it when the interpreters wear black clothes and sit in front of a white wall," she said. "There is too much contrast in color and it makes me feel sleepy." Another student remembered a time when an interpreter's eccentric appearance was distracting for both hearing and deaf students:

> I find it annoying when the interpreter dresses inappropriately for my classes. For example, I had a male interpreter who wore an earring on his nose and in his tongue, a see-through shirt, and dyed his hair silver. He was attracting attention from other students, and yet at the same time, his appearance was really disturbing to me and other deaf students.

Distracting appearances were also a problem for a graduate student. "One interpreter was a hippie—which is fine with me," he said, "but he should have put a band around his hair to make a ponytail or something so that his hair didn't get in the way of his interpreting."

One college student who depends on both mouthing and signs to understand her interpreters found that lax attitudes led to less accurate interpretations. "Their styles can [create a barrier]," she said. "Like, some are sloppy with their signs and/or speech. Sometimes they would forget to sign something they mouthed or vice versa. Maybe because I usually understand so well, they slack off." One graduate student remembered a time when the interpreter's signing style did not match the educational setting:

> One [interpreter] I had signed in a sing-song way—sort of like singing. That was her style, but it was like she was talking to a child the way she used that sing-song style. She said she grew up with deaf kids and that was where it came from. I said that it wasn't appropriate for graduate level classes.

***Let me make my own decisions; do not make choices for me, coddle me, or discipline me.*** A high school student discussed feeling frustrated that the interpreter would interrupt the teacher during lectures to obtain additional information: "I never ask my interpreters to do that for me." A college student said something similar: "It bothers me when the interpreter repeatedly asks the teacher to clarify or repeat, even if I do not ask for clarification."

A college student remembered her frustration with interpreters in high school acting as disciplinarians. "Interpreters in my high school got mad at me if I wasn't paying attention to them," she said. "I feel like it isn't their right to tell me what to do." A middle school student echoed her comment:

> I don't like it when the interpreters tap on my desk and tell me to pay attention to them. I feel like that is my choice, not the interpreter's. I don't like it when they tell me what to do.

Other students voiced views about wanting equality with the hearing students; they get to attend when they want to, so the deaf students should have the same choice.

One high school student clearly stated his views about interpreters helping him beyond the call of duty. "Sometimes I feel like I am cheating in my classes. The interpreters . . . help me beyond their roles. The hearing kids don't get that type of extra help."

***Please do not rely on us for information, sign instruction, reassurance, or fun.*** One college graduate said that she read her texts before class because she knew the interpreters would get lost and rely on her for clarification. Another college graduate expressed her impatience with interpreters who asked her to teach them signs. "I get bored when interpreters ask me for signs for the words they fingerspell," she said. "It can be a tiring experience."

A high school student talked of feeling like she needed to reassure her interpreters:

> Sometimes the interpreters seem to be under a lot of stress. They will ask again and again if they are clear and I will reinforce them, letting them know they are doing fine. I'll say, "If you aren't clear, I'll let you know and ask you for clarification." It has to do with self-confidence—the interpreter's self-confidence in their skills.

A college student responded similarly: "A pet peeve for me is when the interpreters lack confidence. I end up having to reassure them that they are doing a fine job and telling them to relax and take it easy." Another college student felt one interpreter depended on the students for social interactions: "When I was sitting with my friends, she would get involved. She seemed to be relying on me . . . to have fun."

***Please match your voicing to my style.*** Students asked that interpreters try to match each student's individual style when voicing for them. A college student said that the interpreters' word choices sometimes frustrated her. For instance, when she signs "assimilate," the interpreters voice "come together," making her sound less articulate. "I want them to use the words that make me sound more like an educated person," she said. A graduate student discussed problems that occurred when the interpreters voiced for her, but she was not sure what the specific problem was in each instance:

> Sometimes I am signing and the interpreter talks and then everyone is quiet. It seems like they don't know how to respond to my comment. They are looking at me like they aren't sure that I could have said something like that.

A high school student talked about her love for making jokes and her inability to make them work through interpreters:

> I love to tell jokes and tease other people. My biggest challenge is when I try to tell a joke though an interpreter and the other students aren't laughing. I know the interpreter didn't do it right. They may be speaking too slowly.

***Match your signing to the teacher's style.*** A hard of hearing student talked of the mismatches she noticed in teacher and interpreter styles: "Many times, I can hear the teachers' voices, and sometimes, the interpreters' styles don't match the teachers' tone." One college student talked about how much she likes the interpreters to match the personalities of her teachers—unless the teacher's style is monotonous. "If the teacher is funny, they should show that. I would encourage them to do more of that, and I reinforce them when they do it. If the teacher is monotone, I ask the interpreter if the teacher is flat, and if they say 'yes,' then I ask for more [facial expression]."

***Know your limits, admit to your mistakes, and be open to my suggestions.*** One graduate student shared a positive ending to a frustrating experience with an unskilled interpreter: "Luckily, that interpreter said she had to step out of that role and that was good because she knew her limits." A high school student said that she really appreciates it when the interpreters admit to their mistakes so the errors do not reflect poorly on her: "When the interpreter says 'Interpreter error,' I am relieved." One college graduate clearly stated this stressor: "I hate it when I say something, and students think it is me that said something wrong while it is really an interpreter error."

A graduate student talked about the confusion that can result when either the teacher or the interpreter makes an error, and the interpreter does not indicate who made it:

> If something confusing or erroneous is said, I always get confused as to whether it was an interpreter error or the teacher making the mistake. I'll ask which it was. If it was an interpreter error, as long as the interpreter apologizes, it's OK with me, but how often does that happen? If the interpreter has a personality that can accept criticism, then it works better. I don't mean to say it is all the interpreter's responsibility. Sometimes the teacher is not clear. If the interpreter says that the teacher is just not clear, then I will check in with hearing students to see if they feel the same way. If the teacher was clear according to the interpreter and other students, then the problem is clearly between the interpreter and me.

Students also stressed how much they appreciate it when their interpreters take constructive criticism well. "Sometimes I wish I could tell my interpreters that the signs they make are not correct," said one middle school student. "Sometimes I will tell them, and they take it well. Other times, they tell me not to tell them how to sign and that they will sign the way they do most of the time."

***We know you are human beings and not machines, but please set some boundaries.*** Some students wanted to have friendly relationships with the interpreters whereas others wanted more professional ones. Either way, they all seemed to agree that the interpreter should not try to step into the role of teacher. As one high school student strongly stated, "I have always felt that, if the interpreters want to become teachers, they need to go back to school and work on getting their teacher's certificates."

Others talked about their frustrations with interpreters acting as disciplinarians—of them and of their classmates. One middle school student remembered a time when her interpreter's disciplinary actions embarrassed her. "Sometimes the interpreter yells at my classmates," she said. "I feel embarrassed, and I don't want them to think it has something to do with me."

A graduate student talked about inappropriate interpreter discussions: "At the college level, sometimes interpreters are skilled, but not professional. Some will tell me things, and I have to say, 'That's not my business.'"

***Prepare for class.*** Students in middle school, high school, college, and graduate school raised concerns about their interpreters not being prepared to interpret for classes. To interpret well, most students felt interpreters should have read the readings assigned to the students, skimmed them for new vocabulary and concepts, or talked with the teacher about them. One graduate student clarified: "Having knowledge prior to interpreting is a big help." He noted that, at his level, many terms are used that may be new to the interpreter. "I don't want my interpreters to struggle during the class. I would rather they resolve issues prior to the class."

One middle school student pointed out that preparation might really help interpreters' receptive skills during class. If the interpreters had read the text before class, then when needing to fingerspell, they would be familiar with the subject's specific vocabulary and, thus, would do a better job of fingerspelling accurately. Participants agreed that interpreters should request class texts and all handouts. A college graduate talked about frustrations with this issue: "My interpreters almost never took the time to prepare for my classes, like reading the teachers' notes prior to interpreting." One college student said that even the interpreters who started out committed to preparing for her classes were not able to sustain that commitment. "At first, the interpreters were excited and motivated about the reading," she said. "And then, eventually, they backed off on that and didn't do much."

***Ask me to repeat if I am not clear.*** One high school student expressed this issue well: "Sometimes the interpreter tries to guess what I am saying. I know this when the teacher's comment is irrelevant or doesn't make sense based on my comment. I know I did not ask that question and that the interpreter made a mistake. Often I just give up and feel bad about it."

***Advocate for me when I cannot advocate for myself.*** Although participants generally wanted to be left to make their own decisions, a graduate student described one type of situation when he would like the interpreter to advocate for him: "I wish interpreters would let the professors know if they are speaking too fast since I can't hear the professor's voice."

***Stand so I can easily see you and the teacher.*** One frustration for participants was when the interpreters stood too far from the teacher or too far from the student. One student had a particularly difficult situation in a gym class: "I was taking a weight-lifting class and I wanted the interpreter to stand close to where I was so I knew what the teacher wanted us to do. The interpreter was standing far from me, and when I asked her to move closer, she told me she didn't want to move closer to me because I was sweating and smelled bad. I didn't think that was right."

***Try to give me some space.*** Although students want interpreters by their sides in the classrooms, outside the classes, most said they prefer a little time on their own. One elementary student said that she does not want interpreters with her at lunch and recess: "I'd rather be with my friends and not have the interpreters be in the way." A high school student discussed his relief at not having an interpreter with him in the halls. "If they were with me in the halls, that would be uncomfortable—like your Mom sent someone to watch over you and make sure you don't do anything wrong."

One high school student said she had experienced difficulty getting enough space from her interpreters. "Like in ceramics class," she said. "The interpreter would hover and ask if I needed help, but I just wanted to interact naturally with the hearing students. I could do it with natural gestures." Another student seemed to feel the same way: "Many times I feel like being alone, and I don't want the interpreter to be there. I want to feel like I am a regular student there, just like any other hearing students at the mainstream schools or deaf students at the schools for the deaf."

***Give me eye contact.*** "If they don't give me eye contact," a high school student said, "I get lost."

***Do not become lax with your fingerspelling.*** As one high school student put it, "Fingerspelling is *so* important. Some will just gloss over the fingerspelling and mouth [the words], but I don't know what they are saying. Some will invent signs to avoid fingerspelling."

***Make use of facial expressions.*** Many participants stated that time spent in the Deaf community seemed to correlate with use of appropriate facial expressions, which helped them both comprehend the information and maintain interest. A college graduate stated, "Most interpreters whose skills are really advanced tend to be those interpreters who hang around deaf people and really immerse themselves in American Sign Language and Deaf culture." Another college student explained:

> If interpreters practice sign in Deaf culture, they will have good facial expressions. If they have only practiced with other hearing people, they will not. If they use facial expression, I can see sarcasm and other humor. If they are expressive, it is wonderful. It is more enjoyable and easier to understand. It helps a lot.

One graduate student said, "It is important for interpreters to have good facial expressions. If an interpreter shows no facial expression, I will become bored!" A college student said, "If someone has a rigid, stiff way of interpreting—like a robot with no facial expression—that can be distracting, and I can miss information."

## WISH LIST FOR MAINSTREAM TEACHERS

As with the wish list for interpreters, some items on this list may seem unrealistic to mainstream teachers. Other items should be mandated on Individualized Education Plans (IEPs). Nonetheless, the list offers a look at mainstreaming through the eyes of deaf and hard of hearing students, and can be a springboard for discussions among students, parents, and professionals serving these students in a team effort to make mainstream education as accessible and comfortable as possible.

***Please introduce the interpreter, and when you do, make sure the class knows the interpreter is for everyone, not just me.*** Many students mentioned liking it when the interpreter is introduced to the class. One college student pointed out that, if an introduction is not made, then sometimes students get distracted, wondering why this other adult is in the room. One graduate student stated even more strongly that the interpreter not only should be introduced but also should be presented as being there to facilitate communication for everyone in the classroom:

> I try to emphasize that the interpreter is not just for me, it's for everyone's benefit. They shouldn't call her my interpreter, since the interpreter is really for all of us. In one class, when I explained [that], . . . the hearing students felt more free to use the interpreters to talk to me. So I got the ball rolling. I didn't want to be holding the ball all by myself.

***Do not speak too rapidly or too quietly.*** Many students talked about frustrations either at their having to remind teachers to slow down their speech countless times or at the interpreters having to do so. If teachers talk too quickly, interpreters have difficulty processing the incoming information and relaying it into sign language in a coherent form. Along a similar vein, some students also talked about their interpreters having to interrupt class to ask the teachers to speak more loudly.

***Remember, if I say something that sounds odd, it could be an interpreter error.*** Some students felt that teachers imagined the interpreters to be infallible, imagining all errors to be student errors.

***Think about where you are standing.*** Students mentioned that, when a teacher moves around a lot, it is difficult for them to glance back and forth from the interpreter to the teacher. Other students mentioned problems with teachers walking in front of the interpreters, thus obstructing their view of the incoming messages.

***Remember that I am learning through my eyes, not my ears.*** Because of this reliance on the visual mode, students wanted to emphasize the importance of a note-taker. Students talked about how difficult it is to look back and forth from their notes to the interpreter. Their notes end up being incomplete and confusing, and they cannot fully attend to the interpreter. One high school student said that, for her, the task is especially difficult if she has to take notes with a videotape; her gaze has to be split three ways as she looks at the notes, the interpreter, and the videotape. A middle school student responded similarly: "The most frustrating . . . is when I have to watch a videotape and write down the answers on a worksheet. Even when the videotape is captioned, I miss a lot of information because I have to write down the answers. I wish my teachers would be aware of how difficult this task is for me." Many students mentioned frustrations with teachers not finding videotapes with captioning.

Students also requested that teachers consider writing major points and new words on the blackboard or an overhead projector. They emphasized how helpful visual aids are for them. A graduate student underscored the benefits of charts, graphs, outlines, and diagrams by saying, "If the teacher uses a visual aid, then I can follow. Without it, I would be lost."

***Do not force me to speak.*** A college graduate related a negative experience she had when forced to use her voice in class:

> One day in middle school, my literature teacher told me I had to read aloud. I had no problem with that, thinking the interpreter would voice what I signed. The teacher said, "No, I mean you have to read out loud

> with your own voice." I started to cry. That was a dramatic and hurtful experience for me. No teacher should ever require their deaf students to use their voices if they do not want to.

***Let the person in charge of scheduling interpreters know if you are going to break your classes up into groups.*** In this case, extra interpreters may be needed. One high school student told of a frustrating experience in an American government class:

> We had to get into groups of Democrats and Republicans. The other deaf girl in the class was a Republican and I was a Democrat. The other student had to move to the Democrat group because there was only one interpreter. She didn't get her choice.

***Remember that English is less accessible for me.*** One high school student expressed her wish that teachers would acknowledge that English is a second language for her and, therefore, see that she needs more assistance than hearing students.

***Be patient with the interpreting process.*** As one high school student put it, "Having an interpreter as a third party can be confusing!" Learning through an interpreter was labeled a "struggle" by almost all of the participants.

***Rephrase my comments.*** Many students aired frustrations about the interpreter voicing incorrectly for them. One high school student talked about his positive experience with teachers rephrasing what the interpreter voiced so he could verify or clarify the information before the teacher answered the question or before the class went on.

***Please pause a little between asking a question and calling on students to answer it.*** Many students mentioned frustrations brought on by the fact that interpreting inherently involves processing time. One high school student summed up this issue well: "By the time the interpreter is done interpreting, I raise my hand, but another hearing student has already beat me to it, and the teacher gives them feedback. That can be a frustrating experience."

***Make sure to request an interpreter for conferences.*** Some students need an interpreter for their parents; others, for themselves. One high school student remembered a parent-teacher conference without an interpreter: "I had to write back and forth because there was no interpreter there. It was really hard."

***As often as possible, please treat me like your other students.*** "The teachers all felt sorry for me because I was deaf," said one college student. She continued,

> So I was trying to show that I could do everything, that I could follow everything that was going on. I tried to show them that everything was fine. Sometimes they were overly solicitous because I was deaf. They didn't joke with me like they did with the other students. They just checked to see if I was OK and encouraged me.

***Communicate with me, not my interpreter.*** A college undergraduate quickly jumped at the chance to add this item to the wish list. "I wish my teachers would know not to use the 'Tell her . . .' phrases," she said, "and to speak to me directly." A college student made mention of her frustrations with teachers not maintaining eye contact with her when she said something: "I never worry about what teachers think about me," she said, "because I think they have a hard time seeing me as a student because of the interpreter. They always watched the interpreter."

***Moderate group discussions.*** Almost all the older students discussed the tribulations of group discussions. When conversational turns overlap too much and when more than one person is talking at a time, the interpreter cannot possibly keep up or interpret everything said. Graduate students said they explain this issue to their professors, and they understand it, but then they forget to moderate during group discussions. A graduate student talked about how awkward the process is to go through an interpreter, especially for some hearing students who are new to the process, and she emphasized her wish that teachers would facilitate discussions between deaf and hearing students rather than leave the deaf students' comments without encouraging responses.

***At least in high school, know that interpreters are just interpreters; you still need to teach me.*** This comment was often made by the older participants. Some teachers thought the interpreters were tutors. One college graduate said, "Unfortunately, most of my teachers saw interpreters as responsible for the deaf students."

***Try to connect with me.*** A mix of positive and negative experiences all culminated into the creation of this wish. On a positive note, an elementary school student said she likes the way one teacher treats her as an expert. "My teacher asks me how to sign," she said. "One time she asked me how to sign *stop it*, and I showed it to her. She used it with the hearing students." Some students from middle school through college mentioned appreciating support and interest that came from their involvement in sports, as exemplified by the comments of this college student: "Some [teachers] know I'm on a deaf soccer team and ask me about when the next tournament is," she said. "Or they tell me to keep them posted. They show interest and excitement." Some middle school students greatly appreciated the encouragement they got from their teachers. For example, one middle school student said, "The teachers encouraged me to think positively, especially while I was struggling with English."

When this type of connecting does not happen, then participants reported feeling disappointed and sometimes discouraged. One high school student said, "I wish my teachers would encourage me more to do my best. I don't feel like I am getting enough support from my teachers and interpreters." A college graduate suggested a possible reason for "hands off" kinds of treatment. "Some teachers feel intimidated to approach me," she said.

***Try to establish a solid working relationship with the interpreter.*** One college student remembered when a teacher asked, "Did Mary get that? It is really important." The student remembered feeling great about that, but seeing it as rare:

> I thought "WOW! She really cares!" But most of the time, [teachers] just establish a pattern at the beginning and then follow that. Then, there would be no further interactions between them unless there were problems or if

the interpreter had to tell the teacher to slow down or repeat something. Usually their interactions are limited.

## WISH LIST FOR HEARING PEERS

When asked what they would like to tell hearing peers, deaf and hard of hearing students responded with the following wish list.

***If you try to communicate with us, most of us will appreciate it.*** Some participants talked about hearing students who would write back and forth with them, some discussed students learning a little sign to converse with them. Either way, it was generally appreciated.

***It is fine if you want to ask us questions, and some of us are happy to teach you, but please treat us as individuals, not just as representatives of deafness.*** One high school student voiced an opinion stated by many other students: "I feel like I get a lot of attention from hearing students just because they are curious about my deafness and not my merits." At the same time, one college student said, "I feel impressed whenever the hearing students tell my teacher that they learned something new from me." A graduate student vented her frustrations with being asked questions about deafness that a fifth grader could answer. A college graduate remembered that "very few [hearing students] made the extra effort to get to know [me] as a person." At the same time, she admitted that she should have made more efforts to get to know her hearing peers.

***Do not decide for me what is important to me.*** While signing, writing, or speaking with deaf students, hearing students were quoted as sometimes saying, "Don't worry, it's not important." Participants generally reported responding to them that it was important to be kept abreast of what transpired, no matter how trivial it might seem to another person.

***Do not stand or sit in my sight line.*** Some students discussed frustrations with hearing students when they walked, stood, or sat between the deaf students and their interpreters.

***Are you uncomfortable with talking to me through my interpreter?*** One college student said that she did not have an item for the wish list, but just had a question for hearing peers. "Many times hearing students communicate with me without the interpreter being there. It makes me wonder if they are more comfortable not having the interpreter there."

## WISH LIST FOR INTERPRETER COORDINATORS

When asked what they would like to suggest to interpreter coordinators, participants came up with wishes that make up the following list. As with some of the other lists, some items may seem idealistic and unrealistic. Still, they offer something toward which to strive. Other comments that participants make in this section may surprise parents and professionals, making them question things they thought were given.

***Try to keep the interpreters consistent.*** One middle school student said that he finds it really hard to follow when interpreters change. "It takes me a while to get used to a new interpreter," he said.

***Educate teachers about using an interpreter.*** Students said it was helpful when workshops were conducted to train teachers on how to use interpreters.

***Educate hearing students about ASL, interpreters, and Deaf culture.*** One college graduate who said she was angry about her isolation in the mainstream offered this suggestion: "It would be nice if there were a workshop on ASL and Deaf culture for hearing students. No one explained to hearing students why I was [in the mainstream classes] or how to [talk through] an interpreter. They acted as if I were a student who did not exist."

***Educate deaf students about using interpreters.*** Many students commented that it took them years to become truly adept at using interpreters. One college student shared a positive experience: "My school had a training [program] for deaf students on how to work with their interpreters. That helped me a lot and prepared me well to work with my interpreters. I learned it is important to show respect for our interpreters in order to have a good working relationship." A college graduate said, "I had to learn how to work with an interpreter on my own. No one explained it to me. I hope that is different today."

The deaf college graduate mentioned earlier, who was forced by her teacher to use her voice in class, wished she had known then what she knows now about the interpreter's code of ethics. "I started to cry, thinking, 'why doesn't the interpreter speak up for me?' She was only doing her job by following the code of ethics. I had no idea of her role as an interpreter. Now looking back, I can understand her role better."

***When hiring, be sure to check interpreters' receptive skills.*** Many students pointed out that even interpreters with fine expressive skills do not always have adequate receptive skills. One high school student from a deaf family said that she has noticed that the interpreters understand the deaf students from hearing families better than they understand her:

> So I have to repeat myself again and again and I really hate that. . . . When I fingerspell, I often have to repeat myself very slowly and I have felt people thought I wasn't really smart and then I would speechread the interpreter and realize that wasn't what I said. So I would have to write out my comment and give it directly to the teacher.

***When possible, try to assign interpreters to positions for which they have appropriate background.*** One graduate student said, "Most of my interpreters only have community college level education. In that case, how can they interpret effectively for my graduate level education?" One high school student said that she feels that knowledge of the subject is a more important interpreter quality than signing skills or personality. Many students said that the most important quality in an interpreter is an understanding of the subject matter. One high school student had a positive experience because his interpreter knew the subject matter well: "When I tried out for golf, the interpreter . . . happened to know all the golf vocabulary. That helped a great deal." A graduate student felt very strongly about this issue:

> Especially in graduate school, the interpreter needs to understand the basics of research design. If we could have one interpreter with us throughout our program, that could be great. When a new one comes in, I feel a disconnect, and I really have to work harder explaining everything. In higher-level classes, if interpreters don't understand what the teachers are saying, it is difficult for them to convey the information to the students.

Students from middle school up through graduate school discussed their dreams of having interpreters who had some background knowledge about what they were studying. One hard of hearing college graduate explained the problem:

> Many times, my interpreters would get lost whenever they interpreted for my physics and calculus classes. I always read my textbooks prior to class because I knew the interpreters would get lost. My professor would spend about thirty minutes discussing a physics theory, and my interpreters would get lost during the lecture.

This participant said there is a great need for interpreters who are familiar with engineering, science, and math. Most interpreters she had worked with had educational backgrounds in liberal arts or social work, and "they weren't a good match for my major."

***When possible, try to match the personality of the student with the personality of the interpreter.*** Many students discussed the importance of this match. Some liked interpreters to be more professional; others felt more comfortable if the interpreters were not overly professional. Many talked about wanting the interpreter to represent them accurately and felt interpreters could do the best job of that if their personalities were well-matched to the deaf or hard of hearing person.

***At times, you may need to schedule more than one interpreter.*** Students talked about times when their classes broke up into groups and the interpreters could not be in all the groups at once. One high school student told a story about a time when she was in a psychology class that was to break up into groups by self-defined personality type. She and the other deaf students were all in different groups. "The interpreter had to go around to each of us. I said, 'I'll just take care of it and write.' But why not more interpreters? I can write, but I am not getting all the information from the other students."

Students also stressed the importance of having two interpreters if a class is long (more than an hour, as found in college-level courses). A graduate student clarified one important reason for this need: processing. "The interpreters take everything in and then give us all they can, but I think it is all a problem with processing—trying to get that information receptively from the teacher and then expressing it to the student."

One student stressed the importance of using two interpreters if two deaf students in the same class have really different skills levels. One student discussed the frustrations of having three deaf students in a mainstream class with one interpreter who could not possibly sign at the right level for each of them at the same time. Finally, if group interactions are common in a class, students suggested that two interpreters might be able to do a better job of catching overlapping conversations than one interpreter could do.

***Let us help in the screening process when hiring new interpreters.*** Many participants discussed this wish as a dream. For some, it has been a greatly appreciated reality. Those who had the opportunity to choose said they were always happier with the interpreters that way. For one college student, being involved in interviewing interpreters made all the difference. "College is great," she said, "because I can choose my own interpreters. High school was a bad experience for me because I couldn't pick out the interpreters I was more comfortable working with."

***Listen to our needs.*** A graduate student talked about a negative experience in a high school English class:

> The interpreter was not certified and . . . she really couldn't interpret. I said I needed a different interpreter and they said they couldn't do anything about it. I felt like I wasn't part of the class.

A college student said persistence paid off for her: "Once, the interpreter didn't have the skills," she said, "and so I had to ask them to find someone who could do it. It took about two months to convince the school that that person wasn't adequate for me."

***I need a fluent interpreter, especially for my content courses.*** Many students named art and gym classes as places where they could survive with a mediocre interpreter. For content courses, however, they emphasized the need for fluent interpreters.

## ADVICE TO STUDENTS LEARNING TO USE AN INTERPRETER

As has hopefully become clear, using an interpreter effectively involves much more than just sitting in front of one. As one graduate student said, "As a fluent second-language user [fluent in English and ASL], using an interpreter is easier [for me] than it is for a child still developing ASL and English and still learning how to use an interpreter. How much [the kids] get is in question." She talks about what the student needs to bring to the situation.

> In my MA program, I was serious about my work, but I was also learning about life, so I was busy with that. In my PhD program, I am more focused on my studies, so I work harder to use my interpreters well. I am more careful to make sure I have access to all the information in class. Experience and maturity have made a big difference.

Interview participants shared their insights about using interpreters effectively. What follows is a list of their hints for students new to the interpreting situation.

***Advocate for yourself.*** One college student stated this suggestion well: "Usually, the teachers take the first step of saying, 'I am here if you need help,' but [you] need to take the next step of saying, 'Hey, I do need help *now* and in *this way.*'" A college student talked about the self-advocacy she had to master to obtain a clear message:

> If something wasn't clear, if the interpreter repeated again and it still wasn't clear, I would ask the teacher to say it again. I didn't want to cause too much stopping in class. So if the interpreter could remember it, I would ask them to sign it again. But if they couldn't remember, I would ask them to ask the teachers.

***Establish a good working relationship with your interpreter.*** Many students highlighted the importance of working together as a team. A graduate student explained how she teams with the interpreter when preparing for a presentation: "I try to work with the interpreter beforehand and give them any notes I have. [During the presentation,] I will make sure I pause. I want the interpreter to feel comfortable in voicing for me. I want it to be a win-win situation." A high school student offered the following advice:

> Try to set up a good relationship with the interpreter. [You] can tell the interpreter to do a few things to accommodate [you]. If you are not controlling, usually the interpreter will agree. Like, tell them to teach the teacher and class why you need an interpreter—not to pamper you, but just to communicate.

***Find interpreters who work well with you.*** A college graduate made the following suggestion: "Try to meet as many interpreters as you can. Find out who you feel most comfortable with and who would represent you well."

***Complete assigned readings before class.*** Overwhelmingly, participants suggested that deaf children read the materials for their classes before class to be able to follow the interpreter.

***Know that it will not always feel awkward.*** A college student who used interpreters for the first time in college said, "At first, it was awkward for me. . . . I had to get used to having someone there focused on me."

***Learn to divide your focus.*** A college student said she found it difficult to make her mind act as a split screen. "[At first], I was not sure who to focus on—the interpreter or the teacher."

***Know that it is OK to use interpreting services.*** Some hard of hearing students talked about trying to get by without an interpreter because they did not want to stand out or admit to having the need for interpreting. One college student explained, "I thought, 'I can do it without an interpreter,'" she said. "I would be so tired I couldn't pay attention well enough. Then I realized I needed the support from the interpreters."

***It is hard at first, but it does get better.*** A middle school student offered this advice: "It is challenging . . . to constantly watch an interpreter sign all day long. It is hard on my eyes and it makes me sleepy. It took me a while to get used to watching an interpreter all day long." One high school student who attends both a mainstream school and a deaf school had some helpful advice:

> I would tell other students that it is very hard being in a mainstreamed classroom with an interpreter. If that student feels he or she has the knowledge and ability to go into a mainstreamed school, I would encourage him [or her]. However, if he [or she] doesn't feel he [or she] is prepared for it, then I wouldn't recommend it. It was very frustrating for me at first when I attended the mainstreamed school. I eventually got used to it.

***If you can, work with the interpreters beforehand.*** A middle school student reported, "Sometimes I work with the interpreters ahead of time so they can practice, get used to my style, and be prepared to interpret for me in the future."

***Set up meetings with your teachers outside of class.*** A graduate student talked about a positive experience she had with a teacher, after she got a chance to get to know her a little:

> Some teachers are awkward with the interpreting situation. But in one case, I went in with an interpreter outside of class and [the teacher] was telling funny stories and I realized for the first time that she was really a funny person. And I was able to share some of my own personality with the teacher.

***Know that people have more patience than you may think.*** One high school student said, "If I don't understand, I will be assertive and ask my interpreter to voice my questions for me with teachers or other students. People have a lot more patience than what I thought."

***Consider the best time to start using interpreting services to access education.*** Students disagreed about when it is best to start using an interpreter. One college student said that she was glad she did not use an interpreter before college:

> It would have made me stand out. I might have been made fun of. In college, that's not a problem. By now, kids are more open and accept things easier. In high school, everyone has to be the same, so that is difficult.

A middle school student said he was glad he started using an interpreter before college. "I feel that my experiences in using interpreters now will help me prepare for using interpreters in the future," he said. "It is best that I learn now instead of learning it later on in my life." A high school student explained why that might be: "If you are older when you start using an interpreter, it can be uncomfortable. If you have an interpreter from when you were really young, you don't really worry about it. You are used to it."

## ADVICE TO PARENTS OF DEAF AND HARD OF HEARING CHILDREN

This project's student participants and their parents provided advice to parents of deaf and hard of hearing students new to mainstreaming and the interpretation process.

***Be sure your children get some exposure to deafness.*** From a college student who had a progressive loss but who had not used an interpreter until college: "I would say try mainstreaming, but still be sure to incorporate Deaf culture in their lives, make sure they have a group of deaf friends. So, that way, they have peers more like them—with hearing aids and signing."

***When they are older, let your children be involved in placement decisions.*** Many students underscored the importance of letting them in on these important decisions. When older students were not included, they reported resentment. A parent also agreed that it is best if the child is involved in planning his or her education.

***Get involved.*** The hearing mother of a deaf elementary school student offered the following advice: "Meet with your school principal prior to the first IEP meeting. Meet with the teachers and try to develop a solid working relationship with them. Get involved with family activities at the school. Become aware of how the school functions. Don't be afraid to ask if you have any questions. It is important that you have the answers you want."

***Advocate for your child.*** One mother pointed out the importance of this recommendation with an example: "I feel that the teachers at the mainstream school aren't using resources for my daughter like they should. For example, they should make sure that all videotapes are captioned. There are a lot of things they are not aware of, and I have to educate and help them."

***See if you can secure a helpful resource teacher for your child.*** One mother found that the resource teacher did an excellent job of appropriately helping her child.

***Keep "experimenting and testing."*** One mother used a watch-and-see approach to her daughter's placement. She sent her daughter to various programs, but each time, she carefully watched to see how well the placement worked. If it did not work, she would look into other options.

***Do not accept low expectations for your child.*** One parent of a middle school student said, "I will admit sometimes there is this attitude in the mainstream school, like, 'Oh, she's *deaf*.' I will not accept that kind of attitude."

## CONCLUSION

The deaf and hard of hearing participants who were interviewed for this chapter, along with their parents, presented a variety of reasons for choosing to spend some of their educational careers in mainstream settings with interpreters. Many have found creative ways to reap the benefits of both worlds by spending specific years or specific parts of the day in different placements. According to the students and alumni who were interviewed, academic benefits in the mainstream include a faster pace, a greater variety of perspectives, higher academic expectations, more feedback, and a wider array of educational opportunities. Academic positives in self-contained classrooms and in schools for the deaf include direct communication, easy participation, and more consistent visual access to learning. Students suggested that social benefits to the mainstream setting include a wider pool of potential friends and social groups, greater independence, and a social environment that some found was more conducive to learning. One student said it was important to show that deaf and hard of hearing students can make it in the mainstream. Social reasons for preferring self-contained classes and schools for the deaf included the opportunity to interact with deaf and hard of hearing friends, direct communication with teachers and peers, and stronger connections with teachers.

Responses concerning students' perceptions of interpreter roles uncovered great controversy. Many younger students tended to want their interpreters to tutor them, though not to discipline them. Some even saw their interpreters as role models. Older students tended to want their interpreters to serve only as interpreters. Regardless of age, some preferred interpreters to act more as friends, which is not surprising, given that the interpreters are sometimes the only people in the students' environments with whom they can fluently communicate. Others, however, want their interpreters to act as professionals in business transactions.

Whatever the definition of an interpreter's role, all students agreed that it takes a while to become used to learning through interpretation. In elementary school, the students often do not have the self-advocacy or language skills needed to use an interpreter effectively. As students proceed through the grades, interpreters often do not have the background knowledge needed to generate conceptually accurate interpretations.

Social and academic issues related to attending to and participating in lectures and group discussions arise when a student enters mainstream settings with an interpreter. Interactions with hearing teachers and peers present a host of new social challenges. The expressive and receptive signing skills of the interpreters add another ingredient to the mix. If they are stellar, students are generally highly appreciative. If they are not, students find themselves modifying their own signs to help facilitate communication.

The deaf and hard of hearing students interviewed for this chapter offered their suggestions—their wish lists—for what interpreters, mainstream teachers, hearing peers, and interpreter coordinators could do to make the mainstream setting more comfortable and accessible for them. They, and their parents, also outlined some important advice for other deaf and hard of hearing students and their parents about how to initially navigate the interpreting experience. Each educational interpreting situation is as unique as each deaf and hard of hearing student, each interpreter, and each teacher. Given that fact, this chapter cannot offer information that is well suited for every situation. What it offers instead is information to use as a springboard for important discussions among students, parents, interpreters, administrators, and mainstream teachers. These discussions and ongoing monitoring of the situation are necessary for making mainstream education as accessible as possible for deaf and hard of hearing students.

The field of educational interpreting would find great use in triangulating this issue, that is, in seeing what this experience is like from the standpoints of educational interpreters, mainstream teachers, and a greater number of deaf and hard of hearing students. This chapter makes a few small steps toward that process.

## APPENDIX A

## My Personal Experiences Learning Through Interpretation, by Kim Brown Kurz

Like many other deaf and hard of hearing students who received their education in an interpreted educational setting, educational interpreters played a vital role in my life. I also appreciate the risks special education administrators took when investing in our education, although I truly realized this appreciation only after I became an adult. When I interviewed other deaf and hard of hearing students to get their perspectives of educational interpreters for this chapter, I discovered many similarities when comparing their experiences and my own. In many ways, I was not surprised that, when these students heard about this interview, many of them enthusiastically told me their stories. Most of these students were never given the opportunity to voice their perspectives, opinions, and feelings about their interpreted educational experience. For some students, this interview was an opportunity for them to provide positive and constructive feedback about how to improve educational interpreting in the future, and for other students, it was a chance to vent about unpleasant experiences. After I conducted these interviews, I marveled at how these students had developed a variety of strategies in working with their educational interpreters, whether the interpreters were well qualified or not qualified enough to interpret.

The interviews brought back many memories of the additional work I had to do to receive an appropriate education. Some students call the additional work a "burden," and school administrators and parents may overlook the amount of additional work the student, interpreter, and teacher must engage in to ensure the best learning environment possible. My story about educational interpreters echoed many of those deaf and hard of hearing students' interpreted educational experiences. Of course, students' experiences in some areas were not similar.

I was in a self-contained classroom with approximately twenty deaf children from kindergarten to fourth grade. Total Communication was the communication method we used in our self-contained classrooms during the 1970s. After taking summer courses at Gallaudet University, a liberal arts university for deaf and hard of hearing students, my mother decided that we would use sign language at home so I could access language visually.

My mother often came to my school to observe my self-contained classroom. One day, when she was visiting, my teacher asked a variety of questions. The teacher looked around, pointed at me, and asked me a question in sign language. I answered her question and the teacher said I was wrong. My mother was furious. I had answered correctly, but the teacher did not understand sign language well enough to see that I was correct. The more she observed, the more my mother found that the teachers' signing skills were deficient. Eventually, she approached my teachers about their signing skills. The teachers dismissed my mother's claims and told her that she was expecting too much from me. They discussed research showing that the average deaf child does not read beyond a fifth grade level. As determined as ever, my mother decided she would not buy that. She told my teachers that I could do better than that. My mother wanted to place me in a mainstream classroom with an interpreter who had better sign language skills, but my teachers argued that it would be a mistake. Someone from the U.S. Department of

Education agreed to do an assessment of my situation and fully agreed with my mother that I should be entitled to a sign language interpreter. After several years and many battles, one day when I was in the fourth grade, the teachers finally told my mother that I was ready to be placed in a mainstream classroom with a sign language interpreter.

So at the beginning of my fifth grade year, I was placed in a mainstreamed classroom for the very first time. One other deaf student was placed in my class with me. It was the first time I had ever used an interpreter. Like many other students, it was not easy at first. I eventually became best friends with a couple of hearing girls. They learned sign language quickly. The fact that these girls knew sign language so well gave me access to social life with other hearing children. We had sleepovers, parties, and get-together events outside of school just like hearing children. I never really felt like I was out of place.

Like many other students, I do remember wishing I could communicate freely with my teachers, who did not know any sign language. Whenever I would attempt to talk with my general education teacher through a sign language interpreter, the conversation would often be shorter than I had hoped it would be. I did not get the attention I would have liked. I started to miss the direct communication I had enjoyed in my self-contained classroom.

Because of the indirect communication I had with my teachers, academics were challenging. I knew I was missing some important information, even with the sign language interpreters there. Looking back, I can remember the many times I had to "internally interpret" the messages received by fitting together what I had read, or what I already knew, with the partial or inaccurate information I received. For example, when the interpreter signed a word incorrectly, most of the time I was able insert the correct word, given the context of the sentence and overall topic. Talking to other deaf and hard of hearing students, I have found that this kind of repair work is common. It makes me wonder about all the additional repair work a deaf child in the mainstream setting has to do to receive information from his or her teacher through a sign language intepreter.

Although I was frustrated with some parts of the academic situation, other parts were positive. Like some of the students I interviewed, I felt like I was getting a lot more new information each year in my mainstream classrooms as compared with my former self-contained classroom. In fourth grade, I became impatient with the slow pace in my self-contained classes. In fifth grade, however, things seemed to be passing by too quickly. I felt I would have benefited most from a pace somewhere between the two. But I was determined I could meet the mainstream pace if I could just get used to working with an interpreter.

At one point, my teachers told my mother that they had decided that I did not need an interpreter during recess or physical education class. My mother firmly disagreed, telling them it was necessary for an interpreter to be there so I could learn the rules of games and interact with hearing peers. I agree that I was able to learn the rules of games better, but at the same time, I honestly do not think the interpreters were able to help me bond with hearing students naturally.

My middle school experiences opened my eyes to the world in many ways. I loved middle school and the academic side of school. The interpreters were excellent, and many of them were children of deaf adults (CODAs), so their first language was American Sign Language. These interpreters were also with me in my resource class and would often tutor me. I felt like I had better control of my environment and was getting used to the rapid pace and to working with the interpreters. The interpreters and I would agree that, if I did not understand and if the interpreter had time, he or she would explain what was going on in class or would tutor me right there on the spot.

To give an example, I remember in eighth grade, we were reading Homer's *Odyssey*. Greek mythology was one of the most difficult aspects of my English class. Both in and out of class, my interpreter, who was familiar with Greek mythology, took the time to explain the stories and their meanings. The teacher did not mind. Many faculty of interpreter training programs teach their interpreter students not to discuss homework assignments outside of their interpreting roles because this practice would violate their code of ethics for interpreting. Debate has been ongoing about this sticky role. I have always felt that educational interpreters are an exception; unlike other interpreters in other situations, educational interpreters many times serve as an assistant, tutor, and language model for the student (though not necessarily the best language model).

High school was not what I expected. It was bigger and harder in many ways. The friends I had from middle school started to branch out on their own, and new cliques formed. Students were beginning to date and work at side jobs. Like many of the other students with whom I talked in the interviews, I found that socializing with hearing kids got harder as I became older. As what those interviewees and I wanted to communicate became more complex, we found it limiting and frustrating to interact with hearing peers. This situation created conflicting feelings for me and for many other deaf students. We were hungry for communication with other hearing students, and yet at the same time, we were not comfortable having the interpreters following us outside of class (e.g., to our lockers, hallway, cafeteria, etc.). It was considered uncool.

Unlike my elementary and middle school years when I could communicate through paper and pen or even manual fingerspelling, having a conversation with my peers now through pen and paper became frustrating. I was able to carry on much more rich conversations with the limited number of deaf students and the interpreters at my high school. What I realized is that even the best interpreters could not meet my social needs. There was no way I was going to bring an interpreter with me to a school dance and risk utter embarrassment.

After high school, I attended the National Technical Institute for the Deaf at Rochester Institute of Technology (NTID/RIT). I found their mainstream classes surprisingly easy to access. I was very fortunate in terms of interpreting services; some of the nation's top interpreters were there. Many of the college students and graduates I interviewed expressed their gratefulness for having had the exposure to educational interpreters before their college years. Recently, I received my doctoral degree from the University of Kansas (KU). At KU, whenever I requested an interpreter and an additional accommodation such as real-time captioning for the most difficult classes such as statistics, the university would debate whether or not that request was overaccommodating. That process became a new challenge for me to prove why I did not think it was an overaccommodating request. Having to fight for the accommodations was something most of the college students discussed with me during their interviews. Sometimes, like many other students, I have to wonder exactly what my role is at the college level. No formal training is provided for deaf students and their interpreters at any levels (neither K–12 nor college). Most students expressed the importance of meeting with the coordinator of the student access center to clarify what is expected of the student, interpreter, and teacher before the class. I agree with these students that this meeting is an important stepping stone when working with an educational interpreter.

Being confident to say whatever I wanted through an interpreter in my hearing classes was always a concern for me. Like many other deaf students, I modified my signs or I chose the signs I knew the interpreters would understand. My strategy depended on the quality of interpreters' receptive skills. Like many other students do for themselves, I often rely on the hearing students' and teachers' reactions to my comments or questions. When the hearing students or teachers stare at me or provide comments that are irrelevant to what I have just expressed, then I know the interpreter made an error. Most deaf students are capable of knowing whether their interpreter has interpreted the information correctly or incorrectly. I have always preferred teachers' lectures over group discussions because, for me, fully participating in group discussions is almost impossible. I agreed with most of the students about the importance of educational interpreters being prepared before class. I noticed a huge difference in the quality of their interpreting when they became familiar with the subjects.

After interviewing twenty different deaf and hard of hearing students for this chapter, I found that I could relate to most of what they said about their successful and frustrating experiences with interpreters. Mainstreamed deaf and hard of hearing students seemed most frustrated with the social aspects of life in the mainstream. Often, the social interactions are missing from their lives, unless they are fortunate enough to live close to a large Deaf community or to be placed in mainstream schools that have a large number of deaf and hard of hearing students. Many of us feel that having a less fulfilling social life was a sacrifice we made to earn an education equivalent to the kind hearing students receive. Many of us and our parents, both hearing and deaf, agree that we could not afford to lose that kind of educational opportunity.

In my opinion, each deaf child should be entitled to a top-notch interpreter with excellent skills when direct communication is not an option. For example, data using the Educational Interpreter Performance Assessment (EIPA) indicate that a level-4 interpreter (based on a scale of five levels, with level 5 at the highest skill level) is able to interpret only 80 percent of the information accurately. This finding means that the deaf child gets less accurate information compared with what he or she would get with an interpreter functioning on one skill level higher. Even the best interpreter is not able to provide 100 percent of the information accurately. As a professional, I see that, a lot of times, schools just want to fill the positions regardless of the interpreters' skills. Some of the interpreters may have gotten their training through church or an eight-week American Sign Language class. This kind of training is not acceptable. Hiring top-notch interpreters usually involves more expense for the schools, and school administrators are constantly seeking ways to save money; therefore, our deaf and hard of hearing students end up suffering. That is one of the reasons why many of our best interpreters are not in the educational system. But we need to hire them there. With unskilled interpreters, deaf children may be deprived of a rich language and a full education. I feel strongly that each one of us is entitled to fully accessible information rather than what is considered to be a reasonable accommodation.

Each child is unique and has his or her own needs. What works best for one deaf or hard of hearing child may not be true for another deaf or hard of hearing child. It is imperative that we look at each deaf or hard of hearing child individually and see what works best for him or her.

In my opinion, although many special education program administrators may think that providing an interpreter is the solution, I do not agree that the educational interpreter is the final or permanent solution to the problem in deaf education programs in our mainstreamed schools. I would recommend further studies to understand what is really happening in interpreted educational settings. Are deaf and hard of hearing students truly benefiting from this type of educational approach? How do deaf and hard of hearing students process their thoughts in an interpreted educational setting? What are special education directors, teachers, and parents doing to fulfill the social needs for the majority of deaf and hard of hearing students? These are some factors we need to consider, and I hope we will begin to discover the answers to these questions in the near future.

## APPENDIX B

### Reverse Mainstreamed: A Taste of Educational Interpreting in Graduate School, by Elizabeth Caldwell Langer

Although I am a hearing student, my experiences using interpreters for some of my graduate school courses were surprisingly similar to those of the hard of hearing students interviewed for this chapter. Of course, there are important differences. For example, as an infant, I had full access to fluent language models. My use of educational interpreters was limited to specific classes during two years of a doctoral program. I was working at a sophisticated level with decades of direct education behind me. Most of my interpreters were certified and highly skilled. I had the support of deaf and hearing classmates and professors, who knew about learning through interpreters. At the end of the day, I could relax with easy communication in the hearing world. Yet, even with all of those advantages, I still found learning through interpreted lectures and discussions to be a serious challenge.

In some of my classes, the professor and the other students communicated in ASL. I am an intermediate signer whose initial exposure to signing was Signed English. In a social situation, one on one, I can understand my professor and most of the other students most of the time. Their use of codeswitching, the simpler conversational topics, and my ability to control at least part of the discussion all probably facilitate communication in that kind of setting. Like many hard of hearing students, if the stars are all aligned—if no one turns away from me, if no one is backlit, if everyone keeps a steady pace, if my sightline is not obstructed, if no one has an unfamiliar accent or dialect, and if conversational turns do not overlap—then I can understand the majority of what transpires. But in the classes conducted entirely in ASL, when discussions became most interesting, I became hopelessly lost. My head could barely turn fast enough to follow the sea of hands before me.

The first tough step was to admit that I needed an interpreter. Like so many hard of hearing students we talked to, I was reluctant to use an interpreter, wishing I could make it on my own, not wanting to bring attention to my deficient skills. I did not want to be singled out as needing special help. But I found that I had to make a choice: Either I was going to appear to fit in or I was going to get the vital information I needed from my classes. Even after realizing what I needed to do, I still did not always do it. At times, I said I did not need an interpreter when really I did. When you can get along fine most of the time, it takes a leap of maturity to admit that, in this case, you just cannot do it. For me, the springboard for that admission finally came from the fact that some academic situations were just too exhausting without an interpreter. Trying to follow the class without an interpreter meant that I had to allocate cognitive resources not only to understanding the material covered in the class but also to participating in the communicative process. It was absolutely draining.

An educational interpreter seemed to be the obvious solution to the problem. However, just like most of the hard of hearing students we spoke with, I quickly found that an interpreter still left me without full access. Unlike some children in the schools, I was lucky enough, for the most part, to have highly skilled interpreters. Nevertheless, because of processing time, linguistic differences, and human limitations, interpreting is far from perfect, even with the best of interpreters.

I quickly realized the crucial role that self-advocacy plays in learning effectively through an interpreter. As so many of the students we interviewed said, succeeding with interpreting means learning to advocate for yourself. Even with all of my background and support, I often failed at that. I understood the importance of self-advocacy in theory, but putting it into practice with an interpreter was another story. Sometimes, the interpreters had trouble keeping up with the pace of discussions, and they did not always ask people to slow down or repeat. I knew I should remind people to slow down or pause between turns in group discussions. But I did not always do it. I feared that enforcing a deliberately slow tempo and vigilant pauses between comments would alter or destroy the dynamics of the conversation. I also did not always ask for a repetition or clarification when I needed one. Not wanting to interrupt the flow of a conversation or lecture and, again, not wanting to bring attention to my deficit, I hoped I would figure out what I missed by piecing together what I eventually got. That kind of recursive linguistic work drained my cognitive and attentional resources, often leaving me, yet again, confused and exhausted. As an adult, I was embarrassed to have to ask for the help I needed. I applaud the students in our study who talked about feats of self-advocacy. I also understand completely those students who talked about an inability—or even, at points, a resigned sense of apathy—in this regard.

To feel more connected to the other students in my classes, I often signed for myself. In some ways, that approach seemed to help me feel less isolated. But as many hard of hearing students found when speaking for themselves, haunting questions arose each time I signed. Were students listening to what I had to say, or were they distracted by how I said it? Did I come off as I intended? I wondered how I appeared to them but also felt some resignation about it, knowing I could never really know.

This resignation also arose because many aspects of the interpreting situation could not really be controlled—things that are just inherent to this process. First, even if people were reminded countless times to slow down and pause between conversational turns, they quickly forgot to do so because that behavior is just unnatural. Second, although in situations allowing for direct communication I was often an active participant, with an interpreter, by the time I got the interpreted message and picked up my hands to respond, I realized the conversation had turned in a new direction. Finally, use of an interpreter resulted in limited eye contact with professors and other students. This limitation magnified the feeling of being a detached observer rather than a full participant in the class.

Another inevitable problem that typically arises for students with some residual hearing, and that also arose for me, is the challenge of dual input. In my case, when watching signers and listening to interpreters, I had two modes and versions of input. They were similar, but the interpreted message necessarily came seconds after the original one. For those using residual hearing and watching a signing interpreter, the same thing happens. Two versions of the message are almost simultaneously presented, but with the lag of processing time between them. It leads to an echo effect. That describes the best-case scenario—when the messages from both sources match in content. When the two messages differ (if the interpretation does not quite match the message), the result can be confusing and can lead to focus on the linguistic mismatch rather than the content of the discussion at hand.

Even with all of the advantages I had walking in, I was often overwhelmed by the interpreting process. I can only imagine the academic and social challenges that mainstreamed deaf and hard of hearing children learning through educational interpreters must face. Far from pitying these children, however, I found their resilience and insightful comments inspirational and helpful. I could definitely have benefited from much of their advice and knowledge as I tried to learn through an interpreter. In this chapter, the reader will get a rare glimpse at the advice, wishes, frustrations, and successes of deaf and hard of hearing students who are learning through interpreters.

I conclude this essay with a wish list of my own. I hope that we can all learn from those who have been on the receiving end of this process and that what we learn will influence our efforts to make those situations that necessitate interpretation as accessible as possible. I hope that those involved in placing children in educational settings consider what these students say about what it takes to effectively learn from an interpreter (please see the students' wish lists in the body of this chapter). I hope that deaf and hard of hearing students who are new to the interpreting situation find the words of these savvy students helpful. And I hope that those who interact with deaf and hard of hearing students in the mainstream—their teachers, interpreters, peers, parents, and interpreter coordinators—listen to all that these students and their own students have to say and do all they can to offer them the academic and social access they deserve.

## REFERENCE

Woodward, J. 1972. Implications for sociolinguistic research among the deaf. *Sign Language Studies* 1:1–17.

# Language Myths in Interpreted Education: First Language, Second Language, What Language?

Christine Monikowski

Our system has no way to judge whether deaf students in the educational mainstream are afforded an equal education. Between 46,000 and 51,000 deaf and hard of hearing children are in the U.S. public schools at the elementary and secondary level (Allen et al. 1994). During the 1998–99 school year, approximately 59 percent of children with "hearing impairments" in the United States spent more than 40 percent of the day in a regular education classroom; this number increased from approximately 48 percent in 1988–89 (U.S. DOE and NCES 2002). Records show that "most deaf children are now enrolled in regular public elementary schools and receive instruction in English through a sign language interpreter . . . [and] secondary level mainstreamed students use educational interpreters in over half of their classes" (La Bue 1998, 4, 5). Records show that the academic achievement scores of deaf children have not improved much since the early 1900s (Quigley and Paul 1986) when residential schools were the only option.[1] The average deaf student reads at a third to fourth grade level (Schildroth and Hotto 1994, 20). Records show that there are more academic programs for the training of interpreters than ever before (American Annals 2003, 165–70), yet estimates also suggest that the majority of interpreters working in the public schools today are not certified by the Registry of Interpreters for the Deaf, Inc. (RID).[2] However, despite all this information that our records show, our system has no way to determine whether the education of deaf children in the interpreted mainstream is equal to that of their hearing counterparts in the same setting, although many have asked that question since the onset of P. L. 94-142 in 1975.[3]

The success or failure of a deaf child hinges on his or her language proficiency, which, in mainstreaming, most often means English proficiency. For a child whose primary method of communication is visual and manual, proficiency in English can be an unattainable goal (despite La Bue's research, above, that tells us the majority of deaf children in public schools receive instruction in English through interpreters). If, indeed, the interpreter is producing English, the deaf student does not have the necessary English skills and, therefore, cannot comprehend the interpreter's message. Before an "equal education" can be determined, the deaf child's first language (L1) must be identified, a difficult task at best.

> The educational challenge of teaching children who have not acquired a first language is complex. In traditional educational settings, teachers of the deaf, who are most often hearing, are expected to use spoken English along with a signing system derived from English. Yet, most of their students have not yet acquired a fundamental understanding of any natural language. (La Bue 1998, 6)

This educational setting does not afford a deaf student the opportunity to acquire language, and the purpose of placing an interpreter in the classroom should not be to teach that first language.

This chapter first focuses on the individuality of every deaf child and how that individuality affects his or her L1 acquisition. Then, a theory of L1 acquisition is presented with a discussion of the important role that a strong L1 foundation plays in L2 proficiency. The dynamics of a hearing classroom is reviewed and, specifically, the deaf student's role as a participant in that classroom. Finally, the chapter examines the fictitious, assumed, naïve, and mythical role of interpreter as language model.

## THE PARTICIPANTS

Let us consider two important participants in the educational setting, the deaf student and the interpreter, and the language they use in this setting. It would be helpful if we knew the student's primary channel for successful communication. And, it would be helpful to consider what language the interpreter most often uses when interacting with the deaf child in the classroom.

### What Is This Deaf Child's L1?

"As children communicate with those around them, processes of language acquisition unfold, and children come to understand and participate in the social world they inhabit with others" (Ramsey 1997, 6). If the deaf child has Deaf[4] parents who use a visual language such as American Sign Language (ASL) in the United States or Langue des Signes Québécoise (LSQ) in Quebec, the child's L1 is acquired in this natural and spontaneous manner, just as a hearing child acquires L1 from his or her parents. If the deaf child has hearing parents, and the child's hearing loss is such that he or she relies primarily on visual communication, then the question becomes What is the child's L1?

As is commonly known, more than 90 percent of [deaf learners in the United States] have parents who are not deaf (i.e., they are hearing speakers of English) (Marschark, Lang, and Albertini 2002, 43), so a reasonable assumption would be that a child in this type of household does not acquire English naturally and spontaneously. And, as is also commonly known, a variety of hearing loss can be found within the Deaf community; "deaf individuals . . . vary in the degree of their hearing losses, age of hearing loss onset, and the etiologies or causes of the losses" (Marschark, Lang, and Albertini, 44). This variation makes generalizing across the population impossible to do unless we rely on the child's primary method of communication. If he or she relies on visual input, then English cannot be his or her L1 because English is fundamentally a spoken language, and spontaneous and natural acquisition of English does not occur visually.[5] "Deaf children from these environments acquire American Sign Language from other deaf children, usually in school, rather than from the typical language acquisition model (parent-to-child)" (La Bue 1998, 6). This pattern certainly was true before mainstreaming, when residential schools were the overwhelming choice. But, with many deaf children alone in a hearing class today, this method of acquisition is inaccessible, so we again return to the question, What is this child's L1?

Educators reach little agreement on the primary language of most deaf students whose primary channel of input is visual (McAnally, Rose, and Quigley 1987). However, of the utmost importance is not only to identify this L1 but also to ensure that the child acquires that L1 successfully. This language is the means by which he or she is going to access education. Clearly, the L1 foundation is necessary for cognitive development and academic success. If the L1 foundation of this child is problematic or flawed, then problems will surface in the educational setting. Marschark, Lang, and Albertini (2002) affirm the importance of language as "an essential component of normal human development" (111). But they also note that, because most deaf children are "born to nonsigning, hearing parents," they do not, therefore, "have full access to the language of their world until they have passed the most critical ages for language acquisition" (111). Given this information, one might safely say that English is not the deaf child's L1. At best, he or she will learn English later, which we know tends to be an uncertain process, even in ideal situations.

Now, let us expand this discussion to consider the interpreter. The next section takes into account the interpreter's L2, the language he or she most often uses when interacting with the deaf child in the classroom.

## The Interpreter's L2

The native language of most working interpreters today is English; consequently, ASL is their L2. But, just as the variation among deaf individuals makes it impossible to generalize about their language skills, so too, the variation in proficiency levels in interpreters makes it impossible to generalize about their ASL skills. Some interpreters have Deaf parents and learned ASL as a first language or are considered bilingual in ASL and English. (Unfortunately, it is commonly known that most of these skilled individuals work as interpreters in the community and interact with Deaf adults; therefore, young deaf children rarely have access to these interpreters.) Some interpreters complete training/education programs that require ASL courses, and others come from programs that have open admission policies, which allows for little or no quality control over either English or ASL. Problems also arise because of the lack of a standardized ASL curriculum in interpreting programs, not to mention the fact that spending only two years of learning an L2 leaves much to be desired in anyone's skills. Additionally, little research has been done on the ASL proficiency of interpreters, whether they are certified or not.

Research on the ASL proficiency level among interpreters who have acquired ASL as an L2 is scant. La Bue's (1998) research is quite telling; her work "indicate[s] a strong pattern of lexical and grammatical deletions in the interpreted rendition across discourse structures" (xi). The prerequisite for an interpreter's ability to render a successful message is the interpreter's comprehension of meaning. A pragmatic (i.e., holistic rather than discrete) assessment of ASL can actually show how well an interpreter comprehends meaning. The cloze test is a pragmatic instrument for this kind of assessment.[6]

Using a videotaped cloze test to measure ASL (L2) proficiency in interpreters requires the subjects to perform tasks that are fundamentally the same as when they interpret in a real-life situation. Often, interpreters do not see every single sign when a Deaf person is signing, but they do use their cloze skills to fill in missing parts. Swabey (1986) reported on the use of cloze activities in ASL as a skill-building tool for interpreting students. Lambert (1992) discussed using cloze as a "pedagogical tool" for interpreters and translators who work between English and French. In addition, studies have been done in which Deaf subjects participated, but the language has been English (see Reynolds 1986; Odom, Blanton, and Nunnally 1967). Only Monikowski developed and used an ASL cloze test to assess L2 (ASL) skills of interpreters (Monikowski 1994). Her results showed that the ASL proficiency level of interpreters certified by the RID with either a Comprehensive Skills Certificate or a Certificate of Interpretation,[7] although higher than noncertified interpreters, did not match the proficiency level of native or near-native Deaf users of ASL. The mean score for Deaf people was 70 percent, and the mean score for certified interpreters was 57 percent. In addition, this research supports the notion that one's L2 skills cannot surpass one's L1 skills (unless there are extenuating circumstances such as a move to immerse oneself in the minority culture and language).

As reported earlier in this chapter, estimates suggest that most interpreters in the public schools today are not certified. This situation begs the question, What is the L2 proficiency level of noncertified interpreters? In her same research, Monikowski (1994) reported a mean score on cloze tests of 29 percent for noncertified interpreters. Clearly, interpreters working in public schools do not have adequate skills in ASL, their L2. Yet, we expect the deaf student to learn ASL from the interpreter! If successful L2 acquisition depends on first acquiring a strong L1 (and we know that most deaf children do not have access to this kind a process) and if we also know that noncertified interpreters have minimal ASL skills, then we are faced with a frightening scenario to think about what kind of language skills the deaf students are learning from their interpreters. In addition, to say the interpreter is truly using ASL would be doubtful; he or she likely is using more English-like signs, which are more typical of an L2 beginner. This practice has the potential to confuse the deaf child even more.

However, before discussing this situation any further, the reader needs to gain a basic understanding of language acquisition, which is provided in the following section. We will return to the interpreter's L2 later in this chapter.

## LANGUAGE ACQUISITION: L1 AND L2

Acquisition of L2 does not happen in isolation. It is dependent on the level of proficiency in one's L1, which is the foundation for one's educational success.

### Acquisition of L1

Vygotsky saw the demonstration of L1 as the "free, spontaneous use of speech [and signs] and then later, the conscious realization of the linguistic forms" (John-Steiner

1985, 350). A child does not require overt adult "teaching" to process this linguistic information from environmental cues. The L1 is acquired in a natural setting from those present in the child's environment. Vygotsky also believed that language and cognitive development were interdependent (Vygotsky 1986, xviii). Language is a mediator of higher mental functions. It is the understanding of a deeper representation, of generalizations; it is the semiotic (i.e., symbolic) capacity of humans. The primary or native language is the basis for the development of one's semiotic capacity. Oller (1991) cited Peirce, Einstein, Dewey, Piaget, Vygotsky, and others when he said, "The normal development of deep semiotic abilities depends largely on the development of the primary language" (29). If we accept this claim of Oller's, then we can have little doubt about the importance of the successful acquisition of L1. Proficiency in L1 is of the utmost importance; it is the essential foundation for educational success. Proficiency in L2 cannot eclipse proficiency in L1.

Given that 90 percent of all deaf children have hearing parents (as mentioned above), it is questionable whether these children have access to language that is free and spontaneous. Perhaps their parents or primary caregivers are taking "sign language" classes. In many educational settings, the deaf children have learned "sign language"[8] either from their parents (who are not native users) or from the interpreters who are assigned to their classes. Assumptions are made that the child knows either "sign" or English. An important point to understand is that "sign" is not ASL. ASL is a naturally evolving visual-gestural language with grammatical structures, discourse genres, etc., and is as complex as any spoken language, but it does not follow the sentence structure of English. Often, "sign language" classes are a series of vocabulary classes that teach hearing people how to take manual signs and superimpose them onto English words. This use of signs is not ASL. When we talk about language acquisition and the importance of having an L1, "sign language" does not fit the bill. Wilbur (2003) clearly states that "artificially created signing systems . . . do not behave like natural languages" and do not allow for "efficiency" in their production (343). Clearly, the deaf child in this kind of an environment would not be able to fully acquire either language. The child would not acquire English in the home, and he or she could not acquire ASL because the opportunity would not exist to acquire it naturally (i.e., with native users) and exposure to it in natural and spontaneous situations would not occur. Again, quite clearly, English is not the deaf child's L1. In addition, the argument is clear that ASL can be learned only in a "free and spontaneous" environment. Those "sign language" classes for hearing people that focus on vocabulary cannot and do not present a language; therefore, the interpreter or parent who has taken those classes has no foundation in ASL as an L2, and consequently, ASL is not the deaf child's L1.

## Acquisition of L2

Although the primary focus of this chapter is not to review the many theories of L2 acquisition, providing some explanation of the more accepted approaches is important here. According to Lightbown and Spada (2002), "All second language learners, regardless of age, have by definition already acquired at least one language. This prior knowledge may be an advantage in the sense that the learner has an idea of how languages work" (21). A second language learner develops a system, an "interlanguage" (Seliger 1988, 21) that is different, neither "based entirely on his or her first language . . . nor based completely on the [L2]" (1988, 21). In addition, L2 learners attempt to apply what they already know about L1 to the new L2. "Language transfer . . . is the transference of rules from the learner's first language (L1)" that are used to produce the second language (L2) (Seliger 1988, 21).

## Interdependence of L1 and L2

All of the theories of L2 acquisition, despite their intricacies, clearly indicate the importance of an L1 on which to build the L2. John-Steiner (1985) credited Vygotsky as saying that "acquisition of a second language is indeed dependent upon the level of development of the native language" (350). In addition, Vygotsky wrote:

> If the development of the native language begins with free, spontaneous use of speech and is culminated in the conscious realization of linguistic forms and their mastery, then development of a foreign language [second language] begins with conscious realization of language and arbitrary command of it and culminates in spontaneous free speech. But, between those opposing paths of development, there exists a mutual dependency. . . . [T]his kind of conscious and deliberate acquisition of a foreign language obviously depends on a known level of development of the native language. . . . [T]he child acquiring a foreign language is already in command of a system of meaning in the native language which she/he transfers to the sphere of another language. (quoted in John-Steiner 1985, 350)

The "conscious and deliberate acquisition" of the L2 is dependent on "a known level of development" in the L1. Vygotsky said that the child is already "in command of a system of meaning" in his or her native language that supports the acquisition of L2. However, we have already established that a child whose primary method of communication is visual is not in command of English. If the child cannot access spoken English, then he or she cannot gain an age-appropriate command of English. Clearly, identifying an L1 for a child in this situation would seem impossible to do. Consequently, acquiring an L2 would also be impossible. Yet, schools often attempt to use sign language (a questionable L2) to teach classroom content (requiring an L1, which, in this case, is questionable).

If one accepts that language acquisition requires an underlying intellectual ability, then it must be involved in both languages. John-Steiner cautioned that Vygotsky's view of the importance of conscious learning might have been exaggerated because of his focus on learning solely in a classroom. In a more natural second-language setting, the L2 process seems to more closely follow the L1 process. However, the point is made: L1 and L2 acquisition are connected.

The importance of proficiency in L1 is also stressed; L2 builds on the foundation of L1. The L2 acquisition process follows the L1 acquisition process. Thus, if the primary system contains deficiencies or flaws, then the L2 system will have comparable problems. If L1 proficiency is relatively poorly developed, then we cannot expect proficiency in L2 to be more advanced. This reasoning is true for any and all languages. For our discussion, this reasoning maintains that, if a deaf child does not have a strong foundation in English from the home environment, then he or she cannot learn English in the classroom (because the child does not have ASL as an L1) nor can he or she learn ASL from the interpreter (because the child does not have English as an L1 and because the interpreter's ASL skills are questionable). A strong foundation in an L1 is paramount, and we have seen quite clearly that most deaf children do not have that foundation. Yet, in the classroom, educators often assume that the child already has English and, therefore, the interpreter either should sign in English (because it is what the child already knows) or should sign in ASL (because the child is deaf and the visual language is more "appropriate" for him or her). Little thought is given to the development of L1 before entering the classroom.

Vygotsky is not alone in purporting a link between L1 and L2. When Krashen (1982) presented his Input Hypothesis with respect to L1 acquisition, he said "we acquire . . . only when we understand language that contains structure that is 'a little bit beyond' where we are now" (21). This acquisition is possible only by using "more than our linguistic competence" (21) to understand. We acquire by "going for the meaning first" (21) and then acquiring the structure of the language as a result of that comprehension. The child attends to the "meaning and not the form of the message" (21). Krashen (1982) also included L2 acquisition in his hypothesis and noted that input can be "comprehensible" when teachers and students "take advantage of the acquirer's knowledge of the world" (25). Ramsey (2001) clearly related this acquisition to the teacher of deaf children and his or her "powerful role," saying that teachers must be sure they use "accessible and comprehensible" language as "they monitor the learner's engagement with the language and the task" (20). This role involves "intersubjectivity, or joint shared attention," which must be successful if learning is to occur (20).

The deaf child born to hearing parents who do not know ASL does not have access to free and spontaneous use of language (either English or ASL). Children in this situation either develop some kind of pidgin or home signs or adopt an oral approach. One way or another, their language development is seriously delayed. "The underlying fact is that deaf infants do not have sufficient hearing to acquire spoken English in the typical way" (Ramsey 2000, 25). In addition, "many hearing parents who choose to raise their deaf children with sign language do not sign consistently" (Marschark, Lang, and Albertini 2002, 90). When the children enter school, they demonstrate a major deficit in their English and ASL skills, and they spend the next twelve years of education trying to cope with that deficit. This lack of foundation in English (the potential L1 system available in the home) is reflected in the student's struggle to succeed in the classroom. Because English was not acquired as an L1, the child is doomed to play "catch up." An important point to understand is that the presence of an interpreter in the classroom cannot remedy this language deficit.

## THE CLASSROOM

The classroom presents a challenging environment to the deaf student and to the interpreter. Interaction between student and teacher is primary, and it must be successful if the child is to succeed. In addition, the secondary interactions among the students themselves and among the teacher and the other students cannot be ignored.

## Language in the Classroom

According to Marschark, Lang, and Albertini (2002), "the important factor for learning is not the ability to speak, but the ability to communicate through language, whatever its form, from an early age" (92). Cazden (1988) adds that, although "any social institution can be considered a communication system . . . the basic purpose of school is achieved through communication" (2). Communication between the teacher and the student is crucial, as is communication among the students themselves. It is how teachers impart information and how students "demonstrate to teachers much of what they have learned" (Cazden 1988, 2). "Spoken language is an important part of the identities of all the participants" (3). Even among the hearing children, different linguistic backgrounds need to be considered, and the study of classroom discourse is essential for successful teaching. The level of sophistication and the topics discussed certainly change from the elementary school to college, but the structure of the interaction is similar.

Research on success in English as a foreign language supports the importance of L1 in the classroom:

> Academic proficiency in one's mother tongue seems to play a very important role in predicting students' success in [foreign language learning] within a school situation. Even when such proficiency is measured by the teacher's grade, knowledge of L1 is a powerful predictor. The strongest predictor, however, across different student populations, is an external measure of one's academic language ability. (Olshtain et al. 1990, 138)

A number of factors contribute to the complexity of the environment, most notably the "purposes of talk" (Cazden 1988, 54). Talk that occurs in the classroom involves "speaking rights . . . the most important asymmetry," turn taking in discussions, the pace of classroom discourse, and shifts in "speech style." This talk can shift from formal lecture to informal conversation within minutes. In addition, in any classroom there is "considerable variability in the amount of teacher time spent with individuals or groups" (Cazden 1988, 62). In addition, "one of the most important influences on all talk (some say *the* most important influence) is the participants themselves—their expectations about interactions and their perceptions of each other" (67). Students and teachers develop opinions about one another by the way they talk to and about one another in the classroom. An incredible amount of incidental information is shared in the classroom. Children learn how to socialize, how to make friends, how to approach the teacher, how to ignore the nosey classmate, etc. Rarely does the teacher explicitly "teach" the significance of these important tangential events. Yet, these events are the foundation of our social interactions for years to come.

## The Deaf Child in the Classroom with an Interpreter

Deaf children in today's mainstream classroom have "many developmental needs that are not different from those of hearing children. Primarily, they need opportunities to use language to engage with others. These occasions must be embedded in comprehensible social contexts where there are other children and adults who share the language and who can help make the world intelligible" (Ramsey

1997, 3). Intelligibility is an important consideration and, by simply placing an interpreter in the room with the student, naïve participants—administrators, teachers, parents, and many interpreters—think the problem is solved. Why? Placing an interpreter in the class seems to be the perfect answer. The interpreter can communicate with the child, can present the teacher's words in a visual mode, can mediate between the child and his or her classmates. The strategy seems as though it should work, but knowing what we now know about the deaf child's lack of L1 (English) skills and the interpreter's lack of L2 (ASL) skills, we can begin to see the disconnect in this situation.

Winston (1994) clearly presented the dilemma for the deaf child in the hearing classroom, saying that the classroom is "designed to accommodate learning through both visual and auditory channels" (58). The students in Johnson's (1991) study, despite their age differences, exhibit the same "limitation," namely, that it is difficult (perhaps impossible) for a deaf person to visually attend to more than one thing at a time.

Unfortunately, the deaf child receiving his or her information through an interpreter has only the visual channel. We can reasonably assume that the child can, potentially, miss half of the information being presented. What is missed might not be the information coming directly from the teacher; it might be the incidental knowledge that his or her hearing peers are able to "pick up." Remembering the lack of qualified interpreters working in the educational setting, one must question the skills they have and the messages they produce.

In addition, the deaf child has a difficult (if not outright impossible) time actively participating in some of the teacher's activities. Even an extremely skilled interpreter can interpret only one message at a time. Whom does the interpreter choose to follow when several children are talking at the same time? The teacher does not want to stop the energetic discussion, so the interpreter is forced to make a choice, and the deaf student thus lives with someone else's view of the interaction rather than having the opportunity to make decisions by him or herself. However, regardless of the scenario, the important point to realize is that the dynamics of the hearing classroom often make successful interpretation virtually impossible, even when an experienced and competent interpreter is present. In spoken English discourse, for example, turn taking can be a seemingly chaotic event. A classroom of excited and energetic seventh graders includes cross talk, overlap, asides, etc.—all of which is under the direction of the teacher. The interpreter suffers from "information overload" (La Bue 1998, 19), and the subsequent interpretation suffers from multiple missing pieces of information. The result is that the deaf student is overwhelmed and overloaded, and the teacher's attempt to monitor the "learner's engagement" is lost. The participants (i.e., teacher and student) do not share an understanding of the message.

## AN INTERPRETED EDUCATION: THE INTERPRETER AS LANGUAGE MODEL

We know that languages (both L1 and L2) are acquired through exposure to natural and spontaneous models. Regardless of the theory involved—Vygotsky's, Krashen's, Oller's, etc.—there is no doubt of the importance of an L1 language model. Parents certainly know this importance to be true; they can simply watch the language development of their own children. It truly seems that, one day, the child suddenly produces "mama" and the world changes, but we know that countless "conversations" have occurred between mother and child that build up to that moment. The child has had countless opportunities to copy mother's voice intonation, words, head shakes, etc. And, as the child grows, models who are found beyond his or her primary caretaker also become important.

Consider the deaf child with hearing parents, who does not have the opportunity to benefit from those primary models. Then, one day, that child arrives at school and encounters an interpreter who can sign and who can, in the eyes of too many people, function as the language model for that child. Besides the fact that this role involves a tremendous responsibility for a mere interpreter, it is an inappropriate and impossible responsibility.

Earlier in this chapter, "sign language" was mentioned as a commonly taught substitute for ASL. Note that "signed English" and the more structured sign systems (e.g., Signing Exact English) are visual representations of English, an auditory language. This representation causes numerous problems because the systems are not a language, they do not have naturally evolving structure, and they are neither naturally and spontaneously produced nor acquired. In these systems, ASL signs are organized in a way that follows English sentence structure, and initialization is commonly used. The underlying supposition for the use of these systems is that the learner already knows English, a supposition that may be true for hearing people but is not true for deaf children who primarily rely on the visual channel for language acquisition and development. Unless a deaf child has English as his or her L1, it is not cognitively possible for a deaf child to comprehend a signed English system (see Wilbur 2003 for an in-depth discussion of this topic).

We know that many interpreters are signing English in the classroom, and we know that their ASL skills are weak. This situation has resulted in "inadequate access [for the deaf student] to content" in the hearing classroom (La Bue 1998, 232). Deaf students "receive bits and pieces of content through context, and through an interpretation of the discourse" (233). The same is true for older students; Johnson's (1991) work on the university classroom presented data from the deaf students' point of view and reported "significant miscommunication" and "confusion" when working with interpreters (24). In addition, although ASL-English interpreters were not included in his work, Nida's (1976) seminal work on interpreters was quite telling: "Even among experts [working with interpreters] discussing a subject within their own fields of specialization, it is unlikely that comprehension rises above 80 percent level" (63). The lack of a strong L1 for the deaf student (and therefore a weak or nonexistent L2) coupled with a lack of strong L2 (ASL) for the interpreter results in confusion, skewed messages, and substantial miscommunication.

If language acquisition occurs most successfully through natural and spontaneous use of the language, then for two basic and straightforward reasons, deaf children will find that acquiring ASL from their interpreters is difficult if not impossible to do. First, the interpreter is most likely not signing ASL; instead, he or she is probably signing some form of English that may or may not incorporate ASL features. We now know that the relatively high number of noncertified interpreters working in educational settings do not exhibit high proficiency levels in their L2, ASL. However, even if the interpreter is quite proficient in ASL, the second reason comes into play: He or she is interpreting the discourse of another individual, and this communication is not "natural and spontaneous" language use. Rather, it is an interpretation of someone else's thoughts and ideas, and it is potentially an incomprehensible message.

An educational setting does not afford a deaf student the opportunity to acquire language nor should language acquisition be the purpose of placing an interpreter in the classroom. The child is there to learn content. Hearing children certainly are being taught "language" when they are in English classes throughout their education. But the difference is that they already have an English language inside their heads. They cognitively "know" the language they use on a daily basis; English classes serve to expand, to augment, to elaborate on what these children already know. Hearing children also acquire incidental language from their teachers and their peers as a by-product of their education. In contrast, deaf students often do not fundamentally "know" any language; they simply know bits and pieces, but they have no strong foundation on which to build. For example, trying to learn about the Civil War when one does not know the language being used to convey the facts is not only difficult but also unrealistic, and expecting children to learn in this type of scenario borders on cruelty. We would never ask a hearing student to comprehend a lecture in Mandarin if he or she did not have proficiency in the language. Nevertheless, we ask this feat of deaf children every day.

## CONCLUSION

Until changes occur in the education of deaf children, their low reading levels will continue to remain the same. Until changes occur in the education of interpreters, their inadequate ASL levels will remain the same.

Language acquisition, when it occurs naturally, is a seemingly uncomplicated process. However, when a hearing loss affects the communication process to such an extent that use of the auditory channel is not an option, we see what a complex and daunting challenge language acquisition can become.

Many people think that, by providing children with interpreters, we are exposing those children to language. However, language acquisition requires interaction and direct communication. Interaction that occurs through an interpreter is, at best, incomplete. Interpreters who use English signing systems provide only a rough reflection of English. Our deaf children deserve better. Our deaf children deserve real language.

## NOTES

1. Schildroth and Hotto (1994) report a decline in enrollment in residential schools between 1976 and 1993—a loss of almost 9,000 students, or 47 percent of the population.

2. Data exist for several specific states. In 1987, 87 percent of Oregon interpreters working in K–12 public schools were not certified (Jones, Clark, and Soltz 1997, 263). In addition, "almost two-thirds of the interpreters working in public schools in Kansas, Missouri, and Nebraska" were not certified (263). New York State reports 15 certified interpreters out of 983 educational interpreters (Marilyn Mitchell, grant director for the New York State Preparation of Educational Interpreters Project, personal communication, September 5, 2002).

3. This law, also known as the Education for All Handicapped Children Act of 1975, mandates that all children with disabilities have access to the "least restrictive environment" (LRE). Over the years, for deaf children, LRE has come to mean the local public school.

4. The distinction between *deaf* and *Deaf* is made throughout this chapter. The former is the characteristic of not being able to hear, and the latter indicates the group of individuals who see themselves as a culture and a community.

5. An important point to note is that deaf children whose parents' primary method of communication is visual (which accounts for the other 10 percent of deaf learners) compare favorably with hearing children who have hearing parents and that these deaf children "pass comparable milestones at comparable ages" (Meier 1991, 64).

6. Cloze tests have been used in numerous spoken languages to assess the proficiency of native speakers and proficiency of L2 speakers. These tests resemble the "delete every fifth word" activities commonly used in testing signed language proficiency. To administer a reliable and valid test, testers need to approximate the skill level of the students and to reference a complete text because the information from the beginning of the text influences the answers later in the text.

7. These two certificates are commonly accepted to reflect an interpreter's ASL skills. The Certificate of Transliteration is indicative of the interpreter's ability to work within English and does not reflect his or her ASL skills.

8. ASL is the language of the American Deaf community. However, no standardized curriculum for teaching ASL is available like there is in the United States for teaching Spanish, for example. Many hearing people learn a form of "contact signing" (previously called Pidgin Signed English), which is a naturally occurring mixture of ASL and English that occurs when hearing people and Deaf people attempt to communicate manually. However, as Ramsey (2000) noted, contact signing is "generated by people who usually are fluent in both ASL and English" (28), which is not true of most parents of deaf children.

## REFERENCES

Allen, T., K. Lam, S. Hotto, and A. Schildroth. 1994. *Young deaf adults and the transition from high school to post-secondary careers.* Washington, D.C.: Center for Assessment and Demographic Studies, Gallaudet University.

American Annals of the Deaf. 2003. Programs for training interpreters. *American Annals of the Deaf* 148(2): 165–70.

Cazden, C. B. 1988. *Classroom discourse: The language of teaching and learning.* Portsmouth, N.H.: Heinemann Press.

Education for All Handicapped Children Act of 1975, P. L. 94-142, 20 U.S.C. §§ 1400 *et seq.*

Johnson, K. 1991. Miscommunication in interpreted classroom interaction. *Sign Language Studies* 70:1–34.

John-Steiner, V. 1985. The road to competence in an alien land: A Vygotskian perspective on bilingualism. In *Culture, communication, and cognition: Vygotskian perspectives,* ed. J. V. Wertsch, 348–71. Cambridge: Cambridge University Press.

Jones, B. E., G. M. Clark, and D. F. Soltz. 1997. Characteristics and practices of sign language interpreters in inclusive education programs. *Exceptional Children* 63(2): 257–68.

Krashen, S. 1982. *Principles and practice in second language acquisition.* Elmsford, N.Y.: Pergamon.

La Bue, M. A. 1998. Interpreted education: A study of Deaf students' access to the content and form of literacy instruction in a mainstreamed high school English class. Ph.D. dissertation, Harvard University, Cambridge, Mass.

Lambert, S. 1992. The cloze technique as a pedagogical tool for the training of translators and interpreters. *Target* 4(2): 223–36.

Lightbown, P. M., and N. Spada. 2002. *How languages are learned.* Oxford: Oxford University Press.

Marschark, M., H. G. Lang, and J. A. Albertini. 2002. *Educating deaf students: From research to practice.* New York: Oxford University Press.

McAnally, P., S. Rose, and S. Quigley. 1987. *Language learning practices with deaf children.* Boston: Little Brown/College-Hill.

Meier, R. P. 1991. Language acquisition by deaf children. *American Scientist* 79:60–70.

Monikowski, C. 1994. ASL proficiency in interpreters: Assessing L2 with a videotaped cloze test. Ph.D. dissertation, University of New Mexico, Albuquerque.

Nida, E. 1976. A framework for the analysis and evaluation of theories of translation and response. In *Translation applications and research,* ed. R. W. Brislin, 47–91. New York: Gardner Press.

Odom, P. B., R. L. Blanton, and J. C. Nunnally. 1967. Some cloze technique studies of language capability of the deaf. *Journal of Speech and Hearing Research* 10:816–27.

Oller, J. W. Jr. 1991. *Language and bilingualism: More tests of tests.* Lewisburg, Penn.: Bucknell University Press.

Olshtain, E., E. Shohamy, J. Kemp, and R. Chatow. 1990. Factors predicting success in EFL among culturally different learners. *Language Learning* 40(1): 23–44.

Peirce, C. S. 1957. The logic of abduction. In *Peirce's essays in philosophy of science,* ed. V. Tomas. New York: Liberal Arts Press.

Quigley, S., and P. Paul. 1986. A perspective on academic achievement. In *Deafness in perspective,* ed. D. Luterman. San Diego, Calif.: College-Hill/Little Brown.

Ramsey, C. L. 1997. *Deaf children in public schools.* Washington, D.C.: Gallaudet University Press.

Ramsey, C. L. 2000. Theoretical tools for educational interpreters or, true confessions of an ex-educational interpreter. Paper presented at the National Educational Interpreting Conference, August, Kansas City, Mo.

Ramsey, C. L. 2001. Beneath the surface: Theoretical frameworks shed light on educational interpreting. *Odyssey* 2(2): 19–24.

Reynolds, H. N. 1986. Performance of deaf college students on a criterion referenced, modified cloze test of reading comprehension. *American Annals of the Deaf* 131(5): 361–64.

Schildroth, A., and S. Hotto. 1994. Deaf students and full inclusion: Who wants to be excluded? In *Implications and complications for deaf students of the full inclusion movement,* eds. R. C. Johnson and O. P. Cohen, 7–30. Gallaudet Research Institute Occasional Paper 94-2. Washington, D.C.: Gallaudet University.

Seliger, H. 1988. Psycholinguistic issues in second language acquisition. In *Issues in second language acquisition: Multiple perspectives,* ed. L. M. Beebe, 17–40. New York: Newbury House.

Swabey, L. 1986. Cloze skills and comprehension. In *New dimensions in interpreter education: Curriculum and instruction. Proceedings of 6th national convention, Conference of Interpreter Trainers,* ed. M. McIntire, 69–76. Silver Spring, Md.: Registry of Interpreters for the Deaf Publications.

U.S. Department of Education (DOE) and the National Center for Education Statistics (NCES). 2002. *The condition of education 2002* (NCES 2002-025). Washington, D.C.: U.S. Government Printing Office.

Vygotsky, L. 1986. *Thought and language.* Translated and edited by A. Kozulin. Cambridge, Mass.: MIT Press. (Orig. pub. 1934.)

Wilbur, R. B. 2003. Modality and the structure of language: Sign languages versus signed systems. In *Oxford handbook of deaf studies, language, and education,* eds. M. Marschark and P. E. Spencer, 332–46. New York: Oxford University Press.

Winston, E. A. 1994. An interpreted education: Inclusion or exclusion? In *Implications and complications for deaf students of the full inclusion movement,* eds. R. C. Johnson and O. P. Cohen, 55–62. Gallaudet Research Institute Occasional Paper 94-2. Washington, D.C.: Gallaudet University.

# Language Accessibility in a Transliterated Education: English Signing Systems

Kelly Stack

The key question to be asked about the use of English signing systems with deaf children is Do they work? Do children exposed to English signing systems actually acquire competence in English? To answer this question, we must examine how children acquire natural human languages. Are the same processes available to children acquiring English signing systems? What have we learned from the study of English competence in children exposed to English signing systems?

In this chapter, I will argue that English signing systems do not offer children the input needed to trigger development of English grammar. First, after comparing SEE II (Signing Exact English[1]) with English and other natural human languages, we will see that English signing systems intrinsically lack critical characteristics of human language, particularly at the phonological level, which is the level responsible for mapping physical signals received by the ears or eyes to the mental constructs, or phonemes, that constitute the "basic building blocks" of language. Next, the chapter will examine the outcomes of numerous studies of children attempting to learn and use SEE II, and we will see that many of the difficulties children experience learning SEE II can be attributed to "dysharmony" at the phonological level. Finally, we will look at the case of one child who, despite almost perfect circumstances for acquiring SEE II, actually rejects those aspects of SEE II that are least natural, leading her to develop an idiolect that, while linguistically sound, is neither complete nor conventional.

## THE ROLE OF PHONOLOGY IN LANGUAGE ACQUISITION

Phonology imposes psychological order on the chaotic physical world of speech sounds. Although acoustical measurements may show that the physical intervals between a series of sounds that change slowly from [d] to [t] are identical, human beings consistently perceive those intervals quite differently depending on which language they grew up with. Thus, how we perceive the smallest units of language depends on which language we use natively.

In addition to organizing the smallest units of language into rule-governed classes, phonology also regulates the production and perception of entire utterances, grouping words into phrases based on prosody. In general, prosody may be thought of as the underlying rhythm of a language, and different languages use different prosodic indicators; in English, stress plays the prominent role; in French, it is syllable structure; other languages use pitch accent or tone.

For example, compare the syntactic constituent structure of the sentence "He kept it in a large jar," with the prosodic structure (Hayes 1989) in figure 1. The content words (also known as open class or lexical items) are the heads of the three prosodic words (also called clitic groups), and the grammatical words (also known as closed class or functional items) group with the heads within syntactic phrases. So, although, syntactically, the words *in a large jar* form a single phrase, in speech, we place stress on both *large* and *jar*, creating two prosodic phrases, and the entire sentence consists of just three prosodic words: [$_c$he kept it] [$_c$in a large] [$_c$jar].

It is widely accepted that phonology treats open class morphemes differently from closed class morphemes. In general, closed class morphemes, both free (such as *in, he, a*) and bound (such as *-ing, -ly, -s*), are unstressed, undergo phonological reduction (*I am going to* becomes *I'm gonna*), are underlyingly underspecified and subminimal (English past tense is pronounced [t], [d] or [əd] depending on the neighboring sounds), and are subject to cliticization within phonological phrases, as shown in figure 1 (Selkirk 1978, 1980, 1981; Hayes 1989; Nespor and Vogel 1982; Abney 1987).

Considerable evidence indicates that the comprehension of speech depends critically on prosodic structure and on its role in marking lexical and grammatical boundaries in the speech stream. Prosody maps onto and provides cues to linguistic segmentation, and it is essential for comprehension of the message.

Prosody and rhythmic structure also appear to be crucial to language acquisition. There is evidence that children acquiring English use stress patterns in

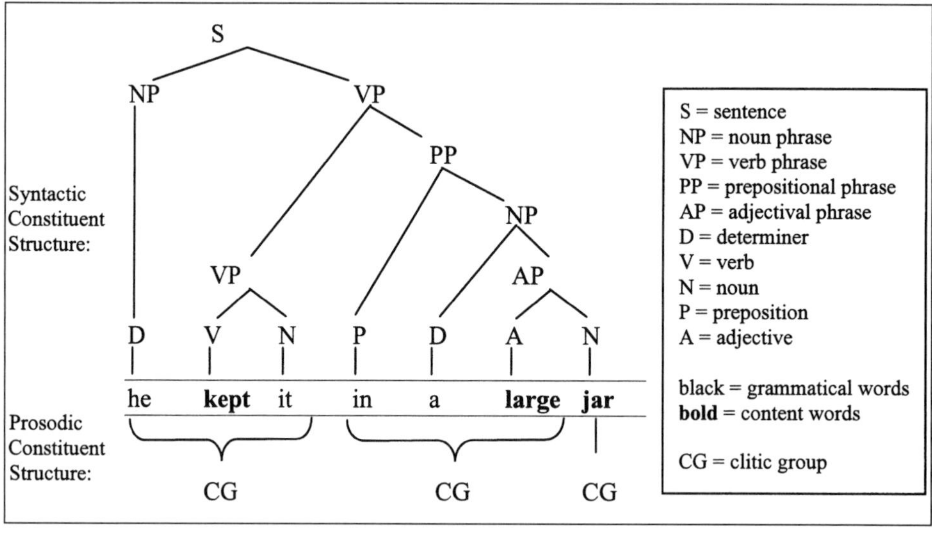


FIGURE 1.

*Source:* B. Hayes, "The Prosodic Hierarchy in Meter," *Phonetics and Phonology* 1 (1989): 201–60.

continuous speech to work out whether to use the grammatical classification of open or closed classes of words and morphemes (Gleitman et al. 1988). In particular, closed class functors serve "as a kind of frame for perceiving and producing content words" (Gerken, Landau, and Remez 1990, 213), even when they do not regularly appear in small children's speech.

## THE STRUCTURE OF ENGLISH SIGNING SYSTEMS

To understand that SEE II's awkwardness is not merely aesthetically displeasing but also fundamentally flawed in comparison with ASL and other signed languages, we need to look at the relationship between the phonetic and phonological domains in language. Considerable evidence shows that English signing systems are incapable of reproducing the prosody of spoken English, particularly its stress patterns. This incapacity appears to be the primary reason why they are unsuitable language models.

In SEE II, the citation-form vocabulary of ASL was used as the basis for developing signs. English word order was followed. Signs were invented to represent inflectional and derivational morphemes such as -ING, -S, -NESS, etc. Initialization was used to create new signs to represent the individual vocabulary items within "families" of English words that "belong together conceptually." For example, the system maintains "the basic ASL sign for BEAUTY, using the P handshape in the same movement for PRETTY, and the L handshape for LOVELY" (Gustason, Pfetzing, and Zawolkow 1980).

The bound and functional (closed class) morphology of SEE II consists of mainly irreducible forms. A reducible form is one in which the underlying structure is not fully specified. In English, for example, we commonly say nouns are pluralized by adding an *-s*. In fact, the *s* sound sounds like an *s* only when the word ends in a nonvoiced, nonsibilant segment, like the *p* in *top*. If a word ends in a voiced, nonsibilant segment, like the *g* in *dog*, then the plural form ends in *-z*. If a word ends in a sibilant, an entire syllable is added, such as *-ez* as in *judges.* The explanation for all this variation is that the English regular plural form is neither *-s* nor *-z*; it is a segment that is not underlyingly specified for voicing. It "borrows" its voicing feature from the neighboring segment in the word to which it is attached.

Like English and other spoken languages, ASL and other natural signed languages contain morphemes with underspecified segments. For example, many verbs in ASL have subject and object agreement morphology; they are signed beginning in one location and ending in another depending on the subject and object. GIVE is a commonly cited example, signed with the beginning location closer to the body in I GIVE-TO YOU but with the ending location closer to the body in YOU GIVE-TO ME. The subject or object agreement morphemes are specified for location but are not specified for hand configuration or movement; those elements are "filled in" by the verb.[2]

Although Gustason and Zawolkow (1993) provide suggestions for incorporating "ASL principles" into English signs, efforts such as these are destined to become mired in the underlyingly fully specified structure of SEE II. For example, in figure 2, the idea of dancing and the grammatical notions of person, existence, negation, mood, and aspect are represented by seven signs in SEE II; two signs in ASL; and two prosodic words in spoken English ([wi ˈarnt] [gənə ˈdæns]). Although speed and fluidity can be enhanced if the SEE II signer follows Gustason and Zawolkow's suggestions and pronounces the signs in closer proximity to one another, no real phonological reduction occurs.

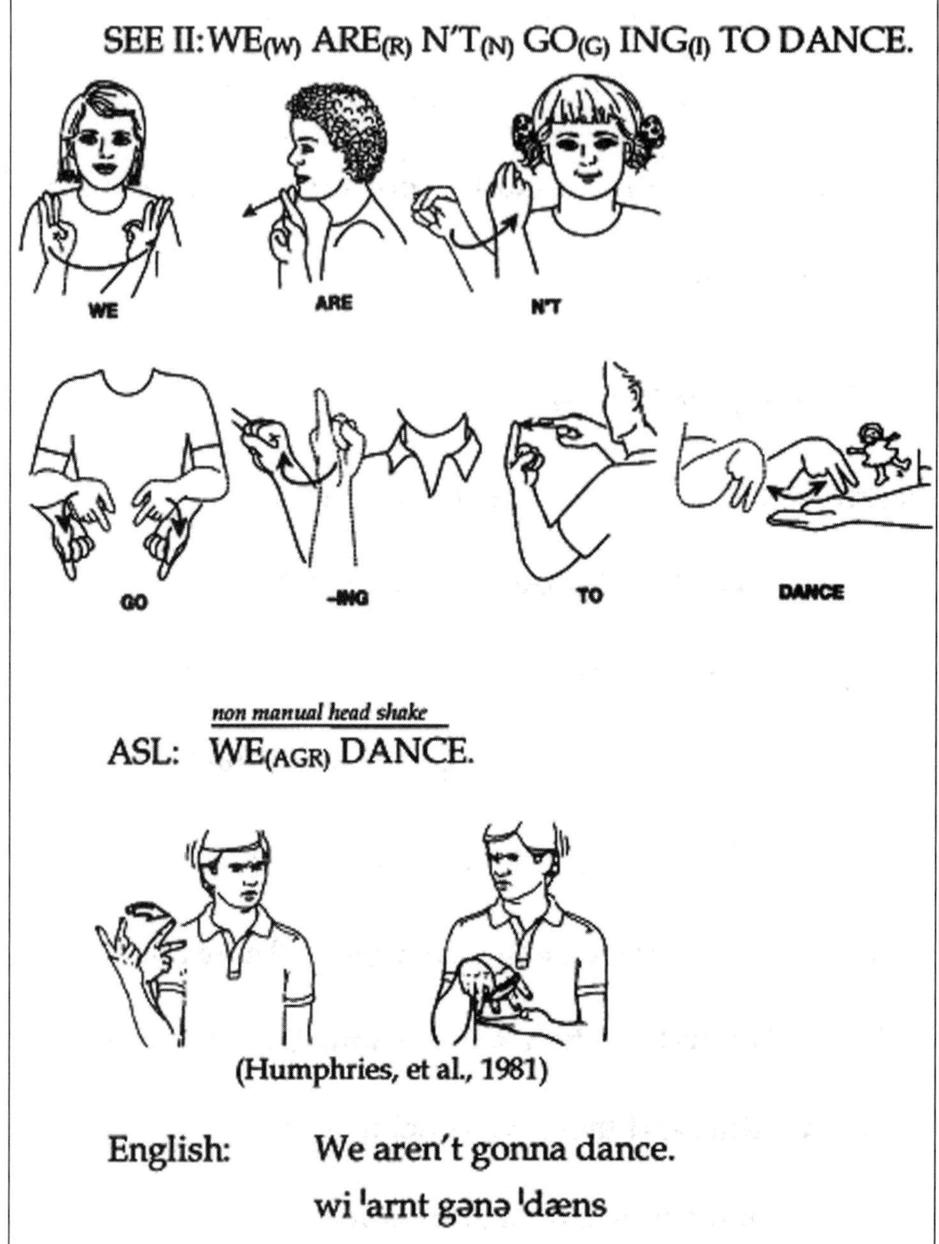


FIGURE 2.

*Source:* G. Gustason, D. Pfetzing, and E. Zawolkow. *Signing Exact English* (Los Alamitos, Calif.: Modern Signs Press, 1990) and T. Humphries, C. Padden, and T. J. O'Rourke, *A Basic Course in American Sign Language* (Silver Spring, Md.: T.J. Publishers, 1981).

In natural languages, the physical phonetic space (acoustic or visual) works in harmony with the psychological domains of language such as phonology, morphology, and syntax. In signed languages, phonologically dependent elements are ordinarily realized as simultaneous morphemes rather than as morphemes occurring sequentially. For example, the marking of aspect in ASL involves the phonologically dependent element, movement. Different aspects are marked by modifying the movement parameter, which is realized simultaneously with the handshape and location morphemes. Put another way, there are no natural languages in which morphological and grammatical processes are not accompanied by phonological processes that are reflected in the physical phonetic signal. SEE II, however, exhibits very little relation between its phonetics and the rest of the language. SEE II grammatical processes are not reflected in the pronunciation of SEE II signs.

## PREVIOUS STUDIES

The literature is clear that children do not acquire English signing systems as first languages. One of the well-known facts about normal language acquisition in children is that it occurs consistently under all but the harshest of conditions; as long as there is access to the ambient language, children who are neglected or even abused attain grammatical competence equal to peers who have been bombarded with nurturing attention. The fact that children do not acquire the ambient language when it is SEE II must be explained.

Children exposed to SEE II are reported to sprinkle signs for inflectional morphemes ad hoc throughout their utterances (Maxwell 1987; Suty and Friel-Patti 1982). These children tend to sign affixes as separate words, even on those occasions when they produce them in the correct order with a root. One child "developed a strategy of signing -ING any time his father indicated that a correction was necessary, whether or not -ING was appropriate" (Maxwell 1987, 332).

Children exposed to SEE II from age three to age six did as well on the GAEL (Grammatical Analysis of Elicited English) Simple Sentence Level Test[3] as deaf children at the same age who had been exposed to no signed language at all (Suty and Friel-Patti 1982). In other words, previous exposure to SEE II did not enhance their ability to understand English.

Another group of children, ages seven to fourteen, from programs very committed to SEE II, "produced roughly half their sentences perfectly ($M = 55\%$, $SD = 20$)" (Schick and Moeller 1992). Their errors mainly had to do with the use of bound morphemes, articles, copulas, and auxiliary verbs (i.e., closed class items). To place these results in context, grammatical competence for native users of a language is normally defined as use of obligatory morphemes in 90 percent of the cases. Children natively acquiring a language simply do not make the quantity and quality of mistakes evidenced by children exposed only to SEE II.

Supalla (1991) found that deaf children who grew up in a strictly SEE II-signing environment failed to acquire the SEE II (and thus the English) pronoun system. They pronounced SEE II verbs correctly only 20 percent of the time, leaving off tense markers and innovating subject-object verb agreement systems. Most disturbing, Supalla found that, although these children were in school together, each child had innovated his or her own verb inflection strategy, which was internally consistent for the child but not shared with peers.

These studies show that children exposed to English signing systems do not make the kinds of errors one expects from a child who is acquiring a natural spoken or signed language. They omit or misuse grammatical morphemes and function words. They treat affixes like whole words. The pattern of errors they make diverges considerably from the error patterns of children who are acquiring natural languages.

## JAMIE'S STORY

Unfortunately, most children using English signing systems are not exposed to the systems very early in life. Therefore, the errors they make may be attributable to lack of access to any language during the critical period for language acquisition (see chapter 2 by Monikowski in this volume). The child in this study, however, was exposed to SEE II at a relatively early age, so any difficulty she might have experienced mastering the system was likely to have been caused by deficiencies within SEE II rather than by declining ability to acquire language because of critical period effects.

"Jamie" is a deaf child of hearing parents, who was exposed to SEE II from the age of eleven months.[4] Both Jamie's parents are avid and skilled SEE II signers, and at the time the study began, when Jamie was four years and three months, she had not been exposed to American Sign Language. At about age five, Jamie began to have contact with deaf children of deaf adults (and therefore began to have contact with ASL) in the context of the SEE II preschool and kindergarten she attended. The study ended when Jamie was five years and five months. Initial testing showed that Jamie possessed an excellent open class vocabulary (i.e., nouns, verbs, adjectives, adverbs) equivalent to that of hearing children her age. Jamie's open class phrase structure was appropriate; moreover, she used open class vocabulary in a wide variety of standard grammatical functions. Noun phrases surfaced in her utterances as subjects, objects of verbs, objects of prepositions, appositives, and complements of determiners. Jamie's use of SEE II verb phrases (except for the copula) in spontaneous conversation was, for the most part, normal. She used intransitive and transitive verbs, including ditransitives and transitives with sentential complements and adjuncts. Analysis of spontaneously occurring conversation revealed strong evidence that Jamie had standard English (i.e., SEE II) prepositional phrase structure; prepositions always appeared with complements, and they served standard adverbial, predicative, complemental, or adjectival functions. Finally, Jamie's use of adjectives and adverbs was, by and large, congruent with standard English.

However, as will be discussed below, when her functional vocabulary (i.e., determiners, complementizers, inflectional elements such as *-ing*, *-s*, etc.) was evaluated, a different picture emerged, one of significant developmental delay. Results of testing using the CYCLE[5] (Curtiss and Yamada 1987) revealed that Jamie at age four years, three months had acquired the closed class vocabulary that one would expect of a normal hearing child age two years, six months.

Jamie's closed class phrase structure deviated remarkably from what would be expected from a child Jamie's age having the same mastery of open class vocabulary and phrase structure. Jamie not only routinely omitted grammatical morphemes in obligatory contexts but also invented her own grammatical innovations. This performance is remarkable given that the literature of normal children acquiring natural spoken or signed languages describes *no* cases of grammatical innovations. Jamie's acquisitional gaps and innovations in this area indicate a profound breakdown in the ability of SEE II to provide children with the tools they need for normal language acquisition.

In spontaneous conversation, Jamie produced the following SEE II pronouns: I, ME, YOU, SOME+ONE, ONE, and IT. When she used them, she used them in the correct context, but Jamie did not always produce a pronoun when there was an obligatory context for one. In addition to the SEE II pronouns, Jamie used an innovated form, a pointing gesture, for third-person references, which I glossed as

FIGURE 3.

*Source:* G. Gustason, D. Pfetzing, and E. Zawolkow. *Signing Exact English* (Los Alamitos, Calif.: Modern Signs Press, 1990).

PROPOINT. Jamie sometimes pluralized PROPOINT by reduplicating it or by tracing an arc in the air. She also pluralized YOU in two instances by reduplicating it, even though the English and SEE II forms of YOU are the same for singular and plural. The SEE II pronominal system is shown in figure 3.

Jamie produced a first person singular pronoun in 74 percent of obligatory contexts. Most of the time, this pronoun was ME. In subject position, she used I only 17 percent of the time, but in object position, ME was always used. An important point to note is that Jamie never used I in object position, which would have been an error unattested in the literature on English child language acquisition. In contrast, her misuse of ME as subject is attested in spoken English acquisition (e.g., "Me do it."), so in this respect, Jamie was not unusual, just immature. All in all, Jamie's performance with first and second person pronouns was comparable with that of a child's early English.

Although children acquiring spoken English tend to master third person singular pronouns by approximately the age of two, Jamie did not master SEE II third person pronouns at any point during the period of study according to her scores on the CYCLE-R subtests involving comprehension of pronouns.

In spontaneous conversation, out of 572 contexts that were obligatory for a third person pronoun, Jamie supplied a SEE II third person pronoun only eleven times (2 percent). In conversational contexts, she used first person pronouns in 69 percent of obligatory contexts and second person pronouns in 93 percent of obligatory contexts, otherwise omitting them. These results are summarized in figure 4.

Why did Jamie do so much better with first person and second person SEE II pronouns than with SEE II third person pronouns? Such a dramatic disparity

| | |
|---|---|
| SEE II 1st Person pronouns supplied in obligatory contexts | 69% |
| SEE II 2nd Person pronouns supplied in obligatory contexts | 93% |
| SEE II 3rd Person pronouns supplied in obligatory contexts | 2% |

FIGURE 4.

involving mastery of different types of pronouns has never been reported in normal children acquiring natural spoken or signed languages. The answer lies not in grammatical person but in the morphophonemic structure of the pronouns. Jamie was able to acquire SEE II pronouns that use phonological location morphemically. Most known signed languages use phonological location for pronominal reference, establishing a point in space as a referent for a noun. But instead of the SEE II third person pronouns that do not make use of space, Jamie innovated a third person pronoun (similar to ASL's third person pronoun): POINT, which she used consistently throughout the period of study. Of those 572 contexts that were obligatory for a third person pronoun, Jamie used the POINT pronoun 40 percent of the time.

In the original version of the CYCLE-R Third Person Object Pronouns subtest, the subject is shown a page with three pictures on it and is told, "Point to them," or "Point to her," etc. I created a revised version in which I briefly described each picture (e.g., "THE GIRL IS SIT+ING ON A CHAIR.") and established a pronominal location in space for it, using SEE II verbs (in this case, SIT+ING) as locational predicates. To eliminate the possibility of copying the locations from the pictures, the pronominal locations I signed were not identical to the position of the pictures on the page. When I asked Jamie to identify the correct picture, I used the POINT pronoun to refer to the pronominal locations. Jamie passed with 100 percent correct responses on the revised version. These results are shown in figure 5.

Jamie's perfect performance on this subtest is particularly remarkable because it shows mastery of the use of arbitrary locations in space for grammatical purposes. Ignoring the case and gender inflection found in SEE II and English, Jamie's developing pronominal system instead used location to mark person, making systematic use of a morphosyntactic feature of natural signed languages that is almost ignored by her target language, SEE II. This pattern also extended to possessive pronouns.

Although exciting from the point of view of a generative linguist interested in child language acquisition, Jamie's innovations were disheartening in terms of acquiring English or SEE II. Instead of learning that pronouns in English are marked morphologically for gender, Jamie had developed a system in which pronouns agree with their referents without regard to gender.

Jamie's innovations did not stop with pronouns. In English, number on nouns is expressed in most cases through the bound plural morpheme, *-s*. In SEE II, the

| | |
|---|---|
| POINT 3rd person pronouns obligatory in contexts (4 yrs, 3 mos–5 yrs, 5 mos) | 40% |
| Results of revised Third Person Object pronouns test (5 yrs, 5 mos) | 5 out of 5 passed (100%) |

FIGURE 5.

regular plural is formed by concatenating an -S to the end of the noun; irregular plurals (such as *man* or *men*) are formed by reduplicating the noun (except in the case of 0-morpheme plurals such as *fish*, which are not marked for number).

Jamie used an overt SEE II plural marker sixteen times in 248 obligatory contexts, two times using –S and fourteen times using reduplication. None of the reduplicated forms were irregulars and, thus, should strictly count as SEE II errors. In testing, Jamie was unable to reliably comprehend or produce the plural morpheme –S. A pretest demonstrated that Jamie understood the difference between singular and plural, but in the absence of the modifiers ONE and MANY, she was unable to distinguish SEE II singular and plural morphology, performing at about the same level as one who is responding by chance.

However, Jamie performed with 90 percent accuracy on an altered version of the CYCLE-R Noun Singular/Plural subtest. This time, instead of using the SEE II –S morpheme, I presented the items using reduplication for plurals. The result suggests that Jamie was not learning to pluralize nouns as SEE II does but was, instead, developing a grammar in which all nouns, not just irregulars, are marked for plurality through reduplication.

Out of a corpus containing 1,122 obligatory contexts, Jamie produced just fifty-six utterances with SEE II inflectional forms in them. Almost all of these inflectional forms were free morphemes such as modals and negatives rather than bound morphemes such as suffixes and prefixes.

Jamie tended to lexicalize grammatical morphemes where possible, omitting bound morphemes. For example, she distinguished between plural and singular nouns by using lexical items such as ONE or MANY without marking the plurality on the noun itself. Jamie never used either of the two SEE II devices for marking past tense (shown in figure 6). She did occasionally use the lexical completive ALREADY instead of a past-tense bound morpheme.

In spoken and signed languages with rich verb agreement systems, overt lexical subjects, objects, or both are frequently optional. ASL is such a language, as

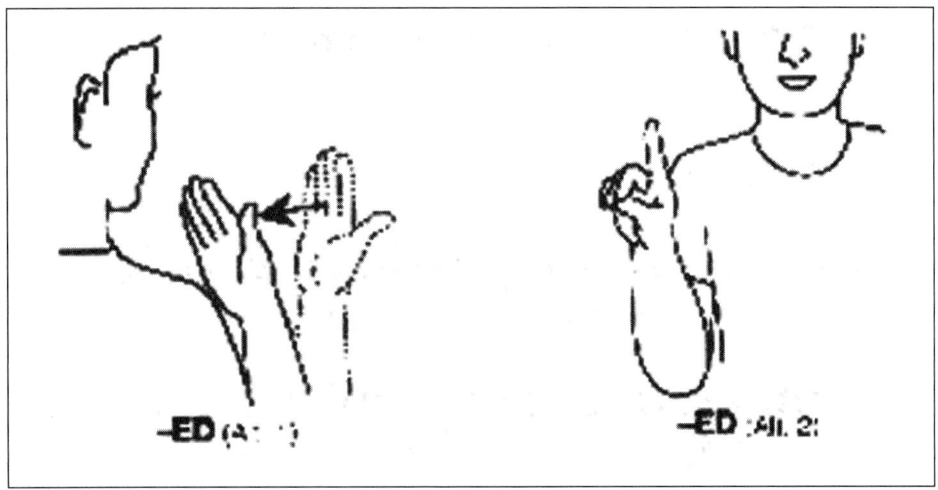


FIGURE 6.

*Source:* G. Gustason and E. Zawolkow. *Signing Exact English* (Los Alamitos, Calif.: Modern Signs Press, 1993).

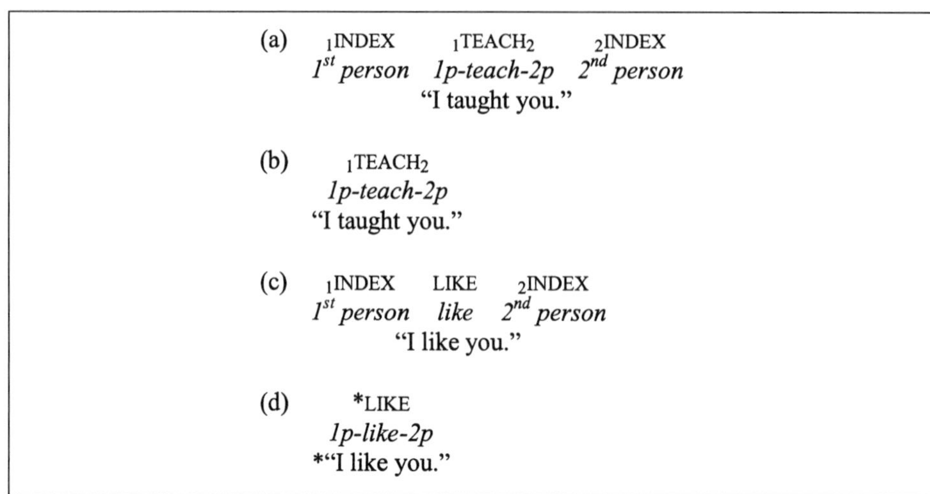

(a) $_1$INDEX $_1$TEACH$_2$ $_2$INDEX
$1^{st}$ person 1p-teach-2p $2^{nd}$ person
"I taught you."
(b) $_1$TEACH$_2$
1p-teach-2p
"I taught you."
(c) $_1$INDEX LIKE $_2$INDEX
$1^{st}$ person like $2^{nd}$ person
"I like you."
(d) *LIKE
1p-like-2p
*"I like you."


FIGURE 7.

illustrated in figure 7, which shows an example where the inflecting verb TEACH may grammatically occur with or without lexical arguments (a) and (b), but the plain verb LIKE may occur only when accompanied by lexical arguments; that is, (d) is ungrammatical, as indicated by the "*".[6]

Jamie produced ten verbs that appear to inflect for person, number agreement, or both and that could be modified in terms of their beginning or ending phonological locations. One might be tempted to view these modifications as ad hoc mimetic extensions, but Jamie's systematic treatment of these verbs with respect to argument structure strongly suggests they were indeed grammatical innovations.

Jamie provided required lexical arguments for noninflecting verbs such as LIKE 83 percent of the time. However, she provided lexical arguments for inflecting verbs such as TEACH only 52 percent of the time (see table 1).

Why would Jamie suddenly "lose track" of subject-object requirements for just the inflecting verbs? The mystery is solved when we include agreement morphology as an additional way to satisfy the requirement for a subject or object, as it is in highly inflected spoken languages. In this case, we find a combined total of lexical and nonlexical arguments appearing 92 percent of the time in obligatory positions, as summarized in table 2.

Jamie's differentiation between inflecting and noninflecting verbs by supplying bound inflectional morphemes as arguments for the former (e.g., $_1$TEACH$_2$; "I taught you") and free lexical items for the latter (e.g., $_1$INDEX LIKE $_2$INDEX; "I like you") is strong evidence that her innovation is principled, not ad hoc.

TABLE 1

| | Noninflecting Verbs | Inflecting Verbs |
|---|---|---|
| Lexical Arguments in Obligatory Position | 83% | 52% |

TABLE 2

| | Noninflecting Verbs | Inflecting Verbs |
|---|---|---|
| Lexical Arguments in Obligatory Position | 83% | 52% |
| Nonlexical Arguments in Obligatory Position | n/a | 40% |
| TOTALS | 83% | 92% |

In contrast, Jamie used SEE II functional elements in unprincipled ways that are unattested in children's normal English language development. All of Jamie's SEE II inflectional structures were fragile, occurring in a very small proportion of obligatory contexts.

In many respects, her acquisition and use of SEE II resembled those of children exposed to language after the critical period of language acquisition, who characteristically acquire relatively large open class vocabularies but little or no grammar. Unlike those children, however, Jamie, who was still within the critical period when exposed to SEE II, additionally innovated a rich but idiolectic grammatical system.

Children who are normally acquiring natural spoken and signed languages never reject entire grammatical systems in the target language and instead innovate their own systems, even though they may play creatively with limited aspects of some systems. With SEE II, Jamie did what normally is not done. Jamie herself is normal, and her acquisitional circumstances were nearly normal (early exposure to language from both parents). We can conclude only that the use of SEE II produced a deleterious effect on Jamie's ability to acquire English and that this use has the same effect on other deaf children.

## NOTES

1. In the late 1960s and early 1970s, three varieties of English signing systems sprouted up in as many years (Gustason 1990). The most widely adopted of these has turned out to be SEE II (Signing Exact English).

2. This discussion of underspecification in signed and spoken languages is intended to introduce the concepts for the nonlinguist, not to make claims based on any particular phonological theory.

3. According to Suty and Friel-Patti (1982), "This test assesses the English language competence of deaf children for basic grammatical categories in simple sentences and for the use of grammatical function words and inflectional affixes" (p. 156).

4. Eleven months is still rather late in terms of language acquisition, but it is well before the age of four, which has been identified by Newport (1990) as being too late for normal language acquisition to occur. Jamie's parents describe a burst of language acquisition by Jamie as soon as she was exposed to SEE II, suggesting that she attained the one-word stage at a relatively normal age, despite her late start.

5. The Curtiss-Yamada Comprehensive Language Evaluation (CYCLE) was developed to provide information about the comprehension and production of specific English grammatical structures and features in semantics, syntax, morphology, and phonology. The

CYCLE consists of many subtests that are divided into CYCLE-R (receptive language) and CYCLE-E (expressive language).

6. Lexical arguments are noun phrases that must co-occur with verbs, usually as subjects or objects; an example would be *it* in *it is raining*. It would be ungrammatical to say *is raining* because the verb *rain* requires a subject.

## REFERENCES


Abney, S. P. 1987. The English noun phrase in its sentential aspect. Ph.D. dissertation, Massachusetts Institute of Technology, Boston.

Curtiss, S., and J. Yamada. 1987. *Curtiss Yamada Comprehensive Language Evaluation (CYCLE).* Los Angeles, Calif.: University of California at Los Angeles (UCLA) Linguistics Department.

Gerken, L., B. Landau, and R. E. Remez. 1990. Function morphemes in young children's speech perception and production. *Developmental Psychology* 26: 204–16.

Gleitman, L. R., H. Gleitman, B. Landau, and E. Wanner. 1988. Where learning begins: Initial representations for language learning. In *Linguistics: The Cambridge Survey, vol. 3,* ed. F. Newmeyer. Cambridge: Cambridge University Press.

Gustason, G. 1990. Signing Exact English. In *Manual communication: Implications for education,* ed. H. Bornstein. Washington, D.C.: Gallaudet University Press.

Gustason, G., D. Pfetzing, and E. Zawolkow. 1980. *Signing Exact English.* Los Alamitos, Calif.: Modern Signs Press.

Gustason, G., and E. Zawolkow. 1993. *Signing Exact English.* Los Alamitos, Calif.: Modern Signs Press.

Hayes, B. 1989. The prosodic hierarchy in meter. *Phonetics and Phonology* 1: 201–60.

Humphries, T., C. Padden, and T. J. O'Rourke. 1981. *A Basic Course in American Sign Language.* Silver Spring, Md.: T.J. Publishers.

Maxwell, M. 1987. The acquisition of English bound morphemes in sign language form. *Sign Language Studies* 57: 323–52.

Nespor, M., and I. Vogel. 1982. Prosodic domains of external sandhi rules. In *The structure of phonological representations, part I,* ed. H. van der Hulst and U.N. Smith. Dordrecht: Foris.

Newport, E. 1990. Maturational constraints on language learning. *Cognitive Science* 14: 11–28.

Schick, B., and M. P. Moeller. 1992. What is learnable in manually coded English sign systems? *Applied Psycholinguistics* 13: 313–40.

Selkirk, E. O. 1978. On prosodic structure and its relation to syntactic structure. In *Nordic prosody II,* ed. T. Fretheim. Trondheim, Norway: TAPIR.

———. 1980. Prosodic domains in phonology: Sanskrit revisited. In *Juncture,* ed. M. Aronoff and M. L. Kean. Saratoga, Calif.: Anma Libri.

———. 1981. On the nature of phonological representation. In *The cognitive representation of speech,* ed. J. Anderson, J. Laver, and T. Myers. Amsterdam: North-Holland Publishing.

Supalla, S. 1991. Manually Coded English: The modality question in signed language development. In *Theoretical issues in sign language research, vol. 2,* eds. P. Siple and S. Fischer. Chicago: University of Chicago Press.

Suty, K., and S. Friel-Patti. 1982. Looking beyond signed English to describe the language of two deaf children. *Sign Language Studies,* 35: 153–68.

# How Might Learning through an Educational Interpreter Influence Cognitive Development?

Brenda Schick

Put simply, educating children with the use of an interpreter is an educational experiment. Although published demographic data documents the number of children who are being educated in classrooms with educational interpreters (Kluwin, Moore, and Gaustad 1992), no studies have been done to document how well these students are doing. For all children, deaf or hard of hearing and hearing, the goal of education is not just to attain and recall factual information. The true goal of education is to develop cognitive skills that will serve as the foundation for later learning and participation in society.

The development of our cognitive systems begins at birth and continues throughout adulthood. As a general concept, cognition can be described as the various forms of knowing: perceiving, remembering, imagining, conceiving, judging, and reasoning (Flavell, Miller, and Miller 2002; Goswami 2002; Kuhn 1988). Cognitive development involves maturation in many domains such as being able to think more abstractly and from multiple perspectives, to integrate knowledge about the world and abstract thought, to solve problems, to imagine, and to empathize.

As children and adults learn, they are organizing and reorganizing their cognitive system. They are learning how to logically reason about the world and people, for example, learning how one's thoughts and beliefs may differ from the thoughts and beliefs of those around them. They develop theories about many domains; for example, related to physics, they learn how things fall, how solids work, and how to figure the velocity and trajectory of flying balls. Many researchers view children as little scientists in that children are accumulating evidence about how the world works and how people interact and are using this evidence to construct theories, much like a scientist would do (Gopnik, Meltzoff, and Kuhl 1999). As children observe patterns of evidence, they formulate theories, and they test those theories on new evidence. If the new observation does not fit their theory, they modify the theory.

As children grow older, they become more adept as problem solvers. Older children view themselves as active, constructive agents, capable of selecting and transforming information (Kuhn 1989, 2000). Throughout the school years, children develop metacognitive skills as they gain a better understanding of the process of thinking and factors that influence it. They are more capable of cognitive self-regulation, the process of continuously monitoring progress toward a goal, checking outcomes, and redirecting unsuccessful efforts, which is a strong predictor of academic success (Joyner and Kurtz-Costes 1997; Zimmerman and Risemberg 1997). They become better able to recognize when they have not understood a message and to identify the source of their misunderstanding (Markman 1977, 1979).

Schools and classrooms provide a rich source of information to children so they can develop these theories and cognitive organizations. Basically, schools are complex social systems that surround children with interaction and modeling that are essential to cognitive development. Both adults and children use the social interaction that occurs among humans and the contexts of the interactions as raw material for cognitive development.

Within theories of education, many educators advocate a Vygotskian-inspired philosophy in which the child is not an independent discoverer of knowledge and theories (Kozulin 2003; Wertsch 1985a). A Vygotskian framework to education promotes assisted discovery in which both teachers and peers can guide a child's learning with explanations, demonstrations, and verbal prompts (Rogoff 1998; Vygotsky 1978; Wertsch and Tulviste 1992). The child's interactions with other individuals, both adults and children who are important to him or her, are central to the child's cognitive development. As stated by Vygotsky (1978), "Each function in the child's cultural development appears twice: first, on the social level, and later, on the individual level; first between people (interpsychological), and then inside the child (intrapsychological)" (57). Often, this philosophy of cognitive development is termed a sociocultural model because cognitive development occurs in the context of social discourse.

Participation in interactions with others is not the only factor that leads a child to construct knowledge and theories of how people and things operate. Language also plays a critical role in this framework (Bruner 1990; Nelson 1996; Wertsch 1985b). According to Nelson (1996), language serves the functions of medium, mediator, and tool of thought, which are all different. First, language is the medium of social interaction. It is the means by which humans interact with one another. It is also a medium of thought, carried out in terms of inner speech. Second, as a mediator, language provides us with categories, relationships, and genres that serve to organize our thinking. Third, as a tool, language is used to manipulate thought, reasoning, and knowledge systems.

Given this framework, cognitive development is the product of sociocultural interaction, mediated by language, in which language becomes a tool to shape and manipulate our thoughts. Deaf and hard of hearing children are capable of the same cognitive development as their typically developing peers. Although research shows that some deaf and hard of hearing children with hearing parents are delayed in aspects of abstract cognitive skills (de Villiers et al. 2000; Peterson and Siegal 1999a; Schick et al. 2000), this delay is because of delayed language skills and lack of access to fluent conversations, both of which occur for various reasons. Deaf and hard of hearing children who are acquiring sign language as an early first language from deaf parents who are fluent in signing exhibit cognitive development paralleling that of hearing children (Marschark 1993).

Cognitive development may be affected in deaf and hard of hearing children who access classroom interaction with hearing students and teachers by means of an interpreter. As Ramsey (1997) showed, providing a child with an interpreter does not provide him or her full access to the classroom. Ramsey followed three eight-year-old deaf children as they spent part of their educational day in a hearing classroom and part in a self-contained classroom with other children who were deaf and hard of hearing. Results of Ramsey's ethnographic study demonstrated that the deaf students were not genuine participants in the hearing classroom and that they seemed much less engaged in the hearing classroom than in the classroom where all the children and the teacher were deaf or hard of hearing. Their interactions with their hearing teacher and hearing peers seemed impoverished. In particular, their hearing peers were unable to sign much more than a few rudimentary signs. The hearing teacher reported that, because the children used an interpreter, an awkwardness affected interacting with the deaf children; she had to "make a concentrated effort" (Ramsey 1997, 59) to have the deaf children answer questions. The teacher felt disconnected from the children because their eye gaze and other behaviors indicated that they were engaged with the interpreter. Even though the teacher understood that the interpreter was simply translating her message, she acknowledged that she often interpreted the children's behavior to mean that they were not engaged in the class.

But probably just as important, some of the hearing children seemed to believe that their role was to help and discipline the deaf children, as if they were not in a peer-to-peer relationship but were apprentices of the teacher. Deaf students' interactions with their hearing peers appeared to be directly related to the context of the lessons or behavior expected in class. In short, the few hearing classmates who interacted with their deaf peers mostly just told them what they were doing wrong. In contrast, the deaf students' interactions with their deaf and hard of hearing peers within their self-contained classroom during part of the day included complex discussions about abstract thoughts, arguments and negotiations, and metalinguistic discussions. The deaf and hard of hearing children indicated that they did not identify with their hearing classmates; they were not friends with them.

In general, Ramsey's (1997) study shows that difficulties are inherent in providing an interpreted education, even with the best of intentions. Given these difficulties as well as the integral relationship among language, interaction with significant others in one's environment, and cognitive development, the challenge to explore potential areas where the use of an interpreter may affect domains of cognitive development becomes worthwhile.

## DEVELOPING A THEORY OF MIND: UNDERSTANDING THE PERSPECTIVE OF OTHERS

In recent years, a great deal of research has been done to find out how hearing children achieve major cognitive milestones that involve understanding how other people view the world. This research, and subsequent research conducted with children who are deaf and hard of hearing, has significant implications for learning within an interpreted setting.

## What Is a Theory of Mind?

As young children mature, they develop an understanding of themselves and other people as psychological beings who think, know, want, feel, and believe. They come to understand that what they think or believe may be different from what another person thinks and believes. They also learn that much of our behavior is motivated or caused by our knowledge and beliefs. These understandings form the basis of a Theory of Mind. The following story might best illustrate what is involved in Theory of Mind:

> Simon and his father made a cake together. But Simon wanted to go play and eat the cake later. So he put the cake in the cupboard. Then Simon left to play. The father thought that the icing on the cake might melt in the cupboard so he moved it to the refrigerator. Then the father left to go shopping. Later Simon came home and he wanted to eat his cake. Where will Simon look for the cake?

You probably responded that Simon would look for the cake in the cupboard. He had put it there, and he did not know that his father had moved it. Your answer shows that you have a Theory of Mind. You can distinguish between what you know and the false belief, based on faulty information, that Simon has.

Children at approximately the age of three, however, will answer this question incorrectly. They typically respond that the boy will look for the cake in the refrigerator because that is where it is. At this age, children have difficulty distinguishing what they know from what others know. They are aware that people have thoughts, but they do not realize that people's thoughts and beliefs can be different from their own.

Major changes happen in the child's understanding of other people's minds by approximately age four. At this age, children can distinguish what they know from what others know, and they can correctly predict that a person's behavior is dependent on what he or she thinks or knows, even when that belief is false. At the age of about four to five years, a child can correctly predict that Simon would look in the cupboard because that is where he left the cake.

Developmental psychologists call this cognitive ability a Theory of Mind because it shows that these children have an integrated set of concepts underlying their understanding of the mind (Astington 1993). This cognitive functioning is much the same as the methodical theories that children develop in areas such as physics and biology. Children develop an understanding that allows them to predict another person's behavior based on what they know about that person's thoughts and beliefs—just like you predicted that the boy would look for his cake in the cupboard. Like a scientific theory, which allows us to predict actions and interactions in our world, a Theory of Mind allows us to interpret and predict other people's actions by considering their thoughts, beliefs, desires, and emotions.

## Research on Development in Deaf and Hard of Hearing Children

Research has shown that deaf and hard of hearing children who have hearing parents have significant delays in their understanding of a Theory of Mind (de

Villiers et al. 2000; Peterson and Siegal 1999b; Rhys-Jones and Ellis 2000; Steeds, Rowe, and Dowker 1997). For example, a recent investigation of Theory of Mind skills in deaf children found that deaf children with deaf parents performed much like hearing children whereas the deaf children with hearing parents (both signing and oral) were significantly delayed in their understanding of a Theory of Mind (de Villiers et al. 2000; Schick et al. 2000). The study also revealed that the language skills in the deaf children were directly related to their Theory of Mind skills. However, what predicted Theory of Mind skills was not the children's general language skills but, rather, their vocabulary skills and their specific ability to comprehend syntactic complements. That is, if a child can understand sentences such as "He thought his cake was in the cupboard," then that child is more likely to understand and predict behavior premised on a false belief, like that of Simon in the story. Children who had more advanced language skills were far more likely to pass the Theory of Mind tasks.

What this finding means is that the language delays that are typically observed in children who are deaf and hard of hearing are causally related to delays in major aspects of cognitive development. Children who are not able to understand complex syntactic forms like complements have difficulty understanding how their own thoughts and beliefs may differ from those around them.

## Accessing the Classroom by Means of an Interpreter May Affect the Child's Development of a Theory of Mind

To express information critical to the development of a Theory of Mind, an interpreter needs to communicate (a) who is speaking, (b) the content of their message, (c) the register of their message, and (d) the communicative stance the speaker has. By receiving all of this information, not just the content, recipients build an understanding of the speaker's beliefs and understandings. Children build this understanding for all of their peers in the classroom and for adults. For example, we know which of our friends and colleagues are prone to exaggeration, a positive attitude, insightful thinking, or a humanistic outlook. We use this knowledge when we are listening and the context of any message includes our understanding of that individual's beliefs, emotions, and knowledge. For children who are still developing a Theory of Mind, if information with respect to speaker intention is missing or distorted, they may miss critical information to help build an understanding of how each mind and individual is different and how understanding someone's beliefs can help us predict behaviors and opinions.

Preliminary evidence indicates that interpreters have difficulty expressing the speaker's register and indicating who is speaking. In a sample of approximately 1,300 interpreters who have been evaluated using the Educational Interpreter Performance Assessment (EIPA) (Schick and Williams 2004), the ability to communicate prosodic aspects of the classroom discourse was difficult for all of the interpreters but particularly those interpreters who were evaluated for interpreting in the elementary school setting; this group scored significantly lower than those who were evaluated for a secondary setting, $F$ (1, 1303) = 6.13, $p$ = .027. The average prosody score was 2.8 for the elementary interpreters and 3.0 for the secondary interpreters. Ironically, elementary-aged deaf and hard of hearing children with hearing families, who are likely to be delayed in their Theory of Mind skills and who are still developing their understanding of how minds work, may have the least amount of information in the classroom interpretation to figure out register and identity of the speaker.

There are several areas where either the use of an interpreter or lack of skills on the part of the interpreter may affect the child's understanding of concepts related to a Theory of Mind. One aspect of all communication is that the speaker's intention may not be obvious from the form of a message. Often, a great deal of information about the speaker's intention, or stance, is communicated through register shifts, discourse markers, and prosodic changes. For example, a teacher might issue a warning to finish seatwork by saying, "It's getting close to reeeeceeesss," meaning "you may not get to go out if you don't finish." If the speaker's intention is obliterated because the interpreter failed to use the appropriate nonmanual devices, then the child could interpret this message literally as an indication that he or she should start looking forward to playing outside rather than as the true intention. The child who interprets this message literally but sees peers working harder could become confused by the resulting mixed message. Without a mature Theory of Mind, the child may not be able to realize this discrepancy, and without the linguistic clues in the interpreted message, the child may also lack the needed information to figure it out.

Another aspect where Theory of Mind may be related to the use of an interpreter is in the area of indicating shifts in who is speaking. The child may not be able to distinguish what information is coming from the teacher in relation to what the interpreter is signing. The concept that information is being processed by the interpreter but the teacher is the person who produces the message may be difficult to understand for young children, especially those with weak Theory of Mind skills. It is probable that young children with delayed language skills confuse these issues continuously. This possibility may be particularly likely because it is impossible for the child to maintain visual contact with both the interpreter and the teacher. In addition, many interpreters who work with young children may alter what the teacher actually says, which may further obliterate the chance to identify which part of the message is from the teacher and which part is from the interpreter. (This point is not meant to conclude that alteration is always incorrect.)

Finally, the possibility exists that interpreters do not fully include information that allows a deaf or hard of hearing child to learn about the personalities and beliefs of the hearing peers in a classroom, information that involves another aspect of Theory of Mind. We use what our peers say to learn about their personal tendencies, for example, whether a particular student tends to be humorous, off-topic, or insightful. When an interpreter does not fully represent who is speaking, the stance of the speaker, and other information often communicated through prosody, the incomplete representation will affect the deaf or hard of hearing child's understanding of his hearing peers as individuals with unique personalities. In addition, not getting this information distances the deaf or hard of hearing child from the collective class culture and may further impede the deaf or hard of hearing child's ability to develop close relationships with the children in the class. Children also use this information to generalize personality traits of friends, a process that is related to their own development of personality and self-esteem (Hartup 1996a, 1996b).

## THE EFFECT OF AUTHENTIC PEER INTERACTION

The fact that childhood friendships are an important part of socioemotional development and social cognition is widely known (Buklowski, Newcomb, and Hartup

1996; Hartup 1996a; Ladd 1990). But increasing evidence indicates that peer interaction, particularly with children who are considered friends, is important to cognitive development, problem solving, and learning in general. For example, research has shown that children conduct more extensive exploration of a new task with a friend than with a nonfriend. Their conversation is more vigorous and mutually oriented. Similarly, children who engage in exploration with a friend are likely to recall more than if exploration is conducted with a nonfriend (Newcomb and Bagwell 1996). Other research shows that children who were engaged in problem solving with friends were more likely to negotiate (rather than simply assert power), to collaborate and elaborate, to offer more suggestions, and to check results—all of which lead not only to better problem-solving results but also to better problem-solving skills (Hartup 1996a, 1996b). When children engaged in collaborative writing with friends, they wrote narratives that were rated higher than when writing with nonfriends. Specifically, their narratives show more evidence of motivating conditions and of solutions, and the texts contain fewer errors.

Rogoff (1990) maintains that "children may be freer to examine the logic of arguments with peers rather than adults" (174). In fact, older children may express more logical arguments with their peers than with their mothers, and their discussions about moral reasoning with peers may have a greater effect on their thinking than discussions with their mothers (Kruger 1993; Kruger and Tomasello 1986). In problem-solving tasks, children who benefited the most from peer interaction were those children who more frequently shared ideas about the logic of the tasks, focusing on solutions and strategies for dealing with the problem rather than focusing on one another's role or behavior. All of this research would indicate that engaging in collaborative and argumentative interactions that require verbal reasoning with peers can foster and support aspects of cognitive growth. However, cognitive growth involves more than simple engagement with peers. As Hartup (1996a, 1996b) notes, cognitive growth occurs, not simply because children interact with knowledgeable peers and adults; it also requires an emotional interdependency that constitutes "closeness" in relationships.

So evidence indicates that peer interaction, particularly with friends, enhances children's problem-solving skills, exploration, and recall. However, peer interaction is an area that is highly likely to be affected by the presence of an adult interpreter. Evidence shows that children will reduce their interaction when adult observers are present (Brody, Stoneman, and Wheatley 1984; Rogoff 1990). Peers are more likely to share their thinking with one another than with an adult. This fact is in direct conflict with the fact that an adult is present during interpreted peer conversations. We should expect that a deaf or hard of hearing child's interactions with peers may be less robust, engaging, and collaborative when an interpreter is present.

Evidence of this lack of quality interactions between deaf and hard of hearing elementary-aged children and their hearing classmates is found in the study by Ramsey (1997). She reported that the deaf and hard of hearing children's interactions with their hearing peers were mostly superficial and often focused on behavior regulation, for example, what the deaf and hard of hearing child should be doing that he or she was not. Research (Newcomb and Bagwell 1996; Hartup 1996a, 1996b; Kruger 1993) shows that the more abstract discussions, negotiations, and opinion-sharing collaborations are what influence cognitive skills in hearing children. Precisely this type of interaction is what was missing in the deaf and hard of hearing children's interactions with their hearing peers in Ramsey's study.

Other researchers have reported that deaf and hard of hearing students who are mainstreamed (a) show strong preferences for interacting with classmates who are also deaf or hard of hearing rather than with their hearing peers and (b) have limited participation in both school and social activities (Foster 1988; Foster and Brown 1989; Greenberg and Kusche 1987; Stinson and Whitmire 1992). The limited quantity and quality in peer interactions between the deaf or hard of hearing student and his or her hearing peers would likely affect more than the child's social development, perhaps also affecting the child's ability to learn collaboratively, to explore problems through discussion, and to engage in complex verbal reasoning. For adults, the ability to socialize effectively is highly related to well-being (Reis, Collins, and Berscheid 2000).

## THE EFFECT OF PEER-TO-PEER ARGUMENTATION AND CONFLICT

According to both Vygotskian and Piagetian theory, cognitive conflict is a positive event in that it can cause cognitive growth in the understanding of complex problems (Rogoff 1990). Piaget believed that, when children of equal status have different beliefs about a problem, the peer interaction can cause children to change their cognitive theories and beliefs. Arguments can be positive rather than negative from a cognitive perspective (Miller 1987). Arguments are basically discussions of divergent understanding in which participants have to resolve what is being talked about before they can proceed. At least three aspects of argumentation benefit children. First is the obvious cognitive growth involved in considering one's own theory in relationship with a peer's, which may result in either strengthening or changing an established theory. Second is a developmental progression involving how well children justify their viewpoints, what are valid points to make, and what is a convincing logical sequence of facts, all of which require both cognitive and linguistic skills. Third, true argumentation, by definition, requires perspective taking, an aspect of Theory of Mind. To argue persuasively, a child must consider the viewpoints of all participants to know what types of arguments would be persuasive.

However, research has focused on arguments between peers of relatively equal social status. Teachers and other adults bring an authority to arguments that can overwhelm a child's sense of what is right or wrong. Probably as important, little evidence indicates that teachers engage children in arguments or even reasoned discussions. Kuhn (1991) notes that students are rarely asked either to develop reasoned arguments to justify a position or to coordinate arguments and counterarguments. She speculates that, most likely, argumentation is more prominent in the out-of-classroom lives of students (and adults). With peers, children can engage in true reasoned arguments about issues and concepts that are meaningful and current in their lives.

The likelihood is that hearing peers will avoid argumentation when an adult is present, in particular, when interacting with a deaf or hard of hearing peer by means of an educational interpreter. Adults give children the message that they should avoid arguments rather than help those children develop argumentation skills. Because of these factors, the deaf or hard of hearing child may experience very little or limited argumentation during development, especially because teachers rarely appear to use argumentation as a method of instruction. So deaf or hard of hearing children may miss argumentation in the classroom and on the playground; moreover, given the sign language skills of many hearing parents, they may also miss it at home. The child would not only miss the benefits to the development of cognition but also would most likely not develop the special discourse skills needed to successfully argue (Grimshaw 1990; Pieraut-Le Bonniec and Valette 1991).

## LEARNING IN THE CLASSROOM: SCAFFOLDING AND APPRENTICESHIP

An important feature of how adults interact with children to support learning is the function of scaffolding (Bruner 1983; Wood 1989). When an individual scaffolds learning during interaction, he or she adjusts the assistance provided to fit the child's current level of performance. As the child gains knowledge of the task or concept, the adult gradually, and often unconsciously, withdraws support, turning over more responsibility to the child. The most effective scaffolding occurs in the Zone of Proximal Development, a term coined by Vygotsky (1978), which refers to a range of tasks that the child cannot yet handle alone but can accomplish with the help of more skilled partners. Adults often break a task into more manageable units or concepts to scaffold a child's learning. Even when adults are not directly teaching, they often guide participation in a cooperative dialogue (Rogoff 1990, 1998). To guide in this way, adults often adjust their language for a younger learner, but the adult selects activities and materials, the context of learning, and other arrangements of the learning environment. As Rogoff observes, guided participation occurs in all cultures; adults all over the world, in literate and preliterate societies, make arrangements for children's learning and revise the children's responsibilities as they gain skill and knowledge. Evidence shows that this fine-tuned support is related to advances in cognitive development.

However, children who are deaf or hard of hearing may not have language or cognitive skills at the same level as that of their hearing peers. Given this possibility, the Zone of Proximal Development for a deaf or hard of hearing child and that for a hearing child in the same classroom may be very different. What would be appropriate scaffolding and guided participation for a hearing child at any point in development may not scaffold the deaf or hard of hearing child's learning. The deaf or hard of hearing child may need interaction and teaching that is more fine-tuned to his or her level of skills and understanding.

Yet teaching approaches basically assume that all the children in a classroom are within a reasonable range of developmental skills. Although this assumption is probably not valid even for the hearing children in the classroom, it is the foundation of our educational system. Given this context, some deaf or hard of hearing children are likely receiving scaffolding that is not well adjusted to their level of skills. Even if the educational team recognizes that the level of instruction is inappropriate for the deaf or hard of hearing child, the educational interpreter often does not have the training to modify the language and content to scaffold that particular child's learning. Interestingly, many advocate that educational interpreters adopt a model of interpreting that was developed by interpreters who work in the adult community where the gold standard is to represent everything the teacher and classmates say. But from an education perspective, it might make more sense to train the interpreter so he or she is capable of working as a member of the educational team to determine and deliver the kinds of modifications that may help the child learn.

Ironically, some evidence shows that communication problems on the deaf or hard of hearing child's part increase the teacher's tendency to control the discourse even more. Wood (1989) found that, when a deaf and hard of hearing child failed to respond appropriately to a teacher's question, the teacher assumed more control of the discourse, further inhibiting responses from the child. Wood describes this process as a spiral of increasing control that consequently inhibits responses from the child. For a child with an interpreter, a question or lesson that is not appropriately adjusted to that child's level may serve to reduce his or her participation or increase feelings of inadequacy.

## THE IMPLICATIONS WHEN THE INTERPRETED MESSAGE DOES NOT REFLECT THE CLASSROOM CONTENT

Although the expectation that the content of the classroom will be interpreted with 100 percent message equivalency is probably theoretically impossible, even with the most skillful interpreters, in most situations, that goal is certainly pursued. Although many interpreters within the larger pool have the skills to provide the highest possible access, many of the working educational interpreters omit and distort large amounts of the classroom discussion. Using the Educational Interpreter Performance Assessment (EIPA), Schick, Williams, and Bolster (2000) evaluated 59 educational interpreters who were currently working in the public schools and who either volunteered to be evaluated or were volunteered by their school district. They found that more than one-half of the interpreters were not able to meet the minimum standards established in the state of Colorado (3.5 on a 5.0 scale). Roughly speaking, a level 3 on the EIPA means that the interpreter is communicating approximately 65 percent to 70 percent of the information. Because specific skills are averaged over a range of skills, an interpreter scoring at a level 3.5 might score below this level in certain areas. In fact, Schick, Williams, and Bolster found that, as a group, the interpreters were significantly better in their sign vocabulary skills than in their grammatical skills or their overall ability to communicate the whole message. Data that Schick and Williams have collected from other states indicate that Colorado is not unique; educational interpreters in all states vary in terms of skills, and many cannot meet what many states consider to be a minimum skill level.

People often discuss the implications of the fact that some educational interpreters are not qualified in terms of how this fact affects the child's learning. But in all probability, the child's cognitive development is affected, too. Interpreters who produce a message that is missing parts of the original message are not typically making principled omissions. That is, many interpreters are not making decisions that will preserve the most important information for the lesson. In addition, information is not just missing; it is also distorted, confused, and sometimes just wrong. The result can be a message that is poorly structured, that is missing major discourse elements, and that contains skewed and distorted facts. This corrupted information then becomes the children's raw material for organizing and developing their cognitive concepts and structures.

A few examples may illustrate this concept. In a lesson that was being interpreted, a teacher announced to the class, "Today, we are discussing mammals, *not* fish or insects." However, the interpreter failed to indicate the phrasal boundary by using prosody to represent the "fish *or* insects" or to emphasize the word *not* prosodically. The interpreted message communicated something more like, "Today, we are discussing mammals not fish-insects." For the hearing children, the teacher's language helped them realize that mammals were but one form of animal life, emphasizing at least three categories: mammals, fish, insects. For the deaf or hard of hearing child, the message communicated that mammals are not fish-insects. The message still communicates the sense of two categories, mammals and something called "fish-insects," but the emphasis is very different. In addition, the message creates confusion about what exactly are "fish-insects." So the information the child now has received to establish a cognitive representation for the lesson is already very different.

Research shows that hearing children are slow to develop the skills needed to recognize when a message is not clear; even hearing 12-year-olds miss obvious inconsistencies (Markman 1977, 1979). So it is unlikely that many elementary-aged deaf or hard of hearing children will be able to recognize unintelligible or distorted concepts. In addition, the child has to use cognitive processing and resources to think about what those "fish-insects" are. Older children may have the metacognitive skills to decide that the interpreter made an error, but that ability also takes cognitive resources. Any time or cognitive resources a child spends thinking about the information that is wrong or confused is time that cannot be spent organizing and thinking about the topic.

The example clearly shows that errors in interpreting affect the child's factual knowledge, and perhaps more important, they affect a child's cognitive structures and processing. They may cause a child to organize a concept in a completely incorrect or inefficient way that directly reduces what we call learning. Then, all new information about the topic is organized using this incorrect or ineffective cognitive structure. Consequently, the child may directly translate interpreting "errors" into poorly organized and badly structured cognitive representations.

## SUMMARY AND CONCLUSIONS

Even when an interpreter is highly skilled and has a good professional relationship with the regular classroom teacher, a deaf or hard of hearing child's education by means of an interpreter is different. A student's access to the classroom discourse and authentic peer interactions and friendships is highly relevant to the development of thinking skills. Access is not just about what the teacher says.

Many professionals have voiced concerns about the potential detrimental effect of these differences on a deaf or hard of hearing child's social development and self-image. However, learning through an interpreted education also may affect a child's cognitive development. A child's development of a Theory of Mind may be affected, especially if the interpreter has difficulty representing register shifts or indicating who is speaking. Without this information, the child has limited data to build an understanding of how other people's minds work or of personal tendencies in teachers and classmates. A child who can access conversations with peers only by using an interpreter may have reduced opportunities to engage in authentic, rich discussions and debate with peers. These kinds of experiences are essential for cognitive development for any child or youth. Also, deaf or hard of hearing children may have difficulty developing close friendships with their hearing classmates, which also can affect the quality of discussions and, ultimately, learning. These potential differences in learning may occur even when the interpreter is highly skilled, which we know is typically not the situation in educational interpreting.

When the interpreter is unable to provide the child access to the classroom content, the information the child receives may distort, negate, or even change concepts. Then the child is faced with the task of trying to determine the real information or concept, which requires a great deal more metacognitive processing than is required by his or her hearing peers.

How can a school ensure classroom access for students who are deaf or hard of hearing? First, recognize that providing access to an educational program means more than providing an interpreter. The educational interpreter cannot make this complex integration happen without help from the deaf educator and the regular classroom teacher. Educational interpreters do not have the training to conduct the kinds of assessments that are necessary to determine the success of the placement. However, educational interpreters can provide critical observations about the student. Each member of the educational team contributes a unique perspective and expertise. Of course, the educational interpreter should also be trained to be a true member of the educational team, which requires knowing more about the learning process than how to interpret. Providing access also involves schools ensuring that the regular classroom teacher strives to make the deaf or hard of hearing student an active participant. It is difficult for an interpreter to "fix" a classroom where the teacher does not have a connection with the deaf or hard of hearing student. The regular classroom teacher should also receive information about what kinds of learning are difficult when a child is using an interpreter.

Second, the educational team should focus on the extent to which the student who is deaf or hard of hearing is truly integrated into the classroom and is learning. The team should base their judgments of the success of this placement on real observations and assessments of learning. Collaborating with the interpreter as a team member, the team should discuss how much the student is included in class participation, how much the student is a respected team member in group projects, and how much the student seems connected with the cognitive life of the classroom. The team should gather evidence of learning. Research shows that children have more difficulty learning with an interpreter than from a teacher who signs, even when the interpreter is highly skilled (Kurz 2004). If a student is having difficulty learning basic facts and concepts using an interpreter, then likely, many aspects of classroom discourse are also not being learned.

Third, all educational interpreters must be qualified to provide access according to external standards. Schools should employ only interpreters who have skills that meet some external standard (e.g., EIPA > 4.0 or RID-certified). A deaf or hard of hearing student's learning challenge is formidable, even with a highly qualified interpreter. In addition, when a deaf or hard of hearing student is not making adequate progress, schools should not assume that the student is the source of the problem. Schools should also consider that the student may not have sufficient access to the classroom content because of the interpreter's limited qualifications.

In summary, many aspects of classroom discourse are essential for children to learn. We should look beyond the provided services of a qualified interpreter to consider how well a student can learn and participate in a particular educational setting. In addition, because peer and friend relationships, class participation, and engagement in learning is essential for all students, we should focus on these elements when assessing the success of an interpreted education placement. Schools need to ensure that students who learn through educational interpreters are active participants in the cognitive life of the classroom. Ensuring this participation is not the educational interpreter's responsibility; rather, all members of the educational team should work to make this engagement happen. Anything less compromises learning and cognitive development, essential goals of education.

## REFERENCES


Astington, J. W. 1993. *The child's discovery of the mind.* Cambridge, Mass.: Harvard University Press.

Brody, G. H., Z. Stoneman, and P. Wheatley. 1984. Peer interaction in the presence and absence of observers. *Child Development* 55(4):1425–28.

Bruner, J. S. 1983. *Child's talk: Learning to use language.* Oxford, U.K.: Oxford University Press.

———. 1990. *Acts of meaning.* Cambridge, Mass.: Harvard University Press.

Buklowski, W. M., A. F. Newcomb, and W. W. Hartup. 1996. *The company they keep: Friendships in childhood and adolescence.* Cambridge, U.K.: Cambridge University Press.

de Villiers, P., J. de Villiers, B. Schick, and R. Hoffmeister. 2000. Theory of mind development in signing and non-signing Deaf children: The impact of sign language on social-cognition. Paper presented at the Seventh International Conference on Theoretical Issues in Sign Language Research, Amsterdam, The Netherlands.

Flavell, J. H., P. H. Miller, and S. A. Miller. 2002. *Cognitive development.* Upper Saddle River, N.J.: Prentice Hall.

Foster, S. 1988. Life in the mainstream: Reflections of deaf college freshmen on their experiences in the mainstreamed high school. *Journal of the American Deafness & Rehabilitation Association* 22(2):27–35.

Foster, S., and P. Brown. 1989. Factors influencing the academic and social integration of hearing impaired college students. *Journal of Post Secondary Education and Disability* 7:78–96.

Gopnik, A., A. N. Meltzoff, and P. K. Kuhl. 1999. *The scientist in the crib: What early learning tells us about the mind.* New York: Perennial.

Goswami, U., ed. 2002. *Blackwell handbook of childhood cognitive development.* Malden, Mass.: Blackwell.

Greenberg, M. T., and C. A. Kusche. 1987. Cognitive, personal, and social development of deaf children and adolescents. In *Handbook of special education: Research and practice.* Vol. 3, *Low incidence conditions,* ed. M. C. Wang, M. C. Reynolds, and H. J. Walberg, 95–129. New York: Pergamon.

Grimshaw, A., ed. 1990. *Conflict talk: Sociolinguistic investigations of arguments in conversation.* Cambridge, U.K.: Cambridge University Press.

Hartup, W. W. 1996a. The company they keep: Friendships and their developmental significance. *Child Development* 67(1):1–13.

———. 1996b. Cooperation, close relationships, and cognitive development. In *The company they keep: Friendships in childhood and adolescence,* eds. W. M. Buklowski, A. F. Newcomb, and W. W. Hartup. Cambridge, U.K.: Cambridge University Press.

Joyner, M. H., and B. Kurtz-Costes. 1997. Metamemory development. In *Memory performance and competencies: Issues in growth and development,* eds. W. Schneider and F. E. Weinert, 275–300. Hillsdale, N.J.: Erlbaum.

Kluwin, T. N., D. S. Moore, and M. G. Gaustad. 1992. *Toward effective public school programs for deaf students: Context, process, and outcomes*. New York: Teacher's College.

Kozulin, A. 2003. *Vygotsky's educational theory in cultural context*. New York: Cambridge University Press.

Kruger, A. C. 1993. Peer collaboration: Conflict, cooperation, or both? *Social Development* 2(3):165–82.

Kruger, A. C., and M. Tomasello. 1986. Transactive discussions with peers and adults. *Developmental Psychology* 22(5):681–85.

Kuhn, D. 1988. Cognitive development. In *Developmental psychology: An advanced textbook*, 2d ed., eds. M. Bornstein and M. Lamb. Hillsdale, N.J.: Erlbaum.

———. 1989. Children and adults as intuitive scientists. *Psychological Review* 96(5):674–89.

———. 1991. *The skills of argument*. Cambridge, U.K.: Cambridge University Press.

———. 2000. Theory of mind, metacognition, and reasoning: A life-span perspective. In *Children's reasoning and the mind*, eds. P. Mitchell and K. J. Riggs. Hove, U.K.: Psychology Press.

Kurz, K. B. 2004. A comparison of deaf children's learning in direct communication versus an interpreted environment. Ph.D. dissertation, University of Kansas, Lawrence.

Ladd, G. W. 1990. Having friends, keeping friends, making friends, and being liked by peers in the classroom: Predictors of children's early school adjustment? *Child Development* 61:1081–1100.

Markman, E. M. 1977. Realizing that you don't understand: A preliminary investigation. *Child Development* 48(3):986–92.

———. 1979. Realizing that you don't understand: Elementary school children's awareness of inconsistencies. *Child Development* 50(3):643–55.

Marschark, M. 1993. *Psychological development in deaf children*. New York: Oxford University Press.

Miller, M. 1987. Argumentation and cognition. In *Social and functional approaches to language and thought*, ed. M. Hickman, 225–49. San Diego, Calif.: Academic Press.

Nelson, K. 1996. *Language in cognitive development: The emergence of the mediated mind*. Cambridge, U.K.: Cambridge University Press.

Newcomb, A. F., and C. Bagwell. 1996. The developmental significance of children's friendship relations. In *The company they keep: Friendship in childhood and adolescence*, eds. W. M. Buklowski, A. F. Newcomb, and W. W. Hartup. Cambridge, U.K.: Cambridge University Press.

Peterson, C. C., and M. Siegal 1999a. Deafness, conversation, and theory of mind. *Journal of Child Psychology and Psychiatry* 36:459–74.

———. 1999b. Representing inner worlds: Theory of mind in autistic, deaf, and normal-hearing children. *Psychological Science* 10(2):126–29.

Pieraut-Le Bonniec, G., and M. Valette. 1991. The development of argumentative discourse. In *Language bases to discourse basics*, eds. G. Pieraut-Le Bonniec and M. Dolitsky, 245–67. Amsterdam: Benjamins.

Ramsey, C. L. 1997. *Deaf children in public schools: Placement, context, and consequences*. Washington, D.C.: Gallaudet University Press.

Reis, H. T., W. A. Collins, and E. Berscheid. 2000. The relationship context of human behavior and development. *Psychological Bulletin* 126(6): 844–72.

Rhys-Jones, S. L., and H. D. Ellis. 2000. Theory of mind: Deaf and hearing children's comprehension of picture stories and judgments of social situations. *Journal of Deaf Studies and Deaf Education* 5(3): 248–65.

Rogoff, B. 1990. *Apprenticeship in thinking*. Oxford, U.K.: Oxford University Press.

———. 1998. Cognition as a collaborative process. In *Handbook of child psychology.* Vol. 2, *Cognition, perception, and language,* 5th ed., eds. D. Kuhn and R. S. Siegler, 679–744. New York: Wiley.

Schick, B., R. Hoffmeister, P. de Villiers, and J. de Villiers. 2000. American Sign Language and Theory of Mind in deaf children with deaf or hearing parents. Paper presented at the Seventh International Conference on Theoretical Issues in Sign Language Research, Amsterdam, The Netherlands.

Schick, B., and K. Williams. 2004. The Educational Interpreter Performance Assessment: What are children receiving? Paper presented at the Office of Education Personnel Preparation Conference, March 24, Washington, D.C.

Schick, B., K. Williams, and L. Bolster. 2000. Skill levels of educational interpreters working in the public schools. *Journal of Deaf Studies and Deaf Education* 4(2):144–55.

Steeds, L., K. Rowe, and A. Dowker. 1997. Deaf children's understanding of beliefs and desires. *Journal of Deaf Studies and Deaf Education* 2(3):185–95.

Stinson, M. S., and K. Whitmire 1992. Students' views of their social relationships. In *Toward effective public school programs for deaf students: Context, process, and outcome,* eds. T. N. Kluwin, D. F. Moores, and M. G. Gaustad, 149–74. New York: Teachers College Press.

Vygotsky, L. S. 1978. *Mind in society: The development of higher psychological processes.* Cambridge, Mass.: Harvard University Press.

Wertsch, J. V. 1985a. *Vygotsky and the social formation of the mind.* Cambridge, Mass.: Harvard University Press.

———, ed. 1985b. *Culture, communication, and cognition: Vygotskian perspectives.* New York: Cambridge University Press.

Wertsch, J. V., and P. Tulviste. 1992. L. S. Vygotsky and contemporary developmental psychology. *Developmental Psychology* 28(4):548–57.

Wood, D. 1989. Social interaction as tutoring. In *Interaction in human development,* eds. M. Bornstein and J. S. Bruner. Hillsdale, N.J.: Erlbaum.

Zimmerman, M. A., and R. Risemberg. 1997. Self-regulatory dimensions of academic learning and motivation. In *Handbook of academic learning: Construction of knowledge,* ed. G. D. Phye, 105–25. San Diego, Calif.: Academic Press.

Part 2

# Interpreting and Interpreters

# Perspectives on Educational Interpreting from Educational Anthropology and an Internet Discussion Group

Elizabeth Caldwell Langer

Between being relatively new to the school setting and serving a low-incidence population, many interpreters in school settings are facing virtually uncharted territory. With expectations as ambiguous as they are varied and with roles poorly defined, interpreters—and the students and teachers with whom they work—are often left without a template for responding to the day-to-day circumstances they face.

The purposes of this chapter are twofold and intertwined. The first purpose of this study is to investigate issues raised by interpreters, in this case, by means of an Internet discussion group. Information was gathered from the group's archives and from interviews with its participants to gain insight into three of the most passionately discussed issues raised on the subscriber list. Specifically, list archives were consulted and participants were queried to collect interpreters' views and experiences related to (a) identity and role formation for educational interpreters in schools today; (b) communication breakdown between teachers and interpreters; and (c) control of bodies and spaces in classroom settings. After discussing these issues, the participant interpreters offered suggestions for implementing improvements. Of course, the information in this chapter can neither represent the views of all interpreters nor present solutions that will work in all situations. The hope is that it will offer a glimpse at the perspectives of educational interpreters, that it will provide a look at some of the situations they face, and that it might serve as a springboard for further discussion. This chapter addresses the perspectives of the participant interpreters, but not of the teachers with whom they work. Another study addressing teacher perspectives about these issues would also greatly benefit this discussion.

The author would like to express gratitude to the moderators and participants of the Internet discussion list for K–12 educational interpreters. Without their volunteered time and critical insights, this chapter would not have been possible.

The second purpose of this study is to investigate this online venue as a means for providing educational interpreters with new lines of communication. An Internet discussion group is one place where issues can be discussed in a candid, potentially anonymous, straightforward way. This study investigates what members gain from participation in an online discussion list particular to their occupation. Participants were asked what purposes the list serves, why they believe there is a need for a list of this kind for educational interpreters, and what they see as the advantages and disadvantages to meeting online.

Clearly, the Internet has become a popular forum for social interaction and information exchange. Barnes (2001) reports that more than 70,000 discussion groups operate on the Internet. The first moderator and creator of the list that was studied for this chapter started his group to fill a perceived need in the interpreting community. When he started the list five years ago, other Internet discussion groups related to interpreting were already operating, but he thought they were best suited for interpreters working in community settings, typically working with adults. Given the unique issues that arise when working with students in school settings that range from kindergarten through high school, he felt educational interpreters might benefit from a list of their own. The group now includes more than 350 members. In four years, the site has accumulated more than 8,000 postings in its archives. (The list has existed for more than five years, but only the last four years are currently archived.) The members posted an average of ninety messages per month in 2002.

Averaging across two randomly selected months from two recent years, discussions can be classified into four basic types. Thirty-five percent of the discussions involved information exchange (e.g., discussion of signs, facts about the field, job openings); another 35 percent pertained to issues and opinions related to interpreting (e.g., views about sign languages versus sign systems, suggestions for dealing with child behaviors, ethical discussions, and questions about job definitions); 15 percent of the discussions were written for fun, social-emotional support, or both; and a final 15 percent involved logistical issues related to the site or clarification of earlier messages posted to the list.

## METHODOLOGY

This author read five months of postings at the end of 2002 and postings from three randomly selected months from previous years. This reading brought to light insights about the group itself as well as insights about three major issues facing educational interpreters today. Next, nineteen interviews were conducted with educational interpreters on the discussion list to verify and extend the perceptions made by this author in reading the postings. Participants were recruited by means of responses to a posting on the discussion list.

### Participants

Participants include those who were interviewed and those who entered into discussions on the list within the time periods included in the archive analyses. Twenty-five discussion list members responded to the posting requesting participant interviews for this study. Nineteen of them completed the interview. Two of these respondents are the list moderators; for this study, however, they are referred to as participants to maintain confidentiality.

The interviewees represented great diversity in interpreting experience and in length of time as members of the discussion list. On average, the participants had worked as educational interpreters for 8.8 years, with a standard deviation of 5.7 years. The minimum number of years of educational interpreting was 1.5 and the maximum was twenty. The average number of years on the list was 2.5, with a standard deviation of 1.6. Some had been on the list since its inception (approximately five years), and some had been a part of it for only six months. The majority were working mainly with students in kindergarten through high school, though some either had worked previously with or were working concurrently with preschool students, college students, or both. Most reported serving students in a variety of grades throughout their careers. Fifteen percent had at some point worked in preschool settings; 79 percent, in elementary schools; 90 percent, in middle schools; 90 percent, in high schools; and 42 percent, at the college or graduate school level.

### Procedures

Each participant chose a preferred mode of communication for the interviews. One participant responded to questions by fax, two were interviewed over the phone, and the rest of the participants responded to questions by e-mail attachment. All sent signed consent forms to the author by postal mail or fax. Phone interviews lasted approximately sixty minutes. Written interviews ranged from three to five single-spaced pages. First, participants were asked general questions about their interpreting backgrounds and number of years on the list. Next, participants were asked twenty-two questions divided into two sections. The initial eleven questions related to the discussion list itself, focusing on what the members gain from participation on the list. The remaining eleven questions pertained to issues that surfaced frequently on the discussion list. The questions were written to further probe issues that arose in the list's archives. These interview questions often recapped list dialogue and then requested related commentary. See the appendix to this chapter for the full list of interview questions.

## THE ISSUES

This section addresses three main issues that were repeatedly and passionately discussed not only on the Internet list but also by its subscribers in the interviews for this chapter. These three issues are (a) identity and role formation, (b) communication breakdowns, and (c) control over bodies and space in the classroom.

### Interpreter Identities within Schools

On the discussion list, interpreters talk frequently about their roles as professionals. In Interpreter Preparation Programs (IPPs), list interpreters said that they are often told to act as professionals. In community settings, interpreters reported that they are seen as professionals. In school settings, however, interpreters reported that they do not always sense that they are seen as professionals. Instead, some said they sense that their roles are misunderstood, at times leading to a reduction in status.

Educational anthropologist Mehan (2000) suggests that "there is often a competition over the correct, appropriate, or preferred way of representing objects, events, or people" (259). He exemplifies this competition with a discussion of the various ways nonresident workers can be represented—some of which reduce the power and status of the individual so labeled. In a similar way, many interpreters reported that, at times, they are represented in the schools in ways that negatively affect status, respect, prestige, and power. A survey conducted by Taylor and Elliott (1994) highlighted some of the discrepancies between mainstream teachers' and interpreters' views of the roles of interpreters. Teachers tended to see interpreters' responsibilities as including duties often relegated to aides. For example, a majority of teachers believed interpreters should serve as not only as interpreters but also as tutors and note-takers. Only a small minority of interpreters agreed. According to 84 percent of the interpreters interviewed for the current study, treatment of interpreters can be negatively affected when teachers misunderstand interpreters' roles and mislabel them.

Mehan (2000) discusses various ways in which people engage in the "politics of representation"—trying to order what they find on horizontal planes into vertical hierarchies. Whether or not it is deliberate, interpreters reported that some teachers and administrators refer to them as "aides," "assistants," "helpers," and "signers," suggesting that they may misunderstand interpreters' roles and responsibilities. According to the participants in this study, these representations that are found in the language of teachers and administrators become "social facts" produced from what Mehan refers to as the "ambiguity of everyday life" (260).

Mehan (2000) explains that he is concerned with "the ways in which the stable and enduring features of our everyday world are assembled through historical processes and in concrete social settings" (261). In his chapter, he describes the way students earn the label "Learning Disabled." He demonstrates how this process is not objective and does not seek information equally from all concerned adults. Routine bureaucratic practices conducted by means of written and oral social interactions (initial referral, standardized testing, and team meetings) lead to a child's school identity. This identity then opens or closes educational options for the student.

In the case of interpreters, we see that, historically, either educational interpreters were nonexistent or those performing the task of interpreting in educational settings were parents or friends of the deaf child. Later, aides were often asked to try to help deaf children in hearing classrooms, and sometimes, this help involved signing with them. More recently, interpreter training and standards for interpreters have improved. In many cases, however, school terminology has not caught up with these changes in the field of interpreting.

Mehan (2000) discusses the ways these social facts can constrain immediate social situations. Many interpreters who are frequently referred to as paraprofessionals reported that they are not invited to conferences about the child; they are asked to perform the duties of aides, disciplinarians, tutors, lunch monitors, and janitors; they are not informed about lesson plans (so cannot prepare adequately); they are asked to complete students' work; they are reprimanded if "their" students are late or have not completed their work; and their contracts are often the same ones used for custodians and aides. Mehan writes about "mutually constitutive relationships" between thought, discourse, and action. Some list interpreters reported that sometimes when interpreters are both thought of as aides and called aides, they are then asked to perform the duties of aides. Although the participant interpreters clarified that aides play an important role in school settings and hold an important set of skills, many interpreters highlighted the need for a clear distinction between the roles of interpreters and the roles of aides.

According to Barnes (2001), an important part of a person's acquiring and sustaining an identity is finding others to confer the identity that the person would like to hold. She states that our interactions with others are important partly because they help us more clearly define ourselves. Communication with others evokes a response to our own statement of who we are. For people to be identified as teachers, others around them must act as their students. In the case of educational interpreters, many on the list reported that, for them to identify themselves as professionals, they need, among other things, to have those around them treat them as professionals. On the list, educational interpreters discuss various ways to encourage teachers to treat interpreters as professionals. At the same time, their obvious acknowledgment of one another as professionals seems to allow them to feel more assured (at least while on the list) that they are, in fact, professionals.

According to Eisenhart (1997), another educational anthropologist, an important part of being a professional is an ongoing drive to improve. She makes the suggestion that "building or claiming an identity for self in a given context is what motivates an individual to become more expert; that developing a sense of oneself as an actor in a context is what compels a person to desire and pursue increasing mastery of the skills, knowledge and emotions associated with a particular social practice" (370). One can imagine that, for interpreters, the need to build a professional identity is not merely engendered by a desire to adhere to their job descriptions. Given their specific set of skills and responsibilities, they also may need to feel a sense of themselves as experts.

Before delving into speculations about teachers' motives for using labels such as "aide" in referring to interpreters, some participants wanted to clarify four points. First, they do not lump all teachers together. As one interpreter put it, "Teachers are human. Some are stubborn; some are pretty ignorant; many are terrific." Second, the participants clarified that this discussion is not to denigrate aides but, rather, to make clear the differences between the roles and responsibilities of aides and interpreters. One interpreter felt strongly about making this difference clear. "I have incredible respect for what [aides] do," she said. "I don't want to get into the comparison that we are professionals and aides are not. However, having said that, I think it is important to the profession that people clearly understand what we do and what we do not do and why. . . . [O]thers need to understand our roles and our autonomy." Third, many interpreters understand that teachers may confuse the two occupations because many in this group either used to serve both roles or still do serve both functions. Finally, interpreters said that sometimes the blame falls back on them for not clearly clarifying their roles and needs from the outset. Nearly all interpreters made mention of the need to start the year by clearly communicating about their roles and needs and then to continue to remind teachers of these roles and needs periodically thereafter. After all, one interpreter explained, "They're probably thinking anyone brought into a classroom other than the teacher is the teacher's helper. Mainstreaming is a fairly new concept and has been dumped on teachers without any training." It could also be that teachers just honestly forget. "Our job is not at the forefront of the teachers' minds," explained one interpreter. "So they easily forget how we need to do things." Another interpreter sympathized by saying, simply, "Old habits die hard."

Having clarified these points, many interpreters expressed concern about some teachers' continued use of labels such as "helper," even after multiple reminders that they are "interpreters." Some interpreters pointed out that teachers are overburdened, and regardless of formal roles and responsibilities, teachers just need a helping hand. Some suggested that, because of that overload, wishful thinking might lead to the use of the term "aide" in referring to interpreters. Some interpreters said that they believe it is interpreters' lack of higher levels of formal education that leads teachers to see them as aides. One interpreter lamented, "Sometimes when teachers discover that an interpreter does not have a teaching degree, communication stops totally!" On the reverse side, an interpreter with an education degree said that once teachers know of her background in education, they tend to be far more willing to share their lesson plans and make her part of the team.

More than half of the respondents believed that the use of these labels may come from teachers' negative feelings about having interpreters in the room. A quarter of the respondents used the word *threatened* to describe how they think some teachers feel about having another adult, or another professional, in the room. "Maybe if teachers acknowledge another professional in the room, it feels threatening," explained one interpreter. "Sometimes when you first introduce yourself and explain that you will be there all day, every day, all year long, teachers freak out. Some walk out and come back with the principal." One interpreter views it as a combination of intimidation and need for control. "Some teachers have control issues," she said. "They either feel threatened by the interpreter or they feel intimidated by the inability to communicate with the deaf students. This can cause some teachers to be stubborn."

Finally, some respondents mentioned issues related to the field of interpreting that might lead to the continued use of labels other than "interpreter." Some mentioned the lack of consistency from one interpreter to the next—some serving as aides, others not. A highly experienced interpreter said that, until interpreters see themselves as professionals, they may not be able to convince anyone else that they are professionals. "We are looked on by [our national organization] as being lesser interpreters, so we may look upon ourselves that way," she said. "But you are working with the future of the deaf community; you have a large impact on children's lives. I feel I worked my way *up* to kindergarten. The younger the child, the larger the impact you can have." Others echoed this comment, agreeing that interpreters first need to fully convince themselves that they are important team members and professionals, and then others will be more likely to see them as such. "As a profession we are still trying to figure out who we are," said one interpreter. "So we can't yet explain it well enough for it to stick."

Regardless of why some teachers continue to refer to interpreters with labels other than "interpreter," when it happens, interpreters reported feeling "misrepresented" and "misunderstood." Many also said that they feel "degraded," "demeaned," "devalued," "unimportant," "unskilled," and "disempowered." They also described feeling less like team members. "Even if it is not meant to demean the interpreter," explained one respondent, "many interpreters will be negatively affected by it." Many interpreters mentioned that, beyond demeaning interpreters in the school setting, these terms also misrepresent the profession as a whole.

Eighty-four percent of respondents agreed (many of them with exclamations) that the use of these terms probably leads to undesirable treatment of interpreters.

"If the interpreter is seen as an aide, he or she will be treated as an aide," stated one respondent. With teachers, this perception can lead to lack of access to lesson plans and team meetings. "If they see me as a professional," said one respondent, "they won't hesitate to offer lesson plans. If they perceive me as someone who just waves his arms around, they won't see why I would need to understand classroom goals." Respondents stated that, coming from administrators, these inaccurate terms and perceptions can lead to lower pay as well as to fewer opportunities and less funding for professional development. To an extreme, one interpreter suggested that, in some cases, a job description that includes "other duties as assigned" can lead to skill loss if one consequently interprets only infrequently.

Some respondents stated that students and interpreter-student relationships can also be negatively affected by these labels. Some respondents mentioned a concern that, when interpreters are referred to as "aides" and "assistants," students are disempowered. "It assumes that the deaf student needs a personal helper when what they really need is just access to communication." Moreover, teachers who see interpreters as aides may not respect their code of ethics. "If we are not seen as professionals," one respondent said, "then people seem to think it is OK to ask us to snitch on our students, leading to lack of trust from students." One interpreter pointed out that interpreters can perpetuate and exacerbate the situation by talking about the child they work for as *their* child. "If you do that," explained one respondent, "it starts to sound like the student is your responsibility and not the teacher's." Some interpreters further discussed concerns that mislabeling interpreters as "aides" and "assistants" might have negative effects on students as future consumers of interpreter services. "It is important that students learn how to use an interpreter professionally and treat their interpreters really well when they go on to college and into the professional world. We are educating consumers."

It should be noted that 15 percent of the respondents did not think that the labels teachers use for interpreters are a problem. They reported that these labels are products of poor communication, poor education, and in some cases unprofessional behavior on the part of interpreters. "Initially [these labels] may be a problem," stated one interpreter. "But if we behave in a professional way, what we are called should not matter. It is our actions that matter. Actions speak louder than words." One respondent said that even if the labels have some negative effects, interpreters need to learn to pick their battles. "There are people who will never learn the word *interpreter*," she said. "So let go of that." Another interpreter seconded that and added some related thoughts of her own:

> I do not think these terms should affect the educational interpreter at all. Our conduct will begin to show what our roles are, and I believe educators will begin to see us appropriately. After all, we have only just begun to understand our own roles, so the trickle down effect will take some time.

## Communication Breakdown

Educational anthropologists McDermott and Gospodinoff (1979) investigated possible reasons why various groups in schools have difficulty interacting with one another. They suggest that the difficulty lies not only in a question of differences among the groups but also in vested interests to maintain boundaries between groups. In their case, McDermott and Gospodinoff studied a classroom scenario where a teacher from a majority group and a student from a minority group were shown to gain in immediate ways by miscommunicating with each other. These researchers uncovered ethnic and political issues at stake—and ways in which both groups benefited from maintaining the boundaries between them. For the minority population under study, these immediate benefits were maladaptive in the long run, serving to maintain an unfavorable status quo.

From the perspectives of the majority of respondents and those in the discussion list archives, the long-term academic goals of teachers and interpreters match up well while their social goals often conflict. Similarity in long-term academic goals of both groups are clear: Teachers strive to teach students the classroom material, and interpreters strive to offer students access to that material. Short-term academic goals for these two groups are also similar: Each day, they both strive to see the student succeed with the lessons of the day.

Divergent social goals are what may lead some teachers and interpreters to miscommunicate. As many of the list's interpreters stated as they described their situations, teachers' social goals are often to maintain control over their classrooms. Of the interpreters interviewed, 95 percent agreed that, for their part, they intermittently answer to conflicting short-term and long-term social goals. Their long-term goals—to be seen and treated as professionals—sometimes lock horns with their short-term goals—to establish and maintain good rapport with teachers and students, to help teachers in a bind, and to not disrupt classroom flow. As many stated it, the more they act as aides or, as one respondent put it, "do things to keep the peace," the more they are seen and treated as aides. Thus, some interpreters reported allowing misunderstanding about their roles to persist out of a desire to meet those short-term goals. Perhaps, then, here as in McDermott and Gospodinoff's study, vested interests of these groups can, in some cases, lead to perpetuation of communication breakdown.

## Bodies and Spaces

The discussions of this group also bring to mind the work of another anthropologist who studies school settings. For the purposes of his study, Nespor (1997) discusses bodies and spaces in terms of the teachers' control of the classroom space and students' bodies. He then described the students' consequent lack of control over classroom spaces and their own bodies (e.g., they are required to walk rather than run in the halls, they are not allowed to go to the restroom at will, their natural bodily functions are frowned on, they are told where to sit or stand). If teachers control bodies and spaces in the classroom, where do educational interpreters fit in?

On the discussion list, various postings have addressed where interpreters should stand or sit in classes, assemblies, concerts, plays, and sporting events. They have discussed possibilities of using different spaces to signify different aspects of their jobs. For instance, some said they wished they could sit in one place when they are interpreting and sit in another if they are tutoring. Interpreters on the list have aired frustrations with being seated next to children who do not control their bodily functions, use profane language, and exude displeasing bodily odors. Questions have been posed to the group about whether or not interpreters should insist that the children they interpret for sit in the front row, to ensure visual access. A controversy broke out on the list about whether or not interpreters should remain in a classroom when a teacher leaves the room. If they stay, they are suddenly the disciplinarians and could be held responsible for whatever happens in class. If they leave, the children they are interpreting for will miss out on critical information—especially if the class has been left with instructions to work in small groups. Many interpreters also mentioned frustration with not having a secure space for their belongings. Others discussed frustrations with students and teachers walking in front of them while they sign.

Of those interviewed, 90 percent stated that lack of control over bodies and spaces made them feel frustrated, devalued, or less respected. The fact that interpreters' positions in space are often either ambiguously defined or mainly controlled by others seems to some interpreters like a reduction in status and loss of respect from teachers, students, and administrators. If they were important, these interpreters asked, wouldn't they have defined spaces for their materials, their bodies, and the bodies of their students? These body and space issues are clearly important to the group, are highly controversial, and further reflect the new and ambiguous status of educational interpreters. Excerpts from the interpreters' general comments about these issues follow:

- "I call it classroom homelessness."
- "It makes [me] feel all the more like an outsider."
- "Sometimes, you are led to believe that you are in the way or are a burden to the classroom and teacher."
- "When we feel in the way, we feel less empowered. We feel we are bothering people."
- "It gives students the impression that, if the interpreter is not important enough to be granted their own space, they are not important enough to be respected."
- "It reduces us to the position of a child to a parent."

## *Space for Materials*

Some of the interpreters were frustrated by not having a reliable, secure place to store their possessions and materials. Some of their thoughts follow:

- "It is difficult to feel professional if you are just floating with no place to keep your purse or papers."
- "A specific, secure place for our things would give us validity."
- "Having a designated place to put your things makes you feel like a part of the staff."

## *A Place for Preparation and Downtime*

In addition to a place for their materials, many interpreters also talked of the desire for a designated place to work during preparation time or to be during downtime. Some of their comments follow:

- "We often get a desk far from the classroom or a student desk in the classroom—not a good situation."
- "Interpreters need a place where they can go to relax and prepare. Not having a place to prepare can make the interpreter feel unimportant."

- "As far as seating goes, that goes back to our credibility overall. One tends to forget whom they don't value!"
- "Having a desk makes you feel like a part of the team . . . it's part of being accepted as a professional."

## *A Place to Work*

Perhaps the most basic question with respect to space issues for interpreters is where to be while interpreting. Interpreters said the following about this issue:

- "In the school where I work, overcrowded classrooms often create problems for me when I have to fight for a chair everyday and sit next to the teacher's elbow."
- "Sometimes the interpreter needs to go against the wishes of the teacher . . . in order to make sure students can see the teacher, any visuals, and the interpreter at the same time."
- "Being unable to find a space that does not block other people's views is very frustrating and I do not try to obscure the chalkboard, but often it is difficult not to."
- "Within the classroom, positioning can be a real hassle because we inconvenience the teacher and other students."
- "Having a teacher complain about space can make the interpreter feel unimportant."
- "If we are told to be somewhere that is not appropriate, we are less effective and do not feel like part of the educational team."

One interpreter shared a poignant experience she had because of this type of space issue.

> I once was in a math classroom where the teacher wrote all over the board. I would stand next to him because he often said "this goes there, that goes here" and I could not sign that to the student and have him understand what "this" and "that" were. He [the teacher] picked me up by my elbows and moved me to the other side of the room!

Even once placement decisions are made within the classroom, those involved must then consider all the exceptional situations. For instance, many said that finding and keeping an appropriate space during field trips, assemblies, and concerts can be challenging.

## *Ownership of the Classroom*

The language that some of the interpreters used in talking about space issues painted a picture in which teachers own the classrooms and interpreters are their uninvited guests. Some respondents implored other interpreters to tread lightly with teachers because "after all, it really is their classroom," "you are the one being forced onto them," and teachers "need to feel that the room is still under their control." Others talked of inconveniencing teachers. Issues of control over the room came up repeatedly, as when interpreters said that some teachers seem to feel "territorial."

These perceptions of ownership and infringement were not confined only to space concerns. Some interpreters saw classroom *time* as also belonging to teachers. For example, one interpreter said, "We feel we are bothering people . . . like when we have to take the time to set the captioning on the TV before the teacher shows a video." Other respondents talked about dealing with problems before or after class in an effort "not to take up class time." Some interpreters, looking at the situation historically, see that each teacher had his or her own room before the interpreter came onto the scene. However, other respondents argued that rather than think of the classroom as being owned by one person, it is best to think solely in terms of what is best for students and for the facilitation of classroom interactions. To these latter interpreters, this approach involves thinking of the classroom as a teaching tool that is molded by its occupants to optimize its effectiveness.

## INTERPRETERS' SUGGESTIONS

At first, the most logical approach in writing this chapter seemed to be one that listed at the end of each preceding section the suggested solutions for each of the individual, though related, problems being described. This approach led to redundancy, however, because the solutions interpreters offered for one problem were quite similar to those they suggested for another, which highlights how interrelated these issues truly are. Consequently, the following sections list the suggested solutions in terms of those for interpreters, for teachers, for administrators, for teacher training programs, and for interpreters' professional organizations.

### Suggestions for Interpreters

The suggestions the participant interpreters offered to those in their own profession involved acting in a professional manner, communicating clearly, serving as an advocate, and working to fit into "school culture."

***Act professionally.*** Respondents suggested that, to be seen as a professional, interpreters need to view themselves as professionals and then act professionally. What this suggestion involved, of course, varied greatly. It included considering teachers' perspectives and needs, coming to meetings and classes well prepared, separating personal issues from work-related issues, treating teachers and administrators with respect, dressing appropriately, and putting students first. For a great majority of the respondents, it also meant practicing diplomacy. They suggested being "gentle," "nonconfrontational," "patient," "nonjudgmental," "friendly," "full of humor," and "approachable."

Some also pointed out that proof of skills and education are also critical to being a professional. Many recommended continuing with education or striving for certification, regardless of state requirements. Some said that they hope to push the profession in the direction of requiring an associate's or a bachelor's degree. Some expressed the view that part of being a profession is working together to improve pay issues as well as to standardize state requirements and job descriptions.

***Communicate clearly about your role from the outset.*** The first step in clearly communicating one's role, said many interpreters, is clearly understanding it yourself.

Some suggested that interpreters rehearse a way to clearly articulate their roles and needs. Next, respondents suggested meeting with students, administrators, and teachers before school starts to discuss the needs of all parties. Providing an example of the benefits of this approach in terms of space needs, one respondent said, "Allowing the teachers to explain why they think their placement is best allows the interpreter to get a better feel for how the classroom operates."

***Advocate for yourself, students, and the interpreting process.*** Many interpreters reported that advocating for the student, themselves, and the interpretation process is a critical part of their jobs. As one interpreter said, "You need to take control of the situations you are in to ensure that your students get the best access possible. You are not *just* the interpreter; you are *the* interpreter. If you don't advocate for the child, it is possible no one else will." Other respondents' comments followed suit:

- "School culture is about the kids, make this about the kids, too—not what I need personally, but what is needed for me to give this child the input he or she needs."
- "We are responsible for the communication process between the students and teachers. Therefore, we are the ones who should be making the decisions about how that happens. I try to work as a team with the teacher and student. But I also try to balance the imbalance of power by giving most of the weight to the desire of the student."
- "You have a right to speak up. You have a large impact on the child. Part of your job is to be a team member and to maintain communication with the child and the rest of the team."

Although advocacy is crucial, one respondent warned that interpreters need to pick their battles: "We need to know when to advocate for ourselves and when to let it be. Life is not perfect."

***Try to fit into school culture.*** One participant stated that many interpreters do not put out enough time and effort to try to fit into school culture. "Some interpreters walk into a classroom and start listing what they will and will not do. We need to learn to match the cultural environment in which we work. We need to do a perspective shift to try to see this from the viewpoint of the teacher in specific, and school culture in general." Another interpreter echoed that participant's views and further suggested that interpreters watch to see what teachers do for one another and then use that example as their model for what they will or will not do, realizing that flexibility and adaptability are critical in any work setting.

## Suggestions for Teachers

When the participant interpreters listed their suggestions for teachers, they included learning more about the interpretation process, recognizing their responsibilities to deaf and hard of hearing students, acknowledging interpreters as part of the educational team, and playing their part in fostering clear communication with interpreters.

***Take an active role in learning about the interpretation process.*** Some interpreters expressed a dream that teachers would take an active part in facilitating the interpretation process. Those whose teachers did so spoke glowingly of the results.

***Recognize that the students are your responsibility.*** Respondents clarified the position that, ultimately, deaf and hard of hearing students are students. They need to benefit from the teacher's skills and experience as much as the hearing students do.

***Recognize interpreters as part of the educational team.*** Interpreters discussed the fact that they know students well and can, when breeches of confidentiality are not involved, offer important insights and feedback to teachers. They also mentioned that it is helpful for interpreters to be aware of IEP goals and objectives of the students for whom they interpret.

***Communicate clearly and diplomatically with interpreters.*** Respondents were quite clear in stating that power struggles and miscommunication between teachers and interpreters can lead to negative results not only for the interpreter-teacher relationship but also for the students.

## Suggestions for Administrators

Participant interpreters' suggestions for administrators included requiring teachers and students to learn more about interpreting, recognizing interpreters as part of the educational team, ensuring that interpreters have what they need to effectively perform their jobs, and treating interpreters like professionals.

***Require teachers and students to attend in-service training about the interpretation process.*** Overwhelmingly, interpreters suggested more in-service training for students, teachers, and administrators with respect to educational interpreting. Some interpreters suggested that the in-service training should be conducted by outside interpreters so discussions do not become too personal. Others suggested that deaf, hard of hearing, and hearing students should all be required to attend in-service training along with administrators, teachers, and interpreters. Respondents suggested that deaf and hard of hearing students would benefit not only from in-service training to learn how to work with interpreters but also from meetings with deaf adult mentors to guide them in day-to-day interactions with interpreters. One interpreter suggested that older students be asked to do "mini in-services." She suggested that, if students explained the role of the interpreter to the staff, their effort would demonstrate to the staff that the students have high-level expectations, and it would also foster student empowerment.

***Consider interpreters as part of the educational team.*** Interpreters reported that they can do their jobs best if they are included as part of the educational team. To clarify what this inclusion means in terms of everyday behaviors, respondents suggested that administrators include interpreters when disseminating information about students, events, and meetings.

***Make sure interpreters have what they need to do their jobs well.*** Respondents emphasized the importance of teachers and administrators talking to interpreters about space issues. In particular, many mentioned that having a designated place for their belongings and an assigned place for preparation and downtime would be helpful.

***Treat interpreters like professionals.*** Interpreters emphasized that administrators should hire interpreters who are qualified and pay them a professional wage, offer them appropriate resources, and provide them with funding for professional development opportunities.

### Suggestions for Teacher Training Programs

Interpreters highlighted the importance of discussions in teacher training programs about interpreter roles and responsibilities. Initially, one might assume this suggestion refers to mainstream teachers. It definitely does refer to that group, but some interpreters also felt misunderstood by the teachers of the deaf who taught in their buildings. They said that, if the teachers of the deaf are supportive and respectful, then mainstream teachers tend to follow suit.

### Suggestions for State and National Organizations for Interpreters

Some of the interpreters said that state and national organizations for interpreters need to increase attention to educational interpreters' needs. Some expressed hopes that state and national organizations could work on consistency of standards for educational interpreters. "Educational interpreting is a young profession," said one respondent, "and the sooner we adopt uniform standards of behavior and educational requirements nationwide, the sooner we will be considered professional."

## THE DISCUSSION LIST

This section addresses the second purpose of the chapter—to describe the Internet list itself. It examines the ways subscribers use the list, their reasons for needing a forum specific to their subfield, and their views of the advantages and disadvantages to participating on an Internet discussion list related to their profession.

### The Purposes of the List

The results of this study suggest that, for many interpreters, this Internet discussion list is a valuable asset for discussion and resolution of the issues that have been discussed in the previous section.

#### *A Resource for Information Exchange*

The expressed purpose of the group, as written on the list's Web site, is to serve as a resource for information exchange. Ninety-five percent of the respondents reported that the list serves this purpose for them. Many interpreters mentioned that this exchange was their main reason for participating on the list. Some said they felt a need to participate because their interpreter preparation programs (IPPs) had lacked training with respect to work in educational settings. Some reported seeking assistance with signs—especially for specific events, activities, areas of study, and issues of the day. Others reported seeking information about professional development opportunities, contracts, educational CDs, related Web sites, workshops, employment opportunities, research, and information about deaf communities and interpreter gatherings (e.g., conferences, events).

## *A Forum for Discussion*

Ninety-five percent of the respondents also see the list as a forum for discussion of issues relevant to their profession. "It's like a 400-person staff meeting," said one member. This opportunity for discussion seems especially useful for those in rural areas, those who have not had formal training, those whose IPPs did not address issues of educational interpreting, and those who do not work with other educational interpreters.

However, even those who work with other interpreters reported that they rarely get together to discuss controversial issues in their subfield. One said she benefits from being on the list because "I can see other peoples' perspectives on the gray areas of interpreting." Many interpreters mentioned curiosity about how things were done in other places, about differences in urban versus rural settings, and about how other interpreters handle similar, problematic situations. Most prevalent are discussions of role clarification, application of the interpreters' code of ethics to the school setting, and situational advice related to interactions with teachers and students. As one interpreter put it, she gains from the list by getting advice for "navigating the politics of a school system."

Some mentioned that the homogeneity of the group makes communication simpler. "Not many people understand what we do," she said. "It is nice to chat about things that we do without having to explain everything." Others mentioned benefiting from the group's heterogeneity, noting that, besides interpreters, the interpreters' list also consists of teachers of the deaf, deaf and hard of hearing individuals, and IPP instructors.

## *A Support Group*

Eighty-four percent of the respondents reported viewing the list as, in part, a support group. Those interviewed stated that the list is a "nonthreatening," "nonjudgmental," "safe place" that offers them "camaraderie." Being on the list allows them to make friends and connect with colleagues they might never meet otherwise. One respondent said, "I feel connected to interpreters all over the country." For another interpreter, joining the list meant feeling "less alone."

Rheingold (1993) points out that one social purpose of some discussion lists is to help people cope with and normalize difficult experiences. The list seems to serve both of these purposes for its members. One interpreter who works in both community and school interpreting said the following:

> Educational interpreting is tough—sometimes tougher than community interpreting, because we (educational interpreters) usually establish long-term relationships with the students we work with, which can make it

> hard to leave work at the front door at the end of the day. We have to deal with administrators and teachers who have no concept of what we do. The people on the list understand what I experience.

Use of the list as a resource for coping strategies seems evident in archived questions that begin with, "How do you all deal with . . . ?" Efforts to normalize difficult experiences seem apparent in archived postings that start out by saying, "I'm glad to know I'm not the only one who . . . ." As one interpreter put it, "It's nice just to know others are dealing with the same challenges and situations as you are. That's support in itself." Another stated it even more strongly: "This is where I go for my sanity. I see other interpreters are facing some of the same situations as I am." Research pertaining to support groups suggests that they "evoke good feelings by helping members construct new self-understandings" (Denzin 1985). As became clear in the discussion of the issues, interpreters on this list appear to be constructing this type of self-understanding with respect to their roles, responsibilities, and identities at work.

### *Variation in Use of the List*

Clearly, although a great deal of overlap exists, for different people, the list offers different things. As clarified above, most see the list as a forum for discussion and as a resource center for information exchange while some also see it as a support group. Other differences in use of the list are related to levels of experience. A newer interpreter talked about the list this way: "It helps me prepare so that if similar issues come up in the future, I am better able to handle them or to understand other peoples' points of view." For more senior interpreters, the list offers a way to disseminate knowledge accrued from experience. "I am in a stage in my career when I am giving back," said an interpreter who has been working for twenty years. "The list is a good way to touch many people at once." Another experienced interpreter said that she is motivated to answer questions from new interpreters on the list because she feels that every time she helps another educational interpreter, she is also helping another deaf or hard of hearing student. A third seasoned interpreter admitted that, sometimes, she finds comments made on the list frustrating. "But," she added, "I do get ideas about what to teach my students."

## Why the Need for a List Specific to K–12 Interpreters?

Respondents were asked why they thought the need existed for a discussion list specifically designated for educational interpreters in kindergarten through high school settings. Their answers pointed to a need for confidentiality, a sense of isolation from one another, the challenges of situational ethics, the lack of a model to follow, a lack of preparation, and the demands of their multifaceted roles.

***Confidentiality.*** Many respondents mentioned concern with breeching confidentiality as a reason for wanting to communicate anonymously on the discussion list. Although teachers frequently talk informally among themselves about students, some interpreters reported finding themselves concerned about breaking confidentiality in conversations about students or teachers. The discussion list offers these interpreters a place to vent or request feedback without specific people being identified.

***Isolation.*** Unlike community interpreters who sometimes work in pairs or who work out of interpreting agencies, educational interpreters often work in isolation from one another. Many reported being the only interpreter in their schools, districts, or counties. The list offers these interpreters support, feedback, and resources they would have difficulty accessing otherwise.

***Situational ethics.*** Many of the respondents mentioned that the discussion list also helps them deal with situational ethical issues they face on a daily basis. "Although the interpreting process is generally the same in community and educational interpreting, the situations you run into are incredibly different," explained one interpreter. Another said that, because of the nature of the school setting and the fact that consumers are children, "We run into big ethical problems every single day."

***Lack of a model.*** Lack of understanding and vagueness about the role of the educational interpreter seem to make it difficult for many interpreters to find others in their work environments to talk to about work-related issues. One interpreter who has worked in middle school, high school, and college settings said, "All interpreters have challenges, but educational interpreters are confronted with a highly dynamic environment with boundary confusions. You are not the teacher and you are not the principal, but you are an adult. For kids, teachers, and for the interpreter, this is a confusing situation." Respondents added that confusion is exacerbated by the fact that job descriptions vary greatly from school to school and from community interpreting to school interpreting.

***Lack of preparation.*** Educational interpreters reported that their training programs often do not prepare them for the school setting. "Very few IPPs teach you how to be an educational interpreter. So it is trial by fire." Then there's the fact that some interpreters have not attended an IPP. One interpreter reported, "There are far more inexperienced, untrained, or undertrained, uncertified interpreters working in public schools [than in community settings]." Many agreed that the discussion list helps by filling in gaps created by insufficient training.

***Multifaceted demands.*** A final reason for the discussion list being of such importance to this group of interpreters is that they have multifaceted roles and do not always feel prepared to handle all of the responsibilities they are asked to juggle. Besides interpreting and explaining their roles as interpreters, they are also often asked to educate families, students, and staff members about deafness, language issues, and the interpreting process. Moreover, they need to learn to navigate school politics and tackle issues that arise when one serves as an educational team member.

## Advantages and Disadvantages to an Online Group

Most respondents found the list highly beneficial. Some members, however, noted some disadvantages inherent to this mode of communication.

### *Advantages to Meeting Online*

Nearly all respondents pinpointed the large sampling from distant geographical regions as an advantage to meeting online—the more members, the more solutions and opinions. Other advantages to the online group—including efficiency, convenience, precision, greater candor, communication across boundaries, and learning from lurking—are discussed below.

***Efficiency.*** Many interviewees mentioned efficiency as part of what drew them to the list. Participants can decide what to read, what to skim, and what to skip. Although responses are not as timely as they would be in person, members said that they are generally quick. One member put it this way, "I have never had a situation where I asked a question and did not receive some sort of answer within a two-day time frame."

***Convenience.*** When asked for advantages to an online group, convenience was an obvious, quick response for many of the respondents. Members mentioned that the list can be accessed from anywhere a computer is available and at any time ("It's open twenty-four hours a day!"). Highlighting the convenience of locale, one member said, "I can deal with the list in the comfort (and the jammies) of my own home."

***Precision.*** Some reported feeling that the online forum encourages well-thought-out interactions. "People can take time to carefully write, read, and edit their questions and answers before sending them," explained one interpreter.

***Greater candor.*** According to Kollock and Smith (1996), prior research suggests that Internet interactions allow for greater candor; participants are less concerned about repercussions given the option of anonymity. In the case of the educational interpreters' discussion list, this possibility seems to be reasonable. At times in the archived discussion list messages, interpreters state that they would not tell those in their schools what they are telling those on the list—partly because they often use the list to gain advice about how to discuss issues with coworkers and consumers.

Those interviewed gave the same impression. In a variety of ways, a great majority of the participants said that the online group allows for greater candor. Members discussed the issue of candor in terms of asking questions (e.g., "You can ask questions without repercussions") and in terms of making statements (e.g., "People can say what they think and feel without worrying" and "It is definitely easier to be blunt with a person you don't know and don't have to look at"). Others agreed, one adding that on line there is "less pressure to conform." Some respondents mentioned that many people are more willing to participate when not in front of a group of people.

***Communication across boundaries.*** Korenman and Wyatt (1996) found that the online group they studied allowed for communication across social, geographical, and hierarchical boundaries. On the list, discussions cross hierarchical boundaries marking highly experienced interpreters (those in the field for decades, those who are now teaching in interpreter training programs), those new to the field, and those who are still students. This boundary crossing has offered some people new to the field some advice they might have had trouble gaining otherwise: "I rarely have any idea of the skill levels or years of experience of those on the list. Hence, intimidation is not a factor." Looking at this issue from another perspective, one participant believes that people are "more likely to take advice at face value" when they do not know who wrote it.

***Learning from lurking.*** Barnes (2001) suggests that "lurking"—reading list material but not participating in the discussions—is a product of the fact that people in our society are now used to being media consumers rather than participants. She also suggests that, although lurking is often considered negative, the possibility may be that those who do not actively participate are learning from the discussions. Those participants who reported reading but not participating said that that the list works in exactly this way for them.

### *Disadvantages to Meeting Online*

Although most respondents' comments highlighted advantages to meeting online, two disadvantages also came to light: logistical limitations and negative aspects to anonymity.

***Logistical limitations.*** Most obvious, perhaps, is the fact that discussing a visual language by means of written description is difficult to do. Additionally, some said they do not respond as often as they might or in as much detail as they would like because they lack computer or typing skills. Others said that, regardless of skill levels on the keyboard, they find typing to be more tedious than speaking, so they tend to keep comments brief. These constraints can limit the information passed among members and can lead to miscommunication of the information that is shared. Respondents also mentioned that lack of intonational cues, body language, and facial expression can lead to miscommunication.

***The negative side of anonymity.*** Some of those interviewed reported that anonymity can lead to reduced participation (because one feels no pressure to join in), rude behavior, and an inability to judge credibility. "Sometimes, you want to see who you are taking advice from," said one interpreter. "It helps you determine their skill level or level of professionalism."

## CONCLUSION

This chapter has explored the perspectives of educational interpreters on an Internet discussion list with respect to three issues important to interpreters. These issues—namely, identity and role formation for interpreters in schools, communication breakdown between interpreters and teachers, and control of bodies and spaces in the school setting—were discussed in terms of their application to similar issues in educational anthropology. Most of the interpreters interviewed, rather than direct frustrations about these issues at teachers, asserted that these problematic issues reflect systems in need of change and boundaries in need of clearer definitions.

Given this perspective, the interpreters offered suggestions not only to teachers but also to administrators, teacher training programs, the state and national interpreting organizations, and fellow interpreters. These suggestions were offered with the hope that, one day, all educational interpreters will become well-respected, well-integrated team members in deaf and hard of hearing children's school careers—a situation with great benefits to offer students and teachers as well as interpreters. One solution that has clearly worked well, at least in part, for many of these interpreters is their discussion list on the Internet. Interpreters noted its many advantages and a couple of its disadvantages as a forum for discussion, a site for information exchange, and a place to gain social support for situations faced by interpreters in school settings.

## APPENDIX

### Questionnaire for Educational Interpreters

Please take as much space as needed to answer each question as thoroughly as you can. If you think of examples that would help to clarify your answers, please include them.

### DEMOGRAPHIC QUESTIONS

- How many years have you worked as an educational interpreter?
- What grades have you interpreted for?
- How long have you been a member of the K–12 terps discussion list?

### QUESTIONS REGARDING THE DISCUSSION LIST

- What made you join the list?
- What do you gain from being on the discussion list?
- Do you feel like the discussion list members have become a cohesive group? How so? Or why not?
- Do you feel the list allows you to communicate with others across hierarchical boundaries within your profession? How so?
- Is there anything characteristic about educational interpreting that makes a discussion list more critical for those in your field?
- In what ways do you participate on the list? In other words, do you tend to initiate discussions, answer questions, reply to comments, or just read others' discussions? Why?
- Do you feel this group works as a support group? In what ways?
- Do you feel this group functions well as an avenue for information exchange? In what ways?
- Do you feel this group functions well as a forum for discussion of issues relevant to your occupation? In what ways?
- What do you see as the role of the moderators?
- What do you see as the differences between an online group and a face-to-face group? Do you think these differences render the online group more or less effective and satisfying? How so? Are participants more candid?

## QUESTIONS REGARDING ISSUES DISCUSSED ON THE LIST

### Concerns about Communication

Concerns about communication between students, teachers, and interpreters have frequently surfaced on the discussion list.

- Why do you think these problems exist?
- Why do you think they persist?
- For instance, it seems educational interpreters sometimes feel they are stuck between their long-term goal of clarifying their roles and making sure people view them as professional interpreters and their short-term need to maintain rapport with teachers and students. Do you think this is the case? If so, what can students, interpreters, and/or teachers do to resolve this?

### Concerns about Role

It is clear from various entries on the list that some educational interpreters do not like some of the ways they are viewed by teachers and other professionals in the school setting (e.g., being called a "signer" or an "aide," being asked to help with students' homework, or being asked to serve as disciplinarians).

- How do you think these terms (e.g., signer, aide, helper) affect educational interpreters and the profession as a whole?
- Do you think the use of these terms leads to certain kinds of treatment of interpreters by teachers (e.g., not sharing lesson plans, requests for disciplinary acts)?
- Why do you think some teachers use those terms—sometimes even after being corrected multiple times?
- If interpreters are seen as equals to teachers, is there a chance that students will feel that they can't be as candid when interacting with deaf and hard-of-hearing students via the interpreter?
- What do you think can be done to improve the way educational interpreters are viewed in the schools?

### Concerns about Space

Some studies discuss the importance of the use and control of space in school settings. On the discussion list, some have voiced frustrations about not having their own space in the classroom or about having to sit in a specific place chosen by the teacher or student. Others have mentioned wishing they had different places to be for different roles they play (interpreter/aide/tutor) to make it clear to the teacher and student which role they are performing. Some have asked about the interpreter's space on field trips, at sporting events, and in assemblies. Some have stated frustrations with teachers and students walking in front of them. One interpreter asked whether she should be in the room if the teacher was not.

- Do you think space/location issues (where to be when) cause problems for educational interpreters?
- Do you think not having control over space in the classroom or not having a clearly defined space of their own leads interpreters to feel less empowered or less important? How so?
- Is there a way to give educational interpreters more control over space/location issues within their classrooms?

## REFERENCES

Barnes, S. 2001. *Online connections: Internet interpersonal relationships.* Cresskill, N.J.: Hampton Press.

Denzin, N. K. 1985. Emotion as lived experience. *Symbolic Interaction* 8:223–40.

Eisenhart, M. 1997. The fax, the jazz player, and the self-storyteller: How *do* people organize culture? In *Schooling the symbolic animal,* ed. B. Levinson. Lanham, Md.: Rowman and Littlefield.

Kollock, P., and M. Smith. 1996. Managing the virtual commons. In *Computer-Mediated communication: Linguistic, social, and cross-cultural perspectives,* ed. S. Herring. Amsterdam: John Benjamins.

Korenman, J., and N. Wyatt. 1996. Group dynamics in an e-mail forum. In *Computer-Mediated communication: Linguistic, social, and cross-cultural perspectives,* ed. S. Herring. Amsterdam: John Benjamins.

McDermott, R. P., and K. Gospodinoff. 1979. Social contexts for ethnic borders and school failure. In *Nonverbal behavior: Applications and cultural implications,* ed. A. Wolfgang, 175–95. New York: Academic Press.

Mehan, H. 2000. Beneath the skin and between the ears: A case study in the politics of representation. In *Schooling the symbolic animal,* ed. B. Levinson. Lanham, Md.: Rowman and Littlefield.

Nespor, J. 1997. *Tangled up in school.* Mahwah, N.J.: Erlbaum.

Rheingold, H. 1993. *The virtual community.* Reading, Mass.: Addison, Wesley.

Taylor, C., and R. Elliott. 1994. Identifying areas of competence needed by educational interpreters. *Sign Language Studies* 83:179–90.

# Competencies of K–12 Educational Interpreters: What We Need Versus What We Have

Bernhardt E. Jones

During the late 1700s and early 1800s, the education of deaf and hard of hearing students and the use of sign language was a common occurrence. Sign language was viewed not only as an educational tool but also as a method of communication. The methods of teaching that used sign language were based on methods used to educate deaf and hard of hearing children in France. Sign language was the mode of communication in the first public school for deaf students, founded in 1755 by the Abbé Charles Michel de l'Epée (Gannon 1981). L'Epée is considered by many to be the father of modern day sign language. L'Epée's purpose was to modify signs that were naturally used by deaf people in Paris (i.e., French Sign Language, or FSL) "in such a way as to develop a visual analog of written French" (Stedt and Moores 1990, 2). In his book, *The Instruction of the Deaf and Dumb by Means of Methodical Signs*, l'Epée (1801) referred to this sign system as "Methodical Signs." These were natural FSL signs produced in the syntax of spoken French (what we in the United States might call "Pidgin Signed English" or "contact signing"). L'Epée wrote in 1801,

> We have only to introduce into their minds by the eye what has been introduced into our own by the ear. These are two avenues at all times open, each presenting a path which leads to the same point. . . . (L'Epée 1801, 1)

In the United States, sign language interpreting (for adults) can first be traced to the year 1816 when Laurent Clerc traveled to the United States as a guest of Thomas Hopkins Gallaudet to establish the first school for the deaf (Lane 1984; Frishberg 1990).

The middle of the twentieth century marked a significant change to public education for deaf and hard of hearing students that has affected sign language interpreting dramatically. In 1954, the U.S. Supreme Court's ruling in *Brown v. Board of Education of Topeka*, 347 U.S. 483 started a major trend toward the removal of barriers to educational access heretofore erected to exclude minority groups (Turnbull 1990). Although the minority group in 1954 was African American, all minority groups benefited from this decision, including individuals with disabilities.

Soon after *Brown*, Congress commissioned what later became known as the Babbidge Report (Babbidge 1965), which showed an overall weakness in the education of deaf and hard of hearing students, primarily in the residential schools for the deaf throughout the country. These findings, coupled with the Vocational Education Act Amendments, vocational rehabilitation funding of postsecondary deaf and hard of hearing students during the 1960s, Section 504 of the Rehabilitation Act of 1973 (equal access to communication, interpreter training), PL 94-142 (Education for All Handicapped Children Act of 1975), and now the Individuals with Disabilities Education Act of 1990 (IDEA) all contributed to the expanded changes in educational options for deaf and hard of hearing youngsters of public school age.

K–12 educational interpreting has a relatively short history. In 1975, Public Law 94-142 (the Education for All Handicapped Children Act of 1975), which later became the Individuals with Disabilities Education Act of 1990 (IDEA), placed the primary responsibility of educating deaf and hard of hearing students, with necessary related services (IDEA Sec. 140 (22)) in the hands of K–12 local education agencies (LEAs). To accomplish this goal within the least restrictive environment (LRE) (IDEA Sec. 12 (a) (5)), namely, the mainstream, LEAs have employed educational sign language interpreters to facilitate the communication between the deaf or hard of hearing student and the teacher or teachers as well as other students in the class who are unable to use sign language. As in *Brown* in 1954, IDEA upheld the ruling that segregation based on immutable traits was illegal and unacceptable.

Nationally, Moores (1987) reported that, between the years of 1974 and 1984, the residential school population of deaf and hard of hearing students dropped 18.3 percent while the numbers of these students attending public day classes (public schools) increased by 29.8 percent. Schildroth and Hotto (1991) reported that, between the years of 1985 and 1990, the numbers of deaf and hard of hearing students in "local schools" (public schools) gained in numbers from 62 percent to 67 percent. Today, at least 83 percent (U.S. Department of Education 1999) of deaf and hard of hearing students attend public schools. Deaf and hard of hearing individuals have become a "linguistic minority" (Dolnick 1993) as they have moved from residential schools to public schools. Winston (1985) asserts that, like it or not, this situation is the reality.

With the massive shift in numbers of deaf and hard of hearing students from the residential setting to the LEAs, the need for sign language interpreters for educational settings continued to escalate. Although the need increased, the supply did not. The number of educational sign language interpreters continues to be inadequate; the demand far outweighs the supply (Witter-Merithew and Dirst 1982; Stuckless, Avery, and Hurwitz 1989; Winston 1994; see also Schick and Williams chapter 10). Further complicating problems caused by the inadequate number of sign language interpreters has been the lack of education and skills these interpreters have brought to the job. "Few interpreters had any formal training for working in an educational setting with deaf children, and virtually none had formal preparation as educational interpreters since interpreter training programs were not oriented in this direction" (Hurwitz 1991, 20).

Although the need for interpreters has been documented and the lack of skills demonstrated, educational interpreters have a dearth of education opportunities. Carew (2001) reports in the *American Annals of the Deaf* that only 1 of 74 programs (1.3 percent) is designed to teach interpreting in the K–12 classroom setting. These data are typically underreported to the *American Annals of the Deaf* because program reporting is voluntary. Additionally, this program listing does not represent those programs that may include some type of "special topics" introduction to educational interpreting, with a cursory discussion of settings and requirements in the educational setting.

However, the problem remains: Too few programs are addressing the need to educate interpreters for work in the public schools. And yet the majority of graduates from interpreter preparation programs continue to enter K–12 settings (Battaglia and Avery 1986; Frischberg 1990; Schrag 1991). As early as 1989, the National Task Force on Educational Interpreting (Stuckless, Avery, and Hurwitz 1989) stated,

> [I]t is evident that more than 50 percent of the graduates of interpreter preparation programs nationally become employed as interpreters in educational settings at the elementary/postsecondary levels. (2)

By 1991, Schrag (1991) reported that two-thirds of the graduates of interpreter preparation programs (IPPs) had entered educational interpreting.

## WHAT IS K–12 EDUCATIONAL INTERPRETING?

To be clear about the terminology used in this chapter, some definitions are in order. First, let us define K–12 educational interpreter *qualifications* as the skills, education and training, and experience that are necessary to effectively provide sign language interpretation for school-aged children and young adults. In addition, the following definitions also will be helpful to this discussion.

***K–12 educational sign language interpreter.*** The following two statements clearly describe what is meant by the term *educational sign language interpreter*:

> "Educational Interpreter" means a person who uses sign language in the public school setting for purposes of facilitating communication between users and nonusers of sign language and who is fluent in the languages used by both deaf and nondeaf persons. (Colorado Legislature 2002, 22-20-116 (2), in CDE 2002)
>
> [An educational sign language interpreter] . . . is a professional, who facilitates communication and understanding among deaf and hearing persons in a mainstream environment. The interpreter is a member of the educational team and is present to serve staff as well as students, hearing as well as deaf people, by minimizing linguistic, cultural, and physical barriers. The title, "Educational Interpreter," is recommended by the National Task Force on Educational Interpreting, and is intended to imply that a person holding this title is a professional with specialized preparation in deafness, whose primary role is interpreting, but who is also qualified to provide certain other educational services. (New York State 1998)

***Interpreting.*** Frishberg (1990) and Winston (1989) explain what the term *interpreting* encompasses:

> [Interpreting is] the process of changing messages produced in one language immediately into another language. The languages in question may be spoken or signed, but the defining characteristic is the live and immediate transmission. (Frishberg 1990, 18)
>
> Interpreting . . . refers either to the general process of changing the form of a message to another form, or to the specific process of changing an English message to American Sign Language (ASL), or vice versa. (Winston 1989, 147)

Note, however, that research (Jones, Clark, and Soltz 1997) shows that the term *interpreting* in the K–12 arena refers to transliterating (between two codes of English: one spoken, one signed).

***Transliterating.*** According to Winston (1989),

> [transliterating] is a specific form of sign language interpreting. It is the process of changing one form of an English message, either spoken English or signed English, into the other form. The assumption in transliteration is that both the spoken and the signed forms correspond to English, the spoken form following the rules of standard English and the signed form being a simple recoding of the spoken form into the manual code of expression. (Winston 1989, 147)

Transliteration incorporates features of American Sign Language (ASL) to enhance clarity. Ability to transliterate implies that one has a knowledge of ASL features and can incorporate them into a transliteration.

***Methodical signs.*** Methodical signs are those that are based on the syntax of a spoken national language (L'Epée 1801; Stedt and Moores 1990).

## WHAT ARE THE ISSUES?

From the little research conducted in the area of educational sign language interpreting performed in K–12 public school settings (Hayes 1991, 1992; Jones, Clark, and Soltz 1997; Yarger 2001; Antia and Kreimeyer 2001), two major issues are clear:

1. Qualifications of working K–12 educational interpreters
2. Roles and responsibilities of working K–12 educational interpreters

Let us first look at qualifications (i.e., skills, education and training, and experience). In a statewide survey conducted in the late 1980s, the Oregon Registry of Interpreters for the Deaf found that the vast majority (87 percent) of Oregon interpreters working in K–12 public schools were not certified (Togioka 1990). Also in this survey, 57 percent of the interpreters in K–12 public schools reported that they were not evaluated for their interpreting skills before being hired for their position. A study conducted by the Bureau of Educational Research at the University of Tennessee in 1989 showed that 56 percent of the states in the United States had no minimum standards for interpreters who interpret in educational settings and that 74 percent of the states had no minimum skills assessment for educational interpreting (Bureau of Educational Research and Service 1989).

Jones, Clark, and Soltz (1997) studied all K–12 educational interpreters ($n = 222$) working in public schools in three midwestern states. Qualifications, as defined by skills (measured by means of a certification mechanism), education, and experience, were lacking. Sixty-three percent held no certification; 36 percent of this group had attended some college but had earned no degree. Sixty-five percent had been working in the classroom for five years or less. In addition, 57 percent of the total numbers of interpreters were not evaluated for their interpreting skills before being hired, and 25 percent of the total had never been evaluated for their skills.

The above findings might have been understandable, albeit distressing, in the late 1980s and early 1990s. However, the problem of interpreters lacking qualifications remains virtually unchanged today. This alarming fact begs the question, Why? Why, a decade later, are students still being subjected to substandard services in interpreted education?

In 2000, the state of West Virginia found that 81 percent of the state's K–12 educational interpreters held no certification. Seventeen percent held certification through the National Association of the Deaf (NAD), but 75 percent of those held NAD Level 2 certification, which is classified as "below average performance" (WVCDHH and WVDOE 2002).

Jones (2001) again gathered the same types of information asked for in his previous study (Jones, Clark, and Soltz 1997) of 108 students enrolled within the Educational Interpreting Certificate Program (EICP) at Front Range Community College, Colorado (see Johnson and Winston, 1999, for more information about this program). These students were working interpreters, employed in public school systems in ten states. Fifty percent did not hold any certification; 43 percent had attended some college before EICP admittance but had earned no degree; 40 percent had been on the job for five years or less; and 58 percent were not evaluated for interpreting skills before being hired as K–12 educational interpreters. Further, 31 percent had never been evaluated for their interpreting skills before enrollment in the EICP.

What makes these findings even more distressing is that this group of 108 interpreters was a cohort of individuals who had taken the initiative to improve their skills and knowledge by attending an organized program of study. Although their actions were admirable, the fact that the education system did not require this training is distressing. The encouraging news is that these working interpreters were required to take an entrance exam for the EICP. This exam, loosely referred to as a "modified EIPA (Educational Interpreter Performance Assessment)," did not include the evaluation of sign-to-voice interpreting skills. However, it did measure voice-to-sign interpreting skills, and these interpreters had to obtain at least a level 2.0 (on a five-point scale) to gain admittance to the EICP. Although the level of 2 is somewhat nebulous, it is a beginning point. This beginning point is, unfortunately, somewhat low in the total scheme of things; the "Profile of Skill at Each Rating Level of the EIPA" describes a Level 2 as an "Advanced Beginner" who "demonstrates only basic sign vocabulary and these limitations interfere with communication. . . . An individual at this level is not recommended for classroom interpreting" (Williams and Schick 1999, 4).

Yarger's (2001) study of sixty-three educational interpreters working in two rural states showed that, although none were certified, 73 percent had been evaluated for their voice-to-sign interpreting skills (sans sign-to-voice skills) as a part of the EICP enrollment (minimum score of 2.0) process. At the very least, we can gain some understanding of the skills (or lack of skills) exhibited by these working interpreters and establish a benchmark. Although this minimal step would be somewhat encouraging, one must still be discouraged to note that K–12 interpreters are working with skill levels that are inadequate.

A study of K–12 educational interpreters working in nine western states during fall 2002 (JCCC 2002) found that 83 percent held no national interpreter certification. Clearly, improvement has not happened in the area of interpreter certification. However, some good news is evident. This same study found that 49 percent have, at least, taken the EIPA, 86 percent of that group within the past two years. The time frame is significant because it means that the majority has probably taken the new videotape-standardized version of the EIPA. Of these nine states, the state of Colorado shows the largest percentage of K–12 interpreters having taken the exam (85 percent). Of this 85 percent in the state of Colorado, 70 percent have met or surpassed that state's minimum standard of 3.5 (personal communication, Kim Sweetwood, CDE interpreter standards coordinator, May 18, 2003), which is encouraging progress. Data of this nature for the other eight states are not yet available.

Some progress toward a qualified K–12 interpreter workforce is being made. But what about the interpreters who have chosen not to improve their skills and knowledge? Yarger (2001) found that every interpreter she studied self-reported a higher level of interpreting skill than was later actually found to be true by means of interpreting performance testing. From these data, we surely cannot say that interpreters who have chosen not to improve their skills would be more skilled than interpreters already evaluated for skill.

Yarger's study clearly shows the need for standards of quality for these important support personnel. Even so, what benefits are there to placing a student in an interpreted education with unskilled interpreters? Ramsey (1997) has suggested,

> The mere placement of deaf and hearing children in the same room is a waste of deaf children's developmental time and a thoughtless burden to place on them. . . . Unless a school principal and teaching staff [and interpreting staff] can make a commitment to preparing themselves to communicate with and understand the educational needs of deaf children, simply scheduling periods of integration is a fruitless exercise in logistics. . . . If students cannot engage with instruction and with others, it is hard to imagine how they will be able to acquire language and school skills. (113)

"Engaging with instruction" is not possible for deaf and hard of hearing students who use an interpreter with either questionable qualifications or unknown qualifications. One cannot help but wonder how an individual educational program (IEP) team can make an appropriate educational placement of a deaf or hard of hearing student without knowing whether that student's communication needs are being met. At least 50 percent of the time, we cannot know the answer to this question because the empirical data show that at least half of the K–12 educational interpreters in the United States are not certified, or have not been tested for their skill.

According to Sanderson (1991), "Ninety percent of deaf children born to hearing parents will not be fluent during the critical years of language acquisition, so only the best interpreters should be working with them" (67). Affonso (1998) also echoes this notion. Bowen-Bailey (1996) notes, however, that "too often, the interpreters who work with young children are the interpreters most in need of models for their own language development" (16). The reality is that "most often education attracts inexperienced, unskilled interpreters" (Winston 1994, 61).

## WHO ARE THESE INTERPRETERS?

Table 1, compiled from data in Jones, Clark, and Soltz (1997) and Jones (2001), compares characteristics of educational interpreters in 1993 and in 2001 and shows little difference. The educational sign language interpreter working in the public school setting in 2001 had the following characteristics: The interpreter is a White female, averaging 31–40 years of age, with 6–10 years of experience, having attended college, but having earned no degree. She earns $11.01–$13.00 per hour in a full-time job and may be working in a rural or urban setting. She has expressed the need for opportunities to continue upgrading her skills, but those opportunities are not readily available and, if available, are rarely supported by the employer (i.e., the LEA).

The K–12 educational interpreter performs a variety of duties in addition to the primary responsibility of interpreting in the classroom. Traditionally, these have been assigned because there is no one else to do them and not because an assessment has been conducted of the best practices of educational interpreting nor even an assessment of the parameters of interpreting. Some of these duties vary in frequency depending on which state the interpreter works in and whether the interpreter is employed in a rural or urban setting. On the job, the K–12 educational interpreter transliterates using an English-based sign system. This person will primarily sign using methodical signs, although she (sometimes, he) also may use a manually coded English system. The K–12 educational interpreter rarely (by definition) *interprets*.

The notion of the "professional educational interpreter" must be introduced into this discussion to help us view the bigger picture. Mills (1996) states that educational interpreters are professionals. This statement sounds plausible but, in fact, is not based on empirical evidence. We simply do not know about 50 percent of the K–12 educational interpreter workforce and, because no uniform standards exist, we cannot say with certainty how many *professional* K–12 educational interpreters exist. The term *professional* means "conforming to the rules or standards of a profession (Webster's 1996, 1998) and one who "possesses distinctive qualifications" (*WorldNet 1.6* 1997).

Yarger (2001) states that K–12 educational interpreters "need to be viewed as professionals, and as such, held to minimum standards in regard to skill level and other areas" (25). I would suggest that K–12 educational interpreters be viewed as professionals when they have proven, by definition, that they have met at least the minimum standards. If the field of K–12 educational interpreting is ever to be viewed as professional, standards must be in place and evaluation must be the cornerstone. If not, we are subjecting deaf and hard of hearing students to amateur interpreting services. Yarger (2001) also recommends, "Expectations of interpreters' skill levels need to be higher." This recommendation is not enough. For

TABLE 1 Summary of Variables for K–12 Educational Interpreters: Then and Now

| Variable | 1993 Findings | 2001 Findings |
|---|---|---|
| **I. Group Characteristics** | | |
| A. Gender | 95% Female | 99% Female |
| B. Race | 98% White | 94% White |
| C. Median Age | 31–40 Years | Same |
| D. Median Education | Voc. Certificate | College/No Degree |
| E. Median Experience | 2–5 Years | Same |
| F. Median Salary (per hour) | \$9.01–\$11.00 | \$11.01–\$13.00 |
| G. Job Status | 95% Full Time | 88% Full Time |
| H. Experienced Injuries Due to Interpreting | 29% | 34% |
| **II. Sign System Most Used while Interpreting** | | |
| A. Conceptually Accurate Signed English/Pidgin Sign English (CASE/PSE) | 56% | 70% |
| B. Signing Exact English (SEE II) | 33% | 19% |
| C. Signed English (SE) | 7% | 3% |
| D. American Sign Language (ASL) | 3% | 7% |
| **III. Certification, Evaluation, and Training** | | |
| A. No Certification Held | 63% | 50% |
| B. Not Evaluated for Interpreting Skills before Hire | 57% | 58% |
| C. Never Been Evaluated for Interpreting Skills | 25% | 31% |
| D. Interpreting In-Service Training Never Provided | 36% | 38% |
| E. Expressed Need for Continued Interpreter Training | 95% | 90% |

expectations to be higher, we must require that *all* K–12 educational interpreters be measured (i.e., evaluated) for their skills and knowledge. This evaluation needs to happen now.

We have seen some progress with the establishment of standards in some states and with evaluation using the EIPA. This progress is encouraging. However, we do not know about the qualifications of at least 50 percent of working K–12 educational interpreters. This lack of information is damaging not only to the field but also to the deaf and hard of hearing students who depend on interpreting services.

## WHAT ARE THE ROLES AND RESPONSIBILITIES OF THE INTERPRETER?

Let us look at the second issue that remains a concern in our field: the notion of the K–12 educational interpreter's job roles and responsibilities and the timing of these responsibilities. What does this issue involve?

Until the early 1990s, almost every description in the literature was based on individual or group recommendations as to what educational sign language interpreters ideally should be doing (Heavner 1986; Massachusetts Commission and Massachusetts Department of Education 1988; Jones 1989; Brazeau 1991; Contrucci 1991; Wendel 1993). However, in reality, in a small sample of thirty-two educational interpreters in western Pennsylvania, Hayes (1991, 1992) found confusion with respect to what the interpreter, the regular education teacher, the special education teacher, and the interpreter's supervisor reported as the educational sign language interpreter's roles and responsibilities.

Several perspectives (Moores 1984; Mertens 1991; McCreery et al. 1999) articulate these roles and responsibilities. However, both interpreters and educators continue to be confused today with respect to the roles and responsibilities of K–12 educational interpreters (Affonso 1998; Yarger 2001; Antia and Kreimeyer 2001). Stewart, Schein, and Cartwright (1998) describe the misconception:

> Once educational interpreters become members of a team, it is realistic to expect them to share information they may have about the student with the other team members. Realistic, yes, but a violation of the profession's code of ethics. Some interpreters decline to be "members of the team." (194)

This description is stated as if there were an option for team membership. The interpreter is, by law, a member of the educational team. Transliterating-interpreting is one of four roles that the K–12 educational interpreter plays on a daily basis (Winston 1998; Jones 1999). Although interpreting is the primary responsibility of the K–12 educational interpreter, tutoring plays a significant role in the daily lives of deaf and hard of hearing students and is the second most frequent responsibility borne by the K–12 educational interpreter (Jones, Clark, and Soltz 1997; Yarger 2001). The responsibilities do not stop there. Third, the interpreter acts as an aide in the classroom and in the school environment as needed, as all school personnel are expected to do. Finally, and of significance, the interpreter also acts as a consultant. The state of Colorado categorizes the two latter roles within the catchall category of "Team Member" roles (CDE 2002), but the fact remains that aiding and consulting are important roles the K–12 educational interpreter plays.

These four roles may cause confusion in the school setting when roles overlap or seem to conflict with one another. One can rightfully argue that transliterating-interpreting is the most critical function within the responsibilities of K–12 educational interpreting. However, let us not discuss this paramount role to the exclusion of the other three. Interpreting is only one support service (albeit the most crucial). Tutoring may be more appropriate than interpreting for some students, if not many (see chapters 2 and 3 about level of language skills). This use of an educational interpreter is an educational team decision, but it points to the need for K–12 educational interpreters to possess qualifications in addition to transliterating-interpreting.

Winston (1998) and Jones (1999) have identified and clarified the four roles that educational interpreters play in the public school setting. Jones's (1999) Windmill Model presents the framework within which to address potential "dilemmas" faced by interpreters working in the public schools. The dilemma mentioned by Cartwright above with respect to the code of ethics is not a dilemma when properly viewed. Many of the ethical decisions an interpreter makes in the context of the K–12 public school environment are "right versus right" decisions (Kidder 1996) and are of larger magnitude than that of simply interpreting. If the goal is clear (appropriate, equivalent, and accessible education for the deaf or hard of hearing student), then the interpreter role becomes secondary to the role of consultant to the educational team. This adjustment in no way renders the interpreting responsibilities less significant. It is a critical blade of the Windmill Model. Problems continue to arise when the interpreter is unable to categorize the dilemmas into one (or more) of the four roles. However, *professionals* categorize decision making every day.

## WHY SHOULD K–12 EDUCATIONAL INTERPRETERS BE QUALIFIED?

Participation (involvement, communication) and high expectations of deaf and hard of hearing students are indicators of success (Luckner and Muir 2001). It is incongruent to hold high expectations for students and to hold no (or minimal) expectations of interpreters who provide access to education. We are not even discussing maximum potential of deaf and hard of hearing students, as the *Rowley* case (Anthony 1982) has taught us. We are simply discussing equality of access. Deaf and hard of hearing students cannot meet high expectations (or even, heaven forbid, minimum expectations) when we do not even ensure that, at minimum, K–12 educational interpreters can provide equal access. Deaf students, with the help of their parents, school personnel, and peers, will drive themselves to achieve. However, they will not be successful if interpreters are not qualified.

Schein, Mallory, and Greaves (1991) contended that too many educational interpreters are not qualified. They determined that educational sign language interpreter subjects were, by definition, not interpreters, merely "communication aides."

> It would appear that in most schools communication aides choose what to interpret within very loose guidelines, if any, and that there is no ongoing assessment of the appropriateness of these moment-to-moment decisions. (Schein, Mallory, and Greaves 1991, 19)

It would be unconscionable and unacceptable to place any student with a teacher who is not qualified (i.e., certified, educated, and experienced). In fact, a teacher who is not qualified would not be a teacher at all. Yet, the above data show that deaf and hard of hearing students are subjected to unqualified, uncertified interpreters regularly.

## HOW DO WE MEASURE QUALIFICATIONS?

Recommended guidelines and standards for the field are not new (e.g., Anderson and Stauffer 1990; Scheibe and Hoza 1985; Moose 1999). Sanderson and Gustason (1993) have proposed a system for the evaluation of interpreting-transliterating skills specific to the educational environment. Educational interpreter certification has been suggested by many to be necessary to ensure the quality of interpreter services (Witter-Merithew and Dirst 1982; Zawolkow and DeFiore 1986; Stuckless, Avery, and Hurwitz 1989; Contrucci 1991; Schein, Mallory, and Greaves 1991; Sanderson and Gustason 1993; New York State 1998). Certification is one measurement of skills that should be included in an overall system of standards for K–12 educational interpreters.

Many states are addressing this issue by passing legislation that establishes state minimum standards, licensure, or both (e.g., Oklahoma Legislature 2002; Colorado Legislature 1997; Minnesota Legislature 1994; Kansas Legislature 1993; Wisconsin Legislature 1992) and some LEAs are setting their own standards (e.g., Wilcox, Schroeder, and Martinez 1990). These requirements are now finally forcing into the discussion the difficult questions of interpreter qualifications and appropriate placement of deaf and hard of hearing students in LEAs throughout the United States. This discussion is positive for the field. Once we know the qualifications of K–12 educational interpreters, we are better able to improve those qualifications and, therefore, improve access to education.

Accurate measurement of interpreting skills is certainly important. An excellent example of an interpreting evaluation system that addresses these skill areas is the Educational Interpreter Performance Assessment (EIPA), authored by Schick and Williams (1994). The EIPA is not only a measuring instrument that addresses specific criteria of interpreting message equivalency but also one that provides diagnostic results and recommendations for interpreter applicants, guiding them to improved performance (Seal 1998; see also chapter 10). This duality sets the EIPA apart. It is a valid means of evaluating skills (Seal 1998), designed specifically to measure interpreting work in the classroom. The EIPA, a dual-purpose instrument, is the ideal measurement tool to use for exploring the work of K–12 educational interpreters. We are then able to discuss qualifications and skills using the same language. We are then able to discuss remediation of skills using the same language. And we are then able to upgrade specific skills through strategies based on the diagnostics of the interpreters' performance in the educational setting, also provided by the EIPA. As appropriate as this evaluation is, the results are still a "snapshot" of skills on a given day of performance in an elementary or secondary classroom situation. It does, however, specifically address in an organized format the skills needed to interpret in the K–12 setting. In other words, it establishes a benchmark.

Interestingly, even with the use of a testing instrument designed specifically for the K–12 educational interpreter, Schick, Williams, and Bolster (1999) found that 56 percent of educational interpreters did not have the minimum interpreting skills to serve as an interpreter in the classroom. Remember, these interpreters made the effort to take the EIPA and are to be commended, even if their scores were low. Nevertheless, the finding raises concern not only about the group that was evaluated but also about the working interpreters who elected not to be tested for their skills.

There is good news. Almost 49 percent of the respondents in the Johnson County Community College study of K–12 interpreters in nine western states

(JCCC 2002) had taken the EIPA and reported a mean score of 3.7. This finding is encouraging. The percentage of interpreters having taken the EIPA does vary from state to state (13.8 percent to 84.6 percent) as do the mean (average) scores (3.2 to 4.1). The majority of these interpreters have taken the EIPA within the past two years, which is significant because it means that many, if not most, have taken the videotape-standardized version of the EIPA (the new and current test), and therefore, their scores can rightfully be compared with their next test. From these data, we see that the average K–12 interpreter has achieved at least a Level 3.2. However, "average" indicates that just as many interpreters are below the average (3.7) as are above it. Most likely, future EIPA testing will yield lower average scores. The reason for this prediction is that the interpreters already tested had volunteered for the evaluation and were more assertive when it came to measuring their skills. Generally, the interpreters who have procrastinated or ignored the issue will not fare as well (Yarger 2001).

## WHO IS INCLUDED WHEN WE TALK ABOUT FULL INCLUSION?

In light of the previous discussion, I would like to call into question the very notion of "full inclusion" (Wang, Reynolds, and Walberg 1990) of deaf and hard of hearing elementary and secondary students. Qualified K–12 educational interpreters provide a vital support service to a large number of deaf and hard of hearing students who attend their local elementary and secondary schools. Without qualified interpreters, these students are denied access to the mainstream. Without qualified interpreters, "full inclusion" is a myth for these students. Deafness is not a disability within the context that most disabilities are viewed. Deaf and hard of hearing students are a "linguistic minority" (Dolnick 1993). Mediation is achieved through visual linguistic input and output. This visual communication must be accurate to allow equal access to the myriad bits of information, both auditory and visual, with which all K–12 students deal on a daily basis. IEP educational teams attempting to serve the needs of this population have not adequately addressed communication. Qualified interpreters only increase the probability of full inclusion; they do not guarantee it. As language competencies are a prerequisite to interpreting proficiency, qualified interpreters are a prerequisite to accessibility.

The pleas to address these concerns have been, until recently, largely ignored. As long ago as 1988, the Commission on Education of the Deaf stated:

> It is vitally important to students who are deaf that only interpreters possessing appropriate qualifications be employed in regular educational settings. . . . A lack of minimum standards for interpreters and pervasive confusion about their role has compromised the educational services provided to many deaf students. In regular classrooms, hearing students generally communicate by speaking and listening. For many deaf students, however, interpreters are needed to facilitate communications with their teachers and classmates. EHA (Education of the Handicapped Act) requires that deaf students be integrated into regular classroom settings to the maximum extent possible, but if quality interpreting services are not provided, that goal becomes a mockery. . . . Just as a person who

> completes two levels of a foreign language in college would not be qualified to interpret in the United Nations, completing two levels of sign language does not make a qualified sign language interpreter in any setting. (COED 1988, 103–4)

The secretary of the U.S. Department of Education echoed this concern in 1992:

> The Secretary believes that the unique communication and related needs of many children who are deaf have not been adequately considered in the development of their IEPs. . . . Meeting the unique communication and related needs of a student who is deaf is a fundamental part of providing a free appropriate public education (FAPE) to the child. . . . Any setting which does not meet the communication and related needs of a child who is deaf, and therefore does not allow for the provision of FAPE, cannot be considered the LRE for that child. . . . The Secretary is concerned that some public agencies have misapplied the LRE provision by presuming that placements in or closer to the regular classroom are required for children who are deaf, without taking into consideration the range of communication and related needs that must be addressed in order to provide appropriate services. (in Alexander 1992, 49274–75)

Winston is more specific:

> The only way to determine a LRE is to view the environment from the deaf student's perspective; no other perspective can provide an accurate assessment of the setting. (Winston 1990, 61)

Again, if 50 percent of the K–12 educational interpreter workforce is not certified, how do we know whether communication needs of deaf and hard of hearing students are being met? Are parents of deaf and hard of hearing students aware of this situation? It is doubtful.

We have come a great distance since the 1960s when interpreting was portrayed as a paternal "helper" model (Quigley and Youngs 1965). However, a difficult road lies ahead. We presently are facing an underqualified field of K–12 educational interpreters and have been for more than two decades. This underqualified field has done (and is doing) a disservice to deaf and hard of hearing students, those students' parents, and their LEAs in this country.

Standards are here. Expectations are on the rise. This change will strain the system, but it is necessary to reach the goal of equal access for deaf and hard of hearing students attending public school systems in the United States. The question becomes (and has always been), What must we do to meet the expectations that deaf and hard of hearing students deserve and achieve the qualifications necessary to serve this population?

## WHAT MUST THE INTERPRETING FIELD DO?

Interpreting in the K–12 educational setting is a specialization within the field of interpreting. Interpreting for children is not the same as interpreting for adults (Schick 2001). Likewise, evaluation of interpreters who work with children is not the same as evaluation of interpreters who work with adults (Schick and Williams 2001). Specific steps such as those that follow must be taken to address this specialty.

***Standards for K–12 interpreters, with evaluation of skills, must be established and put into practice.*** (See chapter 9.) We have discussed the beginning of this effort, which involves using the EIPA as the cornerstone skills evaluation instrument. Individual states and the Regional Assessment System Project of state departments of education and the Bureau of Indian Affairs (RAS 2002) have begun using the EIPA. This start is commendable, but much more needs to be done. It is appropriate to use an instrument that can be recognized throughout the United States. Qualifications would be reciprocal between the states, and interpreters could move into new districts with less of a disruption for the deaf and hard of hearing students they serve.

***Standards for evaluating the knowledge of K–12 interpreters must be established and put into practice.*** One instrument by which to evaluate this knowledge might be in the form of a written test designed to evaluate the variety of knowledge required to function properly in the public school setting. Fortunately, this type of test is being designed. Through the collaborative effort of Boys Town National Research Hospital (EIPA Diagnostic Center); the University of Colorado, Boulder; and the Regional Assessment System for K–12 Interpreters, the Educational Interpreter Performance Assessment Written Test (EIPA-WT) has been created for this purpose. As with skills qualifications, mentioned above, knowledge qualifications can now be reciprocal.

***Deadlines for compliance must be reasonable and enforced.*** Any practice to grandfather experienced interpreters is inappropriate. Indefinite extension of deadlines for demonstrating qualifications is also inappropriate. Experience alone is not enough to interpret in K–12 public school settings. Experience, with no education-training intervention, will not improve interpreting skill. Good intentions are not enough when dealing with the future of the deaf and hard of hearing population in the United States. Results and accountability (i.e., professional interpreter qualifications) are the keys to success.

***Associate degrees in interpreting are not enough for the specialty area of K–12 educational interpreting.*** The curriculum of a basic interpreter education program simply does not include enough hours to provide adequate preparation for the specialized field of K–12 educational interpreting. Interpreting in the K–12 setting is a specialization with not only requisite skills but also requisite knowledge (see, for example, PDES 1995). Whether interpreting is performed in the elementary setting or the high school setting makes no difference. In a national survey, Burch (2002) reports that all interpreter practitioners and stakeholders realize that a bachelor's degree for K–12 educational interpreters is "essential at all three instructional levels [elementary, middle school, and high school] of students served" (136). We must leave behind the notion that educational interpreters can be "trained." We are not discussing preparation for a circus act. Interpreting requires an in-depth education that builds not only specific interpreting skills but also decision-making skills for professional behavior.

Bachelor-level educational interpreting programs need to be established now. These programs must require students to satisfy exit criteria that measure skills and knowledge. A few bachelor-level models currently in the field can provide examples and guidance: California State University-Fresno, College of St. Catherine, Indiana University and Purdue University at Indianapolis, Kent State University, Northeastern University, University of Arizona, University of Arkansas at Little Rock, University of New Hampshire-Manchester, University of New Mexico, University of Tennessee, University of Wisconsin-Milwaukee, Western Oregon University, and William Woods University. The College of St. Catherine is a specialized program for interpreters wanting to enter the medical field. The Arizona and Kent State programs are designed specifically for K–12 educational interpreters. The other programs are "generalist" programs. Could these generalist programs add programming specialty options to meet the need for K–12 educational interpreters? Could new programs be designed to follow a distance learning model such as the EICP? Of course they could. Interpreter standards will drive the establishment of new bachelor-level programs. Comprehensive delivery and high expectations must be the goals of these new programs. Accessibility for students of interpreting (i.e., distance learning, blended delivery) needs to be evaluated to allow the largest number of qualified students to participate.

***Education and professional development must be part of the in-service training for K–12 educational interpreters within their LEAs.*** The term *in-service* is inclusive, meaning in-service opportunities for K–12 educational interpreters and staff members within a Comprehensive System of Personnel Development (CSPD), as mandated by the IDEA. In-service education must be specifically designed for K–12 educational interpreters, addressing both skills and knowledge, and provided by the LEA or offered by outside agencies contracted by the LEA.

LEAs in the United States must take the above steps. The new No Child Left Behind Act of 2001 (NCLB) makes it clear that the responsibility for regular education lies at the levels of the state education agency (SEA) and the LEA. This responsibility includes "setting standards for student achievement and holding students and educators accountable for results" (Paige 2002, 3). This devolution of power and responsibility is also clear for special education through the IDEA: "(C) developing and implementing a comprehensive system of personnel development needed to provide qualified personnel in sufficient number to deliver special education, *related services*, and early intervention services" (IDEA 1990, 104 STAT. 1114, italics added).

The time has come for partnerships between SEAs, LEAs, regional resource centers, higher education, and others to address these concerns and engage appropriate strategies for taking action. The time is now. The effort is the right thing to do for deaf and hard of hearing students if they are to have any chance of equal access to the public school system in the United States.

## REFERENCES

Affonso, C. 1998. Interpreting with deaf preschoolers. *VIEWS* 15(2): 14.

Alexander, L. 1992. Deaf students education: Policy guidance. *Federal Register* 57(201): 49274–75.

Anderson, G. B., and L. K. Stauffer. 1990. *Identifying standards for the training of interpreters for deaf people.* Little Rock, Ark.: University of Arkansas Research and Training Center on Deafness and Hearing Impairment.

Anthony, P. 1982. The Rowley case. *Journal of Educational Finance* 8(1): 106–15.

Antia, S. D., and H. Kreimeyer. 2001. The role of educational interpreters in inclusive education. *American Annals of the Deaf* 146(4): 355–65.

Babbidge, H. D. 1965. *Education of the deaf in the United States: A report to the secretary of health, education and welfare by his advisory committee of education of the deaf.* Washington, D.C.: United States Government Printing Office.

Battaglia, M., and J. Avery. 1986. *A resource guide to training programs: Interpreting for the hearing impaired.* Rochester, N.Y.: Rochester Institute of Technology and the U.S. Department of Education.

Bowen-Bailey, D. 1996. The challenges of educational interpreting. *VIEWS* 13(3): 16.

Brazeau, K., ed. Spring, 1991. *Oregon guidelines: Educational interpreting for students who are deaf.* Salem, Oreg.: Publications and Multimedia Center, Oregon Department of Education.

Burch, D. D. 2002. Essential education for sign language interpreters in pre-college educational settings. In *2002 journal of interpretation,* ed. D. Watson, 125–49. Alexandria, Va.: Registry of Interpreters for the Deaf.

Bureau of Educational Research and Service. 1989. A survey to determine minimum state and/or local standards for interpreters for hearing impaired students in the United States. Unpublished national study, University of Tennessee, Knoxville.

Carew, M. E., ed. 2001. Programs for training interpreters. *American Annals of the Deaf* 146(2): 192–97.

Colorado Department of Education (CDE). 2002. *Educational interpreter procedures and guidelines manual.* Denver, Colo.: CDE.

Colorado Legislature. *Colorado Act Concerning Standards for Educational Interpreters for the Deaf* (1997) HB 97-1146.

Commission on Education of the Deaf (COED). February, 1988. *Toward equality: Education of the deaf.* Washington, D.C.: United States Government Printing Office.

Contrucci, V. J. 1991. *Educational interpreter license. Exceptional education/pupil services: Information update,* Bulletin No. 91.13. Madison, Wisc.: Wisconsin Department of Public Instruction.

Dolnick, E. 1993. Deafness as culture. *The Atlantic Monthly* (September): 37–43.

Education for All Handicapped Children Act of 1975, Pub. L. 94–142, U.S. Code vol. 20, secs. 1400 *et seq.*

Educational Interpreters/Transliterators of the RID (EdITOR). 1993. Prospective position statement on educational interpreting. Silver Spring, Md.: Registry of Interpreters for the Deaf.

Frishberg, N. 1990. *Interpreting: An introduction* (rev. ed.). Silver Spring, Md.: Registry of Interpreters for the Deaf.

Gannon, J. R. 1981. *Deaf heritage: A narrative history of deaf America.* Silver Spring, Md.: National Association of the Deaf.

Hayes, P. L. 1991. Educational interpreters for deaf students: Their responsibilities, problems, and concerns. Ph.D. dissertation, University of Pittsburgh.

———. 1992. Educational interpreters for deaf students: Their responsibilities, problems, and concerns. *Journal of Interpretation* 5(1): 5–24.

Heavner, J. 1986. *Interpreting in the educational setting: Technical assistance paper number 12.* Tallahassee, Fla.: Florida Bureau of Education for Exceptional Students, Division of Public Schools.

Hurwitz, T. A. 1991. Report from national task force on educational interpreting. In *Conference proceedings: Educational interpreting: Into the 1990s, November 9–11, 1989,* 19–23. Washington, D.C.: Gallaudet University College of Continuing Education.

*Individuals with Disabilities Education Act of 1990* (IDEA), Public Law 101-476, U.S. Code vol. 20, secs. 1400–1485.

Johnson County Community College (JCCC). 2002. *Regional assessment system, K–12 interpreters needs assessment, summer 2002.* Overland Park, Kans.: Johnson County Community College, Office of Institutional Research.

Johnson, L., and E. A. Winston. 1999. The educational interpreting certificate program: New approaches to educating the educational interpreter. *VIEWS* 16(2): 19.

Jones, B. E., ed. 1989. *A handbook for educational interpreters: Elementary settings, secondary settings, post-secondary academic settings, post-secondary technical and vocational programs,* 3rd printing. Overland Park, Kans.: Johnson County Community College.

———. 1999. Providing access: "New roles" for educational interpreters. *VIEWS* 16(2): 15.

———. 2001. Working K–12 interpreter characteristics. Unpublished class study (EDI 234), Educational Interpreting Certificate Program, Front Range Community College, Westminster, Colo.

Jones, B. E., G. M. Clark, and D. F. Soltz. 1997. Characteristics and practices of sign language interpreters in inclusive education programs. *Exceptional Children* 63(2): 257–68.

Kansas Legislature. *Kansas State Act Concerning Interpreters* (1993) HB 2257.

Kidder, R. M. 1996. *How good people make tough choices.* New York, N.Y.: Fireside.

Lane, H. 1984. *When the mind hears: A history of the deaf.* New York, N.Y.: Random House.

L'Epée, C. M. 1801. *The method of educating the deaf and dumb; confirmed by long experience* (translated from the French and Latin). London, U.K.: T. Cadell, Robson, Harding and Longman/Rees.

Luckner, J., and S. Muir. 2001. Successful students who are deaf in general education settings. *American Annals of the Deaf* 146(5): 435–45.

Massachusetts Commission for the Deaf and Hard of Hearing (MCDHH) and Massachusetts Department of Education, Division of Special Education. December 5, 1988. *An information guide related to standards for educational interpreting for deaf and severely hard of hearing students in elementary and secondary schools.* Boston, Mass.: MCDHH.

McCreery, S., K. Feldman, H. Donnel, and K. Davis. 1999. Ethical educational interpreting: Perspectives of multiple members. *VIEWS* 16(2): 6.

Mertens, D. M. 1991. Teachers working with interpreters: The deaf student's educational experience. *American Annals of the Deaf* 136(1): 48–52.

Mills, J. 1996. Educational interpreting at the elementary level. *VIEWS* 13(3): 1.

Minnesota Legislature. *Minnesota State K–12 Educational Interpreter Law* (1994) 122A.31.

Moores, D. F. 1984. Interpreting in the public schools. *Perspectives for Teachers of the Hearing Impaired* 3(2): 13–15.

———. 1987. *Educating the deaf: Psychology, principles and practices,* 3rd ed. Boston, Mass.: Houghton Mifflin.

Moose, M. 1999. Educational interpreting: Raising the standards. *VIEWS* 16(2): 10.

New York State. 1998. *Guidelines for educational interpreters.* Proposed New York State guidelines for educational interpreters. Albany, N.Y.: New York State.

No Child Left Behind Act of 2001, Pub. L. 107–110, 115 Stat. 1425 (2002).

Oklahoma Legislature. *Oklahoma State Educational Interpreter for the Deaf Act* (2002) SB 1328.

Paige, R. 2002. *No Child Left Behind: A desktop reference.* Jessup, Md.: U.S. Department of Education Publications Center. http://www.ed.gov/pubs/edpubs.html (accessed September 15, 2003).

*Professional Development Endorsement System* (PDES). 1995. Winsted, Conn.: Northwest Connecticut Community-Technical College and University of Tennessee.

Quigley, S. P., and J. Youngs, eds. 1965. *Interpreting for deaf people*. Washington, D.C.: U.S. Department of Health, Education and Welfare, Vocational Rehabilitation Administration.

Ramsey, C. L. 1997. *Deaf children in public schools: Placement, context and consequences*. Washington, D.C.: Gallaudet University Press.

*Regional Assessment System for K–12 Educational Interpreters* (RAS). 2002. Overland Park, Kans.: Johnson County Community College, Kansas and State Departments of Education in Alaska, Arizona, the Bureau of Indian Affairs, Colorado, Idaho, Iowa, Kansas, Montana, Nebraska, New Mexico, Utah, and Wyoming. http://www.jccc.net/ras (accessed October 1, 2002).

Rehabilitation Act of 1973, Pub. L. 93-112, U.S. Code vol. 29, secs. 701 *et seq*.

Sanderson, G. 1991. Setting priorities for the 1990s. In *Conference proceedings: Educational interpreting: Into the 1990s, November 9–11, 1989*. Washington, D.C.: Gallaudet University College of Continuing Education.

Sanderson, G., and G. Gustason, eds. 1993. *Model standards for the certification of educational interpreters for deaf students and suggested options for routes to certification*. Silver Spring, Md.: Registry of Interpreters for the Deaf and Council on Education of the Deaf.

Scheibe, K., and J. Hoza. 1985. Throw it out the window! (The code of ethics? We don't use it here): Guidelines for educational interpreters. In *Proceedings of the Registry of Interpreters for the Deaf Convention*, 173–182. Silver Spring, Md.: Registry of Interpreters for the Deaf Publications.

Schein, J. D., B. L. Mallory, and S. Greaves. 1991. *Communication for deaf students in mainstream classrooms*. Edmonton, Alberta: University of Alberta.

Schick, B. 2001. Interpreting for children: How it is different. *Odyssey* 2 (Winter/Spring): 8–11.

Schick, B. and K. Williams. 1994. The evaluation of educational interpreters. In *Sign language in the schools: Current issues and controversies,* eds. B. Schick and M. P. Moeller. Omaha, Nebr.: Boys Town Press.

———. 2001. The Educational Interpreter Performance Assessment. *Odyssey* 2 (Winter/Spring): 12–14.

Schick, B., K. Williams, and L. Bolster. 1999. Skill levels of educational interpreters working in public schools. *Journal of Deaf Studies and Deaf Education* 4(2): 144–55.

Schildroth, A. N., and S. A. Hotto. 1991. Annual survey of hearing impaired children and youth: 1989–90 school year. *American Annals of the Deaf* 136(2): 155–66.

Schrag, J. 1991. Special education in the 1990s, Keynote address. In *Conference proceedings: Educational interpreting: Into the 1990s, November 9–11, 1989*. Washington, D.C.: Gallaudet University College of Continuing Education.

Seal, B. C. 1998. *Best practices in educational interpreting*. Boston, Mass.: Allyn and Bacon.

Stedt, J. D., and D. F. Moores. 1990. Manual codes of English and American Sign Language. In *Manual communication: Implications for education*, ed. H. Bornstein, 1–20. Washington, D.C.: Gallaudet University Press.

Stewart, D. A., J. D. Schein, and B. Cartwright. 1998. *Sign language interpreting: Exploring its arts and science*. Boston, Mass.: Allyn & Bacon.

Stuckless, E. R., J. C. Avery, and T. A. Hurwitz. 1989. *Educational interpreting for deaf students: Report of the national task force on educational interpreting*. Rochester, N.Y.: National Technical Institute for the Deaf at Rochester Institute of Technology.

Togioka, P. 1990. Looking at educational interpreting theory: Course content and rationale used in a training program for educational interpreters. In *The challenge of the 90's: New standards in interpreter education,* ed. L. Swaby. Proceedings of the Conference of Interpreter Trainers, eighth national convention, Pomona, Calif.

Turnbull, H. R., III. 1990. *Free appropriate education: The law and children with disabilities.* Denver, Colo.: Love Publishing.

U.S. Department of Education. 1999. *To assure the free appropriate public education of all children with disabilities: Twenty-first annual report to Congress on the implementation of the Individuals with Disabilities Act.* Washington, D.C.: U.S. Department of Education.

Wang, M. C., M. C. Reynolds, and H. J. Walberg, eds. 1990. *Special education: Research and practice: Synthesis and findings.* Elmsford, N.Y.: Pergamon Press.

*Webster's Revised Unabridged Dictionary.* 1996; 1998. http://dictionary.reference.com/search.

Wendel, T., ed. 1993. *Guidelines for sign language interpreters.* Lincoln, Nebr.: Nebraska Department of Education and the Nebraska Commission for the Hearing Impaired.

West Virginia Commission for the Deaf and Hard of Hearing (WVCDHH), and West Virginia Department of Education (WVDOE). 2002. *Findings of West Virginia educational interpreters in public schools. WVCDHH News,* March 1.

Wilcox, P., F. Schroeder, and T. Martinez. 1990. A commitment to professionalism: Educational interpreting standards within a large public school system. *Sign Language Studies* 68:277–86.

Williams, K., and B. Schick. 1999. *Educational interpreter assessment: Evaluation team summary.* Omaha, Nebr.: Boys Town Press.

Winston, E. A. 1985. Mainstreaming: Like it or not. *Journal of Interpretation* 2:117–19.

———. 1989. Transliteration: What's the message. In *The sociolinguistics of the deaf community,* ed. C. Lucas, 147–64. San Diego, Calif.: Academic Press.

———. 1990. Mainstream interpreting: An analysis of the task. In *The challenge of the 90's: New standards in interpreter education,* ed. L. Swaby. Proceedings of the Conference of Interpreter Trainers, eighth national convention, Pomona, Calif.

———. 1994. An interpreted education: Inclusion or exclusion? In *Implications and complications of deaf students of the full inclusion movement,* eds. R. C. Johnson and O. P. Cohen, 55–63. Washington, D.C.: Gallaudet University Press.

———. 1998. Ethics in educational interpreting. *VIEWS* 15(2): 30.

Wisconsin Legislature. Act Licensing Educational Sign Language Interpreters (1992) Pub. L. 3.305 Educational Interpreter—Deaf or Hard of Hearing—884, PK–12.

Witter-Merithew, A., and R. Dirst. 1982. Preparation and use of educational interpreters. In *Deafness and communication,* eds. D. G. Sims, G. G. Walker, and R. L. Whitehead, 395–406. Baltimore, Md.: Williams & Wilkins.

*Worldnet 1.6.* 1997. Princeton, N.J.: Princeton University.

Yarger, C. C. 2001. Educational interpreting: Understanding the rural experience. *American Annals of the Deaf* 146(1): 16–30.

Zawolkow, E., and S. DeFiore. 1986. Educational interpreting for elementary and secondary level hearing-impaired students. *American Annals of the Deaf* 131(1): 26–28.

# Interpretability and Accessibility of Mainstream Classrooms

Elizabeth A. Winston

After more than three decades of mainstreaming, with little research to support its effectiveness, more and more people are actively questioning the process, wondering to what extent mainstreamed deaf students are being provided illusionary access to a system that is fundamentally biased against their need for visual learning. Turner (2002, 2004) describes this kind of situation as institutional audism, the pervasive bias toward hearing and sound that is found throughout a system like mainstreamed education. The limited research currently available on the effectiveness of interpreted educations is consistently revealing the illusions. Most research about access by means of interpreting has been conducted with adults at the postsecondary level (Marschark, Sapere, Convertino, Seewagen, and Maltzen forthcoming; Marschark, Sapere, Convertino, and Seewagen forthcoming; Livingston, Singer, and Abramson 1994). As Marschark, Sapere, Convertino, and Seewagen (forthcoming) conclude, very little is reliably known about how adults understand interpreted educations. Winston (1990, 1994) has described K–12 classroom activities from the perspective of visual accessibility and resulting interpretability. A published occasional paper (Johnson and Cohen 1994) from Gallaudet University offers several investigations into the social and cultural implications of mainstreaming or "inclusion," repeatedly finding that the practice does not provide adequate access to normal social interaction. Ramsey (1997, chapter 11 of this volume) has described the lot of deaf and hard of hearing children who have been "included" in an elementary classroom:

> In this context, deaf students must struggle to find their own identities as genuine peers of the hearing students who have the advantage of direct and immediate access to the teacher. For some, this identity remains out of reach, discouraging participation in class and making intergrated settings uncomfortable.

The Commission on Education of the Deaf (1988) raised serious concerns about the adequacy of mainstreamed educations for deaf children. Fifteen years later, the NAD (2003) *White Paper: 2003 Reauthorization of the Individuals with*

*Disabilities Education Act* continues to raise these serious concerns about accessibility for deaf children in interpreted educations and presents the fundamental needs of deaf students in education, stating,

> The NAD, consistent with the National Deaf Education Project (NDEP), a collaborative project of the American Society for Deaf Children, the Conference of Educational Administrators of Schools and Programs for the Deaf, the Convention of American Instructors of the Deaf, Gallaudet University, the National Association of the Deaf, and the National Technical Institute for the Deaf, believes that direct and uninhibited language and communication access to the curriculum, and all facets of the schooling experience are essential for a deaf child to achieve equality of opportunity. (NAD 2003)

NAD goes on to express serious concerns about the placement of deaf and hard of hearing children in mainstream settings, stating,

> However, we are profoundly concerned that this provision of the law, intended as a presumption favoring local school placements when appropriate, continues to be interpreted and applied as a mandate for full inclusion. In the case of many deaf and hard of hearing students, the effect of this continued misinterpretation and misapplication of the provision has the net effect of isolating the student from the very things crucial to their development, unimpeded language and communication access to the curriculum and socialization opportunities. The placement decision for deaf and hard of hearing individuals must be communication driven and the LRE for a deaf or hard of hearing child must be the environment that presents the fewest language and communication barriers to the individual's cognitive, social, and emotional development. (NAD 2003)

The chapters in this volume and other research indicate that these concerns are not being adequately addressed. Kurz Brown and Caldwell Langer (see chapter 1) have found that deaf students in their study were often unaware of or confused about the roles of interpreters; Caldwell Langer (see chapter 5) has found that interpreters feel undersupported. In addition, Jones, Clark, and Soltz (1997), Schick, Williams, and Bolster (1999), Schick and Williams (see chapter 10), and Yarger (2001) have documented the sad state of interpreter qualifications in several areas of the country. La Bue (1998) and Caldwell Langer (see chapter 5) have initiated preliminary research about linguistic access available through an interpreted education; each have found tremendous differences between what is available to hearing students and what is interpreted and therefore accessible for deaf students in interpreted education.

No accepted standards exist for determining when a student is ready for placement in an interpreted education. These students are frequently placed with little regard for language skills and background preparation as well as to social, cognitive, and emotional maturity. The field is rife with anecdotal accounts of interpreters who, for example, are forced to interpret to three students, one who is a native ASL signer, one who is a mediocre English signer, and one who is not a signer at all. Although this task is patently impossible, administrators, parents, and teachers all ignore this fact and pat themselves on the back for meeting the letter of the law. Yet, with the ongoing lack of research, deaf students are placed into interpreted educations without an understanding of what can be, might be, or is possible.

The unfounded expectations of teachers, parents, and interpreters abound: that deaf children will learn any language through interpretation; that they will learn English through English signing; and that qualified interpreters can bridge a vast chasm of language deficit, academic disadvantage, and audistic teaching approaches with a Lilliputian rope made up of flapping hands. The failure to require stringent certification and standards for interpreters and, in many cases, to ignore the need for qualifications means that, often, interpreters have even shorter "ropes." These tremendous barriers to interpreted education must be recognized, and anyone choosing this type of education, either for themselves or for their children, must at least make the decision after considering what might be possible rather than placing blind hope in illusionary access.

Nevertheless, it also seems clear that interpreted, mediated educations are going to continue and that, with a number of factors in place, they can provide, not a condition of normalcy, but a potential channel to accessibility. Several factors influence the effectiveness of an interpreted education. These include the skill of the interpreter, the language, the cognitive and academic levels of the deaf or hard of hearing student, the support received from caregivers, and the interpreted classroom environment. Other chapters in this volume address the student and the interpreter; this study investigates the complex interaction between the constraints of interpreting and the classroom environment, especially those characteristics that rely on and reflect the hearing bias of sound-based classrooms. The goal is to analyze whether and to what extent those classrooms and hearing approaches can be made more accessible to deaf students who have adequate language, academic, and cognitive skills to meet the classroom expectations when those students are provided with appropriate, qualified interpreters. Before analyzing whether and how an interpreted classroom can be made accessible through interpreting, this chapter first discusses the unchangeable constraints of interpreting and interpreted educations. Then the following discussion addresses the effect of these constraints on the classrooms, the assumptions about English language learning (implicit and explicit) that are made in hearing classrooms, and the discourse patterns of teachers that are compatible with interpreting an education.

## ISSUES OF ACCESS

Six key issues affect interpretation in the classroom: interpretation's "secondhand" quality, the lag time it creates, the multiple channels of input inherent in the education process, visual accessibility, academic language, and discourse styles of teachers. The following discussion will consider each of these issues in more depth.

### Interpreted Educations as Mediated (Secondhand) Information

For many years, a simplistic definition of interpreting has had a tremendous effect on beliefs about interpreted educations. This definition views the act as a simple decoding and encoding, a one-to-one transformation of words spoken in English into a visual representation of those words through some kind of signing. In this definition, interpreters are simply machines that process this transformation, having no effect on the message, participants, or outcomes. Although most in the field of interpreting have moved far beyond this simplistic definition, the belief that this mechanistic transformation somehow occurs in educational contexts. Interpreters are expected simply to sign what they hear and speak whatever signs they see.

Monikowski and Winston (2003) provide an overview of the history of interpreting and sign language interpreting definitions, ranging from that of Seleskovitch (1978) and Seleskovitch and Lederer (1989) to those of Neuman Solow (1981), Colonomos (1992), Roy (2000), Metzger (1995), and Wadensjo (1998), all of which look far beyond this simplistic definition. Seleskovitch (1978) defines interpreting as a trilogue. Roy (2000), in her early work, describes interpreting as

> a linguistic and social act of communication, and the interpreter's role in this process is an engaged one, directed by the knowledge and understanding of the entire communicative situation, including fluency in the languages, competence in appropriate usage within each language, and in managing the cross-cultural flow of talk. (3)

Wadensjo (1998) describes the interpreting process as a "pas de trois" that must be considered from the perspectives of all the interactants. Metzger (1995) provides insight into the importance of the various frames of the participants, including that of the interpreter, in interpreted interactions. Interpreting is interaction among three or more people; the naïve assumption that deaf students and hearing teachers have access to each other without the filter of interpretation and the interpreter is not true. Yet, the educational system ignores this basic feature of interpreting—that it is always mediated by a third person (the interpreter), with all the language seen or heard by the participants as being, at least in part, the interpreter's language influenced by his or her own filters, knowledge, and experience.

Cazden (1988, 2001) has conducted in-depth analyses of hearing classrooms. Although she does not focus on deaf students or on interpreted education, her observations and insights into the dynamics of interaction in a classroom shed a bright light onto the consequences of an interpreted education. She reminds us of the consequences of both language and timing in a classroom: "In order to be heard as appropriate, a student not only has to speak the right words but also has to say them at the right time" (1988, 185).

The fundamental characteristic of interpreting that cannot be changed is that it is interpretation. It is not direct and certainly is not the mythical "exact word for word, sign for sign" rendition that naïve users of interpreting so often believe happens. Every sign the deaf student sees and every word the teacher and peers hear are those of the interpreter, who is mediating the original intent (Roy 2000; Metzger 1995; Wadensjo 1998). An effective, dynamic interpretation strives to make the interpretation similar in meaning to the original, but no matter how expert, how effective and dynamic, it will still be mediated and different. This characteristic is true regardless of the target language, be it English, ASL, English signing, or cued speech. A deaf student, communicating through the process of interpreting, can never be "heard" as appropriate; only the interpreter is heard. Unfortunately, although the interpreter is the one who is heard, the deaf student is often the one who is judged, and judged as inappropriate, whether it is because the interpreter hesitates and falters when he or she does not understand the student's signing, whether it is simply because the interpreter's voice is an adult female voice like the teacher's acting as if it were a young child, or whether it is because of many other factors that come into play during the interpretation.

An interpreted education is, then, by definition, a mediated, secondhand education, perhaps similar to the education intended for the hearing students, but never the same. To date, no research discusses the added cognitive loads that this process brings to deaf students in interpreted education. And, although watching an interpreted education is commonly accepted as being more tiring, little research actually supports this premise. The understanding that interpreting has an effect on every piece of knowledge and language that goes through the interpreter is of fundamental importance for anyone in a position to place a deaf child into an interpreted education.

## Interpreted Education and Lag Time

One consequence of the processing of the source language to the target language is very clearly measurable and easily understood. Time is essential to the processing of information (as are adequate first and second language skills, skilled interpreting, and understanding of education). This time has been referred to as "lag time," "decalage," and "processing time." Lag time has been used to describe the amount of time that an interpreter "lags" behind the source speaker before producing the target message (Seleskovitch and Lederer 1989; Roy 2000). Depending on the complexity of the source meaning, the lag between the original message and the interpreted message can be less than a second or as much as two to three minutes or more in consecutive interpreting.

The term *lag time* has been discarded by most sign language interpreters as being too focused on the production of messages rather than on the processes that go into the production and as being too negative in its reference to being "behind." The term *processing time* more accurately reflects the need for an interpreter to analyze and then produce a meaningful message. This preferred term refers to a positive activity that should add value to an interpretation rather than imply a negative tardiness in message making.

Nevertheless, *lag time* may still be a more appropriate term for this discussion. From the perspective of the deaf student receiving the message, the student is lagging, is therefore unable to participate on an equal basis with hearing peers, and is judged on his or her social interaction abilities because of this lagging behind. For the purpose of this discussion, I will use the term *lag time* because I am discussing the negative effect that this time difference has on classroom interaction. In effect, the deaf student cannot have normal interaction; the interaction does, by virtue of interpretation, lag behind. Regardless of an interpreter's skill, this characteristic cannot be changed.

However, participants can modify interactions to account for lag time. Roy (2000) discusses participants' learning about the lag involved in interpreted interactions. Hearing participants who are used to interpreted interactions can hold their responses while waiting for an interpretation to be finished. They are, of course, still ready to respond before the deaf person, having that "holding" time in which to process their responses. In an interpreted classroom, however, only the teacher has the authority and power to actually change the interactions to accommodate interpreting. The teacher must actively and consciously hold up the process to allow for deaf student interaction. He or she must do it consistently. Interpreters can help the teacher remember and can actively remind everyone of the need to wait, but unless the teacher is willing to adapt the interactions of the entire class to meet the needs of interpreting, lag time will always be the burden of the deaf student. Thus, educators must understand the serious consequences of both lag time and the mediation of interpreted educations discussed above. Cazden (2001) reminds us that classrooms have been moving from more traditional to less traditional, with more and more focus on student interaction, collaborative learning, and the essential processes of using language through which children learn. These points of focus require direct interaction and, thus, are prohibited through interpreted educations.

## Interpreted Education and Multiple Channels of Input

A related constraint is the fact that interpreters can process and then produce only one incoming message at a time. If two people are speaking or signing at the same time, then someone must decide which message takes priority. With adults, this responsibility is sometimes the task of the deaf person, sometimes the task of the interpreter, and rarely the task of the hearing person. In an interpreted education, where power structures and maturity levels are different, practically speaking, only the teacher can regulate multiple input. An interpreter can (and should) consistently remind the teacher, and theoretically, a student can also do so (if we ignore the power structures ingrained in education). But practically speaking, the teacher is the only person who can effectively manage this responsibility. He or she has the option to decide whether turn-taking will be spontaneous or recognized, whether responses will involve a single student or a choral response from the group, whether he or she will allow a cacophony of different responses or a single one.

The need for a single input, one at a time, leads into the first analysis presented in this study—the presentation of content through a variety of channels. Many hearing classroom activities rely on simultaneous presentation of both visual and auditory information: demonstrating an experiment while describing it, showing a picture while asking about it, watching a video while listening to the narration. Whenever this type of simultaneous presentation of information occurs, interpreting provides access to half of it—the spoken message—and interpreting prevents accessibility to the other half of it—looking at the visual aid (Winston 1994, 2001).

## Interpreted Education and Visual Accessibility

Classroom information is often effectively presented to hearing students by talking and demonstrating things simultaneously. The teacher tries to encourage the involvement of students in the learning process by appealing to their senses, especially those of sight, sound, and touch (seeing, hearing, and doing). And this approach works well most of the time. Of course, hearing students are, at times, overwhelmed when they are asked to listen to directions, watch a demonstration, and do an experiment, all at the same time. But often, describing an action while demonstrating it is very effective for hearing students. This simultaneous presentation of information is the commonplace means of presenting information in the hearing classroom. Hundreds of ordinary examples elucidate the method, including watching a movie (all those educational documentaries with pictures of wildlife and a narrator talking in the background); writing on the board and talking at the same time; asking students to look at a handout while explaining its use to them.

And each of these activities, each of these simultaneous presentations to the eyes and ears, becomes inaccessible by means of interpreting. They are uninterpretable as a simultaneous event. When the spoken part of the activity is interpreted into signs, the deaf student must use the eyes to watch the interpretation. And watching the interpretation means that the student cannot simultaneously watch the demonstration, the movie, the writing, the paper, or whatever else is being watched by the hearing students. In these situations, interpreting, in effect, raises a tremendous barrier to full accessibility in the mainstreamed classroom. We cannot avoid this fact; we cannot ignore this enormous problem created by an interpreted education. At least, the deaf student cannot avoid or ignore it, even if the educators can.

Thus, another fundamental characteristic of interpreting is that it must be accessible. For the most part, accessibility means that interpreting must be visible to the deaf student. If it cannot be seen, then the deaf student cannot have access. Although this need for visibility seems obvious, many barriers block seeing an interpretation: the need to write notes, the need to read from a homework paper, the need to watch a movie or demonstration, the need to read information from the board while the teacher is writing and talking at the same time. Each time the deaf student is forced to look away from the interpretation to see the other required visual input, the interpreting becomes inaccessible. And, each time the deaf student looks at the interpretation, the other required visual input is lost.

In earlier research, Winston (1990, 1994) has identified and discussed five categories of instructional activities that occurred in interpreted fourth-grade classes. The activities in these categories were analyzed for visual accessibility—the ability of a deaf student to access the entire activity visually during the time frame used by hearing peers. Activities allowing access to content visually when interpreted that was equal to the access hearing peers had while listening were considered interpretable without modification. No activity was found to be completely accessible through interpretation.

The categories analyzed were lecture, teacher-led discussion (also labeled as Question and Answer) without and with visual references, reading aloud, independent study, and group work. Lectures, with no other visual aids, no note-taking, and no need to use the eyes for competing visual input, were considered the most interpretable and visually accessible. Lectures that required note-taking, looking at demonstrations, or reading from a text, for example, all added another layer of visual barrier to the activity. Teacher-led discussions, reading aloud, group work, and independent work all added layers of visual barriers that made them difficult to access by means of interpreting. The hierarchy of accessible activities can be compared with classroom activities in traditional and nontraditional classrooms. Traditional classrooms lean toward more teacher-driven lecture; nontraditional classrooms lean toward more student interaction, including collaborative learning and constructive interchanges with group work and peer learning. Interpreting intervenes in these activities, denying to deaf children the direct communication through which and from which hearing children are expected to learn. This tangible effect must be considered when placing students in interpreted educations.

## Interpreted Education and English Ways of Talking

Interpreting involves additional factors that are much more subtle and even more serious than visual accessibility. The process of education involves a way of talking that not only provides content but also provides information about how we talk about that content in English. Those students with adequate language skills learn the subtle nuances of style and vocabulary from classroom presentations. Most important, these students continue to build their English literacy skills. Hearing students are assumed to learn both content and English ways of talking, or academic language (Cazden 2001). Having acquired native language skills, hearing students continue to develop their academic language. Cazden notes:

> For reasons already set forth, students' continued language development throughout their years in school is important. In the short run—here and now—on the path to clarification and new knowledge, articulating ideas more clearly and completely is important for speakers themselves. Moreover, as classrooms change toward a community of learners, all students' public words become part of the curriculum for their peers. In the longer run, oral, as well as written, communication skills are increasingly important in the worlds of work and civil society. (2001, 169)

This language development assumes that basic language acquisition has already occurred. This assumption is an issue that goes far beyond the accepted myths that language acquisition, and specifically English acquisition, can occur by watching an interpretation. Other chapters in this volume (Monikowski, Stack) illustrate this point. Wilber (2003), Schick (2003), and Sofinski (2002) all document the non-Englishness of English signing, discrediting the belief that English acquisition is possible by using interpretation. Winston (2004) discusses some of the language myths of interpreted education, including the issues of acquisition of ASL and English. The language development discussed here is a level of language sophistication that students develop beyond basic acquisition. Language users need to incorporate these levels of language sophistication to appear intelligent and educated in our society. The very fact that education is presented in primarily spoken English makes this need clear. In addition, hearing students are expected to learn how to write English through hearing it. This approach to learning the "talk" of academia is not accessible to deaf students. Whether the interpreted education is in ASL or in a form of English signing, deaf students' only access to English is through writing.

## Interpreted Education and Discourse Styles

Finally, our discussion considers the discourse style of the teacher in the classroom. Discourse patterns of pacing, explicitness, redundancy, and turn-taking are different for each teacher. Some patterns more compatibly fit into interpreting than others. Although one can change a discourse style or pattern for short periods of time, interpreters have long found that teachers who are asked to slow down to accommodate interpreting are able to manage this change for only minutes at most. Although the community wisdom assumes that the hearing classroom teacher is one essential factor for effective interpreted education, this study is the first to relate discourse styles and patterns that are effective for interpretation to the discourse patterns found among classroom teachers. Finding classroom teachers whose styles and teaching approaches are more compatible with the needs of interpreting is an essential first step in choosing an interpreted environment. Then, of course, the teacher must still be willing to seriously focus on further adaptations if the environment is to be even minimally accessible through interpreting.

The constraints and limitations of interpreting need to be recognized and accommodated to achieve minimal education access. A teacher who uses activities that fail to accommodate, whose teaching style does not allow for time and language constraints, who does not recognize that one cannot make direct judgments of language generated by interpreting, and who does not understand that all visual input must be accessible will not be able to provide the minimum requirements for an accessible education. The teacher, whose style and choice of activities recognizes the visual needs of interpreted educations may be able to provide at least the minimum environment required for access to an interpreted education.

An interesting dilemma occurs when a teacher has a style that relies heavily on visual imagery. Although this style might seem to fit well with the visual needs of deaf students, it can, and often does, create even more serious conflicts in the interpreted classroom. Some teachers tend toward a visual style of teaching, using demonstrations, drawings, hand gestures, and so forth to support and supplement their teaching. However, whenever these visual supports occur simultaneously with their spoken input, the result creates an automatic barrier for the deaf student who then must choose which input to watch. A hearing student who watches a demonstration while listening to the teacher talk uses ears and eyes simultaneously. For a deaf student to have adequate and similar access to the same information, the activity must be transformed from being simultaneous to being sequential, where the student can first see the interpretation and then see the demonstration (or vice versa). This constraint is neither changeable nor modifiable. Thus, the accessibility of an interpreted education rests with the ability and willingness of the classroom teacher to transform all teaching and communication activities from being simultaneous to being sequential. Some teachers make this change as a matter of course. Others do not.

## THIS STUDY

This study examines classes being taught about a variety of subjects to a variety of grade levels by a variety of teachers. These situations reflect some of the possible choices that educators and parents have when they decide on an interpreted education. Some of the factors that affect interpretability and accessibility are evident throughout; other factors are evident depending on the discourse and teaching style of the teacher.

### Data Collection

Observing and collecting data in public school classrooms can be problematic. Although one can observe the accessibility and interpretability of classes without using video, for the purposes of research, video is essential. It provides a source for review of linguistic and visual accessibility issues and allows for the inclusion of specific examples in the discussion. Obtaining permission to record classes, however, is problematic. The concerns for student and teacher privacy need to be honored, and the possible disruptions to a class can be considerable. In addition, obtaining permission to share the data with others once it is recorded is often difficult to do.[1]

Because of the issues related to collecting new data, this research takes advantage of a set of classroom videos recorded in 1993 for a U.S. Department of Education grant about educational interpreting (Public School in Action Videotapes 1993). These videos were recorded in a school system, and permissions were obtained to tape and share the videos. They were taped by professional videographers, using multiple cameras, who were able to record adequate sound and to adjust the camera angles and edit the final video so specific speakers are visible. When the teacher is talking, the camera used is one focused on the teacher; when a student or group activity takes precedence, that view is often available. These views are shifted within the actual time frame of the interactions, so turn-taking intervals and rhythms can be observed and noted.

The professional taping provided helpful advantages; in addition, the grant developers prepared a manual to accompany the tapes (Public School in Action Videotapes 1993). The manual provides a brief description of each class, including grade level, subject matter, length of class time, and teacher name, Also included is a list of vocabulary that were considered key for interpreting in the class.

An added benefit to using these materials is that they are available for anyone to order, making the discussion in this study more accessible and providing an opportunity for interpreters, teachers, and parents to practice analyzing interpretability issues using the tapes.

### Data Selection

The study analyzed fourteen classes, with nine teachers. Class choices were based on grade level, subject matter, and teacher gender to have a variety of observations across grade levels and subjects, when possible, and to have both male and female teachers. The courses analyzed are described in-depth in the following section. (See appendix A for a list of specific classes analyzed in this study.)

At least three different teachers were analyzed for each subject. A mix of female and male was chosen when possible; however, in the original taped observations, only female teachers were taped at the elementary level. English as a subject was taught only by female teachers and only at the elementary and middle school levels, and history and science were available only at the middle and high school levels. It was possible to observe at least one person teaching two different classes at each level.

## DISCUSSION AND ANALYSIS OF CLASS ACTIVITY TYPES

The initial intent of this study was to determine the interpretability and accessibility of hearing-sound-based classrooms by analyzing them for the types of activities used to present content and for the length of time these activities were used. Results of this initial analysis led to further questions based on the findings. All of the activities listed in the first section of this chapter were found in at least two classes, with the exception of lectures. None of the teachers used lecture as a way to present content. Instead of lectures, the primary activity used for presentation of content was teacher-led discussion, that is, short periods of talk by the teacher involving no more than eight to ten minutes at a time, followed by questions to the students and responses from them. Most teacher commentary lasted less time, usually between two and three minutes in between student input. Group work in which three or more students collaborated on an assignment was rare in these observations, occurring only during one class as a required main activity. Independent work was also observed in this class, but only when a student's partner or members of a group were absent for that class. One other class had group work of this type; in that class, students had the option of working together, working with a tutor, or working independently while the teacher worked individually with some of them.

## Lectures in the Observed Classes

Lectures that have a single teacher talking without interruption and without the need to refer to other visual input (i.e., demonstrations, overheads, note-taking, etc.) are the most visually accessible and, therefore, the most interpretable environment (represented in Table 1, Row 1). Lecture-style courses of this type would allow the deaf student the most similar access during an interpreted education. The only interpreting constraint that cannot be changed is the lag time required for information processing by the interpreter, which leaves the deaf student perpetually behind the rest of the class.

However, no instances of lecture occurred in the 14 classes observed, classes spanning high school history, math, and science; middle school science and history–social studies; and elementary math and reading. Thus, the most interpretable and

TABLE 1 Analysis of Classroom Activities

| | Lag Time Affects Access | Eyes for Interpretation | Eyes for Interaction | Eyes for Other Visual Content | Eyes for English Form: Written | Eyes for English Form: Sound |
|---|---|---|---|---|---|---|
| 1. Lecture | Yes | Yes | Possible | Possible | Possible | Possible |
| 2. Individual | Yes | Possible | Possible | Yes | Possible | Possible |
| 3A. Teacher-led Discussion (no additional visual content) | Yes | Yes | Yes | | | Possible |
| 3B. Teacher-led Discussion (other visual content) | Yes | Yes | Yes | Yes | Possible | Possible |
| 4. Group | Yes | Yes | Yes | Yes | Possible | Possible |
| 5. Reading Aloud | Yes | Yes | Yes | Yes | Yes | Yes |

accessible form of interpreted education was not available to a deaf student in these classes.

## Teacher-Led Discussion

Cazden (2001) describes teacher-led discussions as the time "in which the teacher controls both the development of a topic (and what counts as relevant to it) and who gets a turn to talk" (30). Typically, a teacher initiates a topic, question, or interaction to which a student (or students) responds in some manner after which the teacher acknowledges the response (or actively ignores it) and evaluates it in some way. This evaluation may be the statement "Right" to an answer, it may be a request to expand or repeat, or it may be an aside related to the student comment. These sets of interactional turns are called topically related sets (TRSs) and make up the structure of many classroom lessons. In these data, teacher-led discussions make up the majority of classroom time. In an analysis of these classroom activities, two subcategories have an effect on access to the discussion for deaf students: (a) activities in which students respond to teacher-led interactions without the use of visual references such as homework papers, text books, or models and (b) activities that require students to refer to some type of visual content.

### *Teacher-Led Discussion without Visual References*

This type of activity is the second most visually accessible activity in an interpreted education. Because a deaf student can watch the interpretation of the teacher's talk and then watch the interpretation of the students' responses, the student theoretically is still able to access the input. The interpreting constraint of lag time is, of course, always present. In addition, the act of turn-taking adds to the level of visual inaccessibility. Hearing students, in addition to accessing the information with their ears, often look at the speaker to identify who is participating as well as to see mood and intent. They then turn back to the teacher.

In the classrooms observed, discussions without visual reference occurred rarely, and when they occurred, they were usually related either to context-related questions (e.g., Where did Andy go?, Who has a question about that concept?) or to side issues arising from the discussion.

However, discussion without visual reference does seem to be a staple of one teacher's class—a second-grade reading classroom—and it poses one of the most interesting mixes of accessible and inaccessible conditions. In this case (discussed in-depth later in the English section), Mrs. B.A.'s class alternated between one and two minutes of poetry reading followed by discussion about what the children understood, liked, thought, or wanted. An example of this interaction is when students are asked to think about whether or not they would like to be a king or queen (Tape 3, 21.00–29.00 min.). When answering, the students had to provide a reason for their answers. For example, various students contributed that the negatives might be going to war and having responsibilities, keeping track of money, needing to dress perfectly all the time. Other students contributed positives such as having money and being rich as well as wearing wonderful clothes. None of these answers required that the students be reading from a paper, taking notes, or checking to see whether they had the "right" answer. A deaf student in this activity would have fewer competing visual claims on his or her eyes than when referring to a paper. As discussed in a later section related to English use, the problems of using sound-based English as a starting point are problematic (e.g., Could the student understand the story when first read to a degree that would allow him or her to respond? Could a story not based on rhymes be used? Could a signed story or a written story—rather than a read-aloud story—be used?). But, in this situation, the activity itself, using open discussion based on felicitous questions is one of the less constrained interpreting activities (see Table 1, Row 3A).

### *Teacher-Led Discussion with Visual References*

Teacher-led discussion with visual references was by far the most frequent type of activity across the classes observed. Visual accessibility for the deaf or hard of hearing student during this activity is limited by the factors that affect both lecture and teacher-led discussions without paper (lag time, turn-taking) and is compounded by the expectation that students will be simultaneously listening to the teacher and looking at a visual reference (e.g., a homework sheet, a text book, etc.) as well as responding in a timely and appropriate manner to questions.

An extreme example of this activity is in a high school math class. Mr. D.O. begins class by standing in front of the class and reading from the homework assignment. This activity lasts for only two minutes but is essential in leading into the rest of the class. He reads the answers, saying (Tape 11, 43.00–45.00 min.),

> 1–18 [questions 1 through 18]
>
> 1—A to the X plus Y
>
> 2 is 1 (*looks up and removes glasses*) Now I think that is by far the best answer to number two because you get P to the 0 and that comes out to be 1. So you really ought to put 1 down as the answer there. OK?
>
> Number 3—B to the X minus Y
>
> Number 4—R to the 2T
>
> Number 5—C to the W plus t minus V
>
> Number 6—P to the S plus Q over Q. Hope I read that right. Did I? (*never looks up*)
>
> Seven— . . .

While he is reading, the students in class are looking at their papers to see whether they have the correct answers. Mr. D.O. does not pause or look up to see whether the students are following; he speaks through the entire two minutes. Only at the end of this reading does he ask what questions they have.

Deaf students can either look at the interpretation or look at the homework sheet or text, but not both simultaneously. They cannot correct their papers and watch the interpretation at the same time. The extent to which this type of activity occurs simultaneously must be a primary concern when choosing an interpreted education (see Table 1, Row 3B).

## Reading Aloud

Reading aloud is also an activity that requires hearing students to listen to auditory input, watch visual input, and at times also perform some type of expressive language. To the extent that reading aloud is part of classroom activities, it is subject to the same interpreting and visual accessibility issues. Deaf students must choose between watching the interpretation of what is being read and reading for themselves from the text. They cannot do both at the same time. Either choice seriously limits the amount of input the deaf student receives in comparison to his or her hearing peers.

If the deaf student chooses to watch the interpretation for the message, he or she is barred from reading the written English that each hearing child is experiencing and is barred, as described earlier, from making any connection between the sounds, or even the signs, and the written word (see Table 1, Row 5). Reading aloud as a class activity is discussed further in the section about English literacy, and an example is provided there.

## Group Work

Group work was not a frequent activity in most of the courses observed, but that is a problem of the data used. The science courses in high school, for example, referred to lab periods when the students would be spending time in groups. The extent to which group work makes up a bigger picture in the educational environment of a class needs further study.

It was possible to observe group work in three classes—one middle school history class as well as the elementary school reading and math classes. Visual accessibility in groups poses a slightly different challenge. As students work together and take turns, the issues involved in question-and-answer interactions come up again. The hearing students can look at the work and can simultaneously listen to the other students talking about it. They can also participate in the flow of discussion. In addition, they can hear the teacher adding comments or directions to the class while they continue to look at the experiment or project under discussion. In one history class at the high school level, students were working on collaborative projects in groups of two to four students (Tape 12). Each group worked on their projects, and the teacher moved from group to group to provide help and guidance. When the teacher stood with a group, either they all looked at her or all, including her, looked at the papers, charts, and books with which they were working. Interaction was much less teacher-nominated, and group members were able to ask or comment spontaneously. This type of turn-taking, combined with intensive use of other visual input, makes access to interpreted group work problematic. Although this type of group work was not available to observe in many courses, teachers did refer to it as a type of activity that had great importance. One science teacher, for example (Tape 11), was presenting information and holding discussions in preparation for lab activities that were to happen on subsequent days.

A variation of group work was also observed. Students, or students and tutors, were paired to work together. Because of the limited number of participants in these situations, the deaf student has easier visual access to the person whose speech is being interpreted, and there is less chance that overlap will occur. This characteristic of paired work makes it somewhat more visually accessible than larger group work. This type of pairing occurred primarily in the elementary school settings, with much of it being adult-student pairing for tutoring. Of the observed classes, most pairing of this type occurred in reading classes, where visual accessibility is confounded by questions of linguistic accessibility, an issue that is discussed in the next section.

## Independent Work

The final activity observed in these classes was independent work. This type of activity would seem to be the most visually accessible for a deaf student, since he or she can attend directly to the project or assignment at hand and not have to mediate access through interpretation. However, independent work as observed in these classes rarely allowed students to simply attend to the assignment. Most often, it was interspersed with teacher instructions or commentary. For example, in one eighth-grade English class, the teacher directs students to get paper and copy some paragraphs from the overhead. As they begin copying, she continues to talk and, among other things, informs them that they will have a quiz the following week (Tape 7, 37.31 min.). Although the independent work did not continue for long, the fact that the students were expected to look back and forth from paper to overhead to do the copying task and were simultaneously being told essential information verifies the problematic nature of individual work.

At other times, the teacher talked to one student while the others worked, but the others had full access to the content of that discussion. If they heard something relevant, they could easily join in to ask a question or participate in the discussion. Deaf students do not have this option. They must choose between (a) focusing entirely on the work and losing all teacher input, (b) being constantly interrupted by the interpretation of teacher input while they are trying to work, (c) attending to only the interpreted input and losing the time required to do the work itself. Independent work time was often a much more social time for the hearing students, an opportunity that is again lost to the deaf student (see Table 1, Row 4).

## Summary of Class Activity Discussion

Each type of interpreted activity imposes constraints to visual access through interpreting. Some activities impose these constraints less than others, and the amount of time each activity occurs in a classroom needs to be an important consideration for choosing a classroom for interpretation. In these observations, lecture, which offers the least constraint, did not occur. Teacher-led discussions without visual references, offering the next least constraint, occurred rarely. The activities that impose the most limitations to visual access were the activities that occurred most frequently. Teacher-led discussions with visual references occurred most frequently, imposing constraints involving visual aids (e.g., paper), turn-taking, and lag time. Although they occurred less frequently, group work and independent work imposed numerous constraints, making them difficult to access visually.

# DISCUSSION AND ANALYSIS OF LANGUAGE EXPECTATIONS

Because all of the activities presented some level of visual inaccessibility, two further analyses were conducted. The first analysis focused on the linguistic accessibility of these classrooms, specifically on the expectations that English—spoken, written, or both—was being learned by the hearing students. The second analysis focused on the discourse patterns of the teachers and the compatibility of those patterns with the constraints of interpreting. For the purpose of building a more complete picture of whole classrooms, I have chosen from the data three classrooms that span the range of potential for interpreted education. I will provide examples from each of these teachers, building a picture of the teacher and classroom as amenable to interpreting or not. The three classes are elementary school English, middle school science, and high school math. All three are primarily interactive exposition and incorporate visual references to support and explain the content. The teachers all have some focus on both written and spoken English. An analysis of only the activities in these classes shows that each would be equal in terms of accessibility or inaccessibility to a deaf student through interpreting.

Notwithstanding, these teachers had a wide range of expectations about English learning and displayed a range of discourse styles that could affect the interpretability of their respective classes. If we relied solely on the activity analysis above, then all three would be considered fairly inaccessible. However, by continuing the analysis, some mitigating factors that might make them more or less interpretable and accessible become apparent. If interpreted educations are chosen, this type of in-depth assessment of the classrooms must become common practice. In-depth analysis of these three classes makes evident that one has the potential to be somewhat accessible with minor modification, one has some undoubtedly modifiable and some particularly nonchangeable aspects that make it problematic, and one requires so many essential modifications that it would not be recommended for interpreting.

## The Classes and Teachers

The three classes chosen from the data for further analysis and discussion represent an eighth-grade science class (Ms. B.I., teacher); a second-grade English class (Mrs. B.A., teacher); and a high school math class (Mr. D.O., teacher). Each is described in more detail here. In addition, the data included observations of six other teachers, which are referred to in general ways to provide perspective to these specific observations.

Ms. B.I. teaches an eighth-grade science class that runs for forty minutes. She is introducing new content to the class during this observation and is requiring that each student assemble a model of a generator at his or her desk during the lesson. At times, Ms. B.I. lets them work independently while she walks around helping individuals. Students are seated in a U shape around the room, with pairs of desks facing each other. At first glance, this environment appears to be quite inaccessible because of the potential conflicting visual input and the fact that many students are not facing the teacher.

Mrs. B.A. teaches a second-grade English class that runs for thirty-five minutes and that is followed by forty-five minutes of independent work. In the first thirty-five minutes, she focuses on creative writing and reads sections of English rhyming stories to the class to begin discussions about how to write their own stories. Students are seated in small groups, then move to sit on the floor for part of the period. After discussion, the students work individually, and she walks around helping them. This class also appears to be notably inaccessible because of not only the environment but also the reliance on English sound and writing.

Mr. D.O. teaches three math classes, two at the high school level and one at middle school level (but the class analysis in this study is of one of the high school classes). His style and approach do not change significantly from one class to the other. He has students check their homework by reading them the answers, then interacts with them as they discuss various problems they are doing for homework or study in the class. He writes on the board, uses overheads, and reads from the students' papers. At various times during the class, he has students work individually while he walks around providing attention to them on an individual basis. Students are seated in small clusters facing a variety of directions. This class appears to be remarkably inaccessible because of the reliance on both visual and auditory input.

Although each class seems fairly similar in terms of activity, the discourse styles of the teachers vary. Thus, although each class is problematic because of the type of activity (interaction with added visual references), the possibility that they might be modifiable, depending on the teacher's willingness and ability to do so, is possible in Ms. B.I.'s class, possible with some concerns in Mrs. B.A.'s class, and possible but unlikely in Mr. D.O.'s class.

Looking only at simultaneous versus sequential styles of presentation (see Table 2), it appears that Ms. B.I.'s presentation of content is closer to being accessible than either Mrs. B.A.'s or Mr. D.O.'s. Further analysis of additional features tends to confirm this observation. However, analysis of these teachers' discourse styles reveals the potential for modifying some classes that have moderate barriers to accessibility.

Analyses of classroom activities like those done in this study can be easily performed by any observer. They do not require a knowledge of sign language, bilingual education, or interpreting. Simply noting which activities are used, to what frequency, and for how long is enough. A watch and a checklist are all that is necessary for any teacher, administrator, parent, or other decision maker to get a clear sense of the number and severity of constraints that will limit visual access to educational content.

However, in analyzing a potential classroom for interpretability, one needs to understand more than just the visual barriers involved. Serious, although less easily recognizable, barriers inhibit language access. The expectations of language

TABLE 2 Simultaneous versus Sequential Presentation of Content

| Content Presentation | Ms. B.I. | Mrs. B.A. | Mr. D.O. |
|---|---|---|---|
| Content is presented primarily through spoken language with no visual references | Seldom | Seldom | Seldom |
| Content is presented sequentially through spoken and visual references | Often | Sometimes | Seldom |
| Content is presented simultaneously through spoken and visual references | Occasionally | Sometimes | Usually |

access for hearing students in education are serious and must be part of the assessment of any interpreted education. The considerations of language are discussed in the next section and in Table 3.

## *English in Ms. B.I.'s Class*

In Ms. B.I.'s science class, much of the class time is focused on helping students understand the concepts of electricity. Little formal modeling of academic English occurs during the class, and many interactions involve more informal, everyday discussions using simple examples (e.g., water pushing through a hose, toast being burned, lightning). A few terms are included as "given," or known, information as she asks students to think about what electricity is. She refers to electrons, but from her use of the term, this use is as a known rather than as a new term.

A few new vocabulary terms are introduced during this observation. One term is *voltage.* The term is not only a new concept for the class but also a new English term. Ms. B.I. is careful to make sure that the students understand the concept, the pronunciation, and the written form as well as other visual representations of the term. She explains the concept with words, drawings, and gestures. As she gets to the end of this explanation, she summarizes the concept and introduces the term itself (Tape 8, 52.42 min.):

> Inside the power source there are electrons. The electrons have to get from the power source out. That PUSH, coming from the source, is called voltage. So you should write this down.
>
> Voltage is the push of electricity coming from a power source. (*Approximately seventeen-second pause occurs while she has them write this information in their notes. During this time, she responds to one student individually—not class directed—by repeating the part of the written English she wants the student to write. Ms. B.I. then repeats the sentence for the entire class.*)
>
> Yeah, electricity or voltage is the push of electricity from a power source to another object or to another source. (*Approximate 10-second pause*)

This example includes Ms. B.I. reinforcing the pronunciation of the English term and the formal English sentence structure. She also reinforces the written form of the English term and structure, requiring that each student write the full English sentence with the term into their notebooks. This emphasis is important enough for her that she leaves two long pauses, walking from student to student to check on their writing to ensure that they have the English form correct.

Although a deaf student would not have access to the pronunciation of the English term, an interpreter could provide the fingerspelled form of this term for the student. If the student is able to understand the fingerspelling and has developed the skill of connecting these handshapes to written alphabetic symbols, then he or she will be able to produce the written term in his or her notes.

Ms. B.I. is aware of the need to make the written form of English explicit for the students, and she writes some vocabulary on the board. Asking her to expand her use of writing would be a modification that would not unduly change either her presentation in the classroom or her discourse patterns.

## *English in Mrs. B.A.'s English Class*

This class presents a dilemma for interpreting. Mrs. B.A. has a moderate discourse pace; uses redundancy and includes explicit references often; regulates turn-taking to one person at a time, identifying students by name and repeating their input often; and tends to present content through various modes sequentially, for example, by first saying it, then showing it.

Yet, her course is English, and it is taught in the fashion that hearing people use to teach English, by basing instruction on sound. Although her discussions focus more on content than on English form, she introduces those discussions through spoken English form, specifically by reading aloud rhyming English poems or stories. The class discussion about whether the students wanted to be king or queen, discussed previously, is an example of this emphasis. She introduces the discussion of royalty by reading aloud from the story, Jonathon Bing (Tape 3, 21.07 min.).

> Poor old Jonathon Bing
> Went out to his carriage
> To visit the king.
> But everyone pointed and said, "Look at that!"
> "Jonathon Bing has forgotten his . . ." (*She points to her head and waits for students to add the rhyming word* hat, *which they do.*)
> (*Students, in a chorus, respond*) "hat."

Mrs. B.A. continues to read through the text in this manner, leaving out rhyming words at the end of sentences and expecting a choral response from the class to fill in the last word. This activity, which occurs daily in English and reading classes, especially at the elementary level, presents some insurmountable barriers to an interpreted education:

1. The deaf student needs to be watching the interpretation to see what the teacher is saying, but the deaf student is also simultaneously required to watch the teacher to see what gesture is used for the visual clue to filling in the blank.
2. The timing of the student responses is essential; they must do it at the same time. The lag time imposed by interpretation would make this kind of response impossible for a deaf student.
3. The purposes of this activity are to help students use rhyme in English to predict the words; to understand more about English form through rhyme; and even more basically, to create involvement in the story by combining the sounds and meanings of English into a pleasant experience—all of which rely on the ability to hear.

Observations of the other elementary reading-English class indicate that the teacher there relies heavily on rhyming stories, on sound-based reading approaches, and on "best guess" spelling in creative writing (i.e., that students are encouraged to sound out the word and figure out the spelling phonically). This approach is used through entire classes. Asking this teacher or any teacher to modify this type of English-based approach would involve imposing serious changes to his or her style and approach, which may not be feasible.

### *English in Mr. D.O.'s Math Class*

The analysis here is of Mr. D.O.'s math class at the high school level. Although English form is not the conscious focus of this class, correct and appropriate English jargon is required to demonstrate competence in math. Students hear the teacher read a formula, an equation, or a format and are expected, implicitly, to repeat it and to talk about it and other formulas according to the model. Like Ms. B.I.'s science class, this ability may be assumed to be given knowledge for these students. However, Ms. B.I.'s use of science jargon was limited to single words and phrases in formal, but usual, English grammatical structures whereas math consists of specific terminology and long strings of nonnormal English grammar. Hearing students see equations and, through years of exposure, implicitly match the corresponding English string of words to the symbols. Access to the pronunciation and to the academic jargon, especially as it becomes more distant from normal formal English, becomes more and more inaccessible through interpretation.

## Discussion of Language Expectations

Hearing students in the classes described above are assumed to learn both content and English as they take in information. The very fact that education is presented primarily in spoken English makes this point clear. In addition, hearing students are expected to learn how to write English through hearing it. This approach to learning the "talk" of academia is not accessible to deaf students. If the interpreted education is in ASL, then their only access to English is through written forms, forms that require hearing ability to learn in most educational activities. If the interpretation is some form of English signing, then the deaf student still has no access to spoken English.

Given the instructions that English signing systems give to users—to condense and delete portions of a spoken English message—even the most fluently signed English interpretation (often called transliteration) does not come close to *being* English. Even if these portions were not deleted, the phonology of English signing is so foreign to that of spoken English that a comparison is impossible. No native English speaker will instinctively recognize *A* for the sound /ay/

TABLE 3 Expectations of English Exposure

| English | Ms. B.I. | Mrs. B.A. | Mr. D.O. |
|---|---|---|---|
| English form is implicit | Seldom | Seldom | Usually |
| English form is explicit but sound-based (spoken only, phonics, rhyming) | Seldom | Often | NA |
| English form is explicit and includes visual reference (English is written in addition to spoken) | Usually | Often | Seldom |
| **Overall, English form is visually accessible** | To some extent | To some extent | Rarely |

without being taught the relationship. Similarly, if they have learned to read, they will not recognize the A handshape for the written letter *A*. For hearing people, the connection between the sound and the written symbol has been reinforced by years of drills, practice, reading, rhyming, spelling tests, and sound-based instruction. For most deaf students, this reinforcement has not been made adequately, certainly not to the extent that hearing students have had access to it. Researchers such as Stack (chapter 3 in this volume), Wilbur (2003), and Schick (2003) make convincing arguments that these signed systems are not English.

Ultimately, deaf students do not have direct access to English in interpreted classrooms. Once again, the presentation of any "English " information must be shifted from simultaneous to sequential and must incorporate visual bilingual approaches to teaching English. For example, when a teacher says, "Voltage is the push of electricity. That is important and you will see it on your test," she means that the students must be able to recognize the written words and possibly produce them. Most hearing students write down this information. Typically, a deaf student cannot write and continue to watch the interpretation. (Some can, but it is hard, it is a learned skill, and it is not comparable to what hearing students do.) In addition, when hearing students write, they match the sounds of a word ("Voltage—what does it sound like?: volt plus age.") to their inventory of sound-to-symbol knowledge of writing. This process is neither possible nor available to deaf students. A deaf student sees a visual symbol or sign with no relation to sound, and must somehow match this symbol to a series of written letters. No adult would expect to see a sign ELECTRIC and automatically know to write e-l-e-c-t-r-i-c. Yet deaf children are expected to do it all day long.

One solution to part of this dilemma might be thought to be fingerspelling in which each letter of a word like *voltage* is presented to the student. Students capable of reading this type of fingerspelling may benefit from this strategy; many cannot. And not all words are spelled. In fact, interpreters frequently invent signs for jargon and technical terms so they do not have to spell them (we will not discuss here the actual skills of interpreters who do not fingerspell because they find it too difficult). Thus, while hearing students repeatedly hear the sounds, a deaf student may see the spelling only once or twice before they have a sign substituted for it. They must learn the spelling through only a couple of exposures compared with the hearing students' repeated exposure.

Thus, every time a teacher expects and assumes that hearing students are absorbing the English way of talking about a subject, the teacher cannot assume that the same is happening for deaf students through interpretation. Nor can the teacher assume that the reading aloud by a deaf student represents anything like the language of hearing students. A deaf student "reading aloud" through signs may or may not demonstrate skilled and competent signing; the teacher has no way of judging the signing skill and hears only whatever the interpreter says. The teacher judges the interpretation, not the deaf student's language. An interpretation of signing cannot exactly represent that signing as speech. When a teacher hears a hearing student stumble on the pronunciation of a word such as *photograph*, the teacher learns that the student may have difficulties with reading *ph*. When the teacher hears an interpreter stumble on the word *photograph*, that teacher has no indication (a) whether the problem is with the deaf student's articulation, which has nothing to do with *ph*; (b) whether the problem is with the deaf student's ability to fingerspell the word, which provides no indication of whether he or she understands it; (c) whether the problem is with the interpreter who either does not know the sign or does not recognize the deaf student's particular articulation of it; or (d) whether the problem is that the interpreter is unable to read the fingerspelling of the child. Neither the deaf student nor the teacher has access to the sign language or English language information needed to teach English.

One observed feature of reading aloud was the reliance in hearing classrooms on rhyming to create interest for the hearing students. This process does not happen for a deaf student through interpretation. First, the deaf student does not hear the sound, so he or she does not learn to associate the sound with the meaning in an interesting and relevant way. Second, a word that rhymes in English is not a rhyme in sign language, so even the idea of rhyme is not expressed through this activity. While the hearing students are getting clues to aid in prediction during reading and writing—and in short, in literacy—the deaf student is not.

Thus, this activity of reading English aloud, especially when part of its importance is rhyming, is pointless for deaf students. In classrooms conducted in sign language by deaf teachers for deaf students, English stories just like the ones in this hearing classroom are used. However, the focus of the rhyme is on the English form of written spelling—not the sound. The fact that *that* and *hat* rhyme in spoken English (and look similar in written English) is a fact that is explicitly taught to these deaf students. It is not implicitly used for the enjoyment of "hearing" it.

The idea of rhyming might well be introduced in a deaf classroom using this story of poor old Jonathan Bing. Signs do have rhymes, and there are specific rhythms that make a signed text enjoyable visually. A signed rhyme relies on the similarity, not of final sounds, but of the use of similar handshapes. A deaf teacher, skilled in sign poetry, could easily give an example of a signed rhyme to explicitly help the students understand the parallels in a spoken language. In other words, the deaf teacher uses strategies of bilingual education to discuss similar functions that are realized differently in signing and in speaking.

This rhyming activity is not interpretable nor accessible. Part of the determination about whether a class like Mrs. B.A.'s could be interpretable would include ascertaining what importance this rhyming activity has in relation to the goals of the class and to the length of time it continues relative to the class whole. Mrs. B.A. uses this activity to introduce each topic but uses it briefly (one to two minutes) and follows it with lengthy discussions based on meaning and understanding, not rhyme. These time periods might be adaptable. Would she be able to substitute other texts that do not rely on English rhyme, for example, texts that could be read silently by the students instead of read aloud? Could she eliminate the chorale responses? And, if she could, would it be advisable, given the learning needs of the other hearing children? These are questions that the educational team must bring to the teacher, and the teacher must decide how or whether to modify his or her presentation accordingly.

## DISCOURSE STYLES AND PATTERNS

The field of education uses various typologies for describing and defining the ways that teachers present information in the classroom. Grasha (1996), for example, describes five types of teaching styles that refer to how a teacher presents him- or herself in the classroom. He labels this style as a teacher's "presence" (Grasha 2004):

- Expert: Possesses knowledge and expertise that students need. Strives to maintain status as an expert among students by displaying detailed knowledge and by challenging students to enhance their competence. Concerned with transmitting information and ensuring that students are well prepared.

- Formal authority: Possesses status among students because of knowledge and role as a faculty member. Concerned with providing positive and negative feedback, establishing learning goals, expectations, and rules of conduct for students. Concerned with the correct, acceptable, and standard ways to do things and with providing students with the structure they need to learn.
- Personal model: Believes in "teaching by personal example" and establishes a prototype for how to think and behave. Oversees, guides, and directs by showing how to do things and by encouraging students to observe and then to emulate the instructor's approach.
- Facilitator: Emphasizes the personal nature of teacher-student interactions. Guides and directs students by asking questions, exploring options, suggesting alternatives, and encouraging them to develop criteria to make informed choices. Overall goal is to develop in students the capacity for independent action, initiative, and responsibility. Works with students on projects in a consultative fashion and tries to provide as much support and encouragement as possible.
- Delegator: Concerned with developing students' capacity to function in an autonomous fashion. Students work independently on projects or as part of autonomous teams. The teacher is available as a resource person at the request of students.

Each of these styles has an effect on the learning of students and reflects a teaching approach of the teacher. However, these descriptions do not truly fit the elements of style that have greatest effect on an interpreted education. Style, in combination with the types of activities a teacher tends to use most often in class, can provide or deny a great deal of access for a deaf student, both visually and linguistically. The two elements of style that are especially important for integrating interpreting into an educational environment are (a) the pacing of the input and (b) the redundancy and explicitness of the input.

## Discourse Pacing

A teacher's pacing is an essential factor for interpreting. Some teachers speak quickly and encourage swift turn-taking as well as immediate, sometimes overlapping, responses from students. They can also encourage choral responses that fit into the flow of the presentation. These teachers expect the presentation time to be filled not only with sound but also, in the observations of the classes in this study, with visual references. If students do not respond immediately to a question, a teacher using this style of teaching rephrases or repeats the question, shifts from student to student without waiting, and leaps to call on those students who respond most quickly. The style seems to challenge students to keep up with the flow of the presentation.

Other teachers talk more slowly, state a question and allow a space of silence while the students process the question, and then regulate the responses by calling on specific students. This style seems to be geared to the processing time of the students, allowing for it rather than challenging them to keep up.

This study makes no evaluation of the quality or effectiveness of either style, which is for educators to discuss. The goal of an analysis related to interpreting is

TABLE 4 Analysis of Discourse Pacing

| Discourse Pacing | Ms. B.I. | Mrs. B.A. | Mr. D.O. |
|---|---|---|---|
| Deliberate and moderate speed | Usually | Usually | Seldom—usually rapid |
| Allows silence through most "silences" | Usually | Usually | Seldom—talks |
| Presents information sequentially (speaks, then writes; speaks then shows) | Usually | Sometimes | Seldom—usually writes and talks, reads and shows |
| **Overall: Modifiable to interpreting?** | Possible | Possible—slow pace and silence makes interpretation more possible | Difficult—probably not |

simply to identify what makes a teaching style more or less interpretable. Table 4 indicates the levels of discourse pacing for each of the three teachers.

### *Ms. B.I.'s Discourse Pacing*

The opening of Ms. B.I.'s class provides a clear example of discourse pacing that may be fairly interpretable with minimal modification needed from the teacher (Tape 8, 48.00–49.00 min.):

> Ms. B.I.: Okay ladies and gentleman, put your bags underneath your desks and get out your notebooks.
>
> (*Approximate ten-second pause while she scans the room*)
>
> Date the page. . . . Feb. fourth.
>
> (*Allowing approximately twenty-five seconds for students to prepare, she gets a paper for one student and scans the room; students who can be seen on camera are getting ready.*)
>
> Everybody set?
>
> (*Approximate three-second pause*)
>
> Here we go.
>
> (*Approximate two-second pause*)
>
> Electricity is invisible.

(*Approximate five-second pause*)

Is that a true statement or a false statement, and when you want to answer, please raise your hand, I forgot to tell you that, so they can zoom in on you, OK?

(*Approximate two-second pause before continuing*)

In this example, Ms. B.I. speaks at a moderate pace and leaves pauses between her utterances, ranging from twenty-five seconds (while students are getting ready) to two seconds (while she begins the actual lesson). During the longer pauses, while she is scanning the room, waiting for students to put bags under desks, get out paper, and get ready, she does not continue to give directions or explanations; she is comfortable with the silence.

An example of presenting input sequentially occurs after she tells them to put the date on the page. She allows a twenty-five second pause during which she scans the room and speaks quietly only to one or two students, asking whether they need paper, etc. No general instructions or directions are given while they are expected to write. A deaf student could watch the interpreter for the instruction ("Date the page."), look down to write the date on the paper, and still have time to look back up to see an interpretation of the teacher's quiet question to one student about having paper.

This pacing is consistent throughout the class, whether she is drawing on the board (first drawing and then speaking), giving directions, or explaining. In the few examples where she expects students to do something while she is speaking, she usually allows time afterwards for the students to finish the activity. Given this teacher's attention to the students' need to process, the modifications needed to accommodate interpreting would probably not be difficult to incorporate.

One point in her class that might raise questions is her comment in this example that the students need to raise their hands because of the cameras in the room. Although the presence of cameras can easily affect participants' behavior, she does not refer to the cameras again. Other teachers refer to this same issue of raising hands and, after the first or second reminder, forget about it. Ms. B.I. does not. Her behavior, which reflects a further positive aspect of her teaching for interpreting, shows that she is cognizant of the need for visual access. A teacher with this awareness already may be much more amenable to the constraints of an interpreted education.

### *Mrs. B.A.'s Discourse Pacing*

Mrs. B.A. presents an interesting mix of interpretable and noninterpretable styles. Although some parts of her class are directly based on English form, which is problematic for interpreted access, many other examples of her pacing are not. During the discussions after short poetry readings, much of the discussion is moderately paced. When she asks a question, she allows silence while she waits for students to raise their hands. At one point in her lesson, she asks students to show the class where contractions occur in the poems (Tape 3, 34.20 min.).

The poem is written on a large paper. After asking the question, she leaves silence while the students look at the written English and raise their hands. She then has various students walk up to the paper and point to the contraction they have found in the written text. Only then does she discuss the specific contraction, its form and its meaning. She does not discuss the contraction while the student is pointing to it, providing some sequentiality in her input. A deaf student would be able to watch peers point out the contraction and then watch the interpretation of the teacher's discussion. Her tendency to leave silences and to focus on one channel of input at a time makes her pacing more adaptable to interpreting.

### *Mr. D.O.'s Discourse Pacing*

Mr. D.O.'s pacing is significantly different from the other two teachers. He speaks quickly most of the time, and even when he gives students time to work individually on a problem, he usually continues to talk about how to solve the problem while they are working. He continues to talk while he is writing on the board or showing overheads. He also expects students to correct papers while he is reading the answers and to take notes while he is discussing solutions to problems. Pauses between comments are rare.

This style of rapid-fire pacing, with continuous talk and simultaneous input for the hearing students leaves little room for accommodation to the constraints of interpreting. A deaf student trying to attend to the class through interpretation would be constantly forced to choose between looking at the interpretation, looking at homework answers, watching the overhead, and taking notes. The entire learning environment would not be accessible. It would certainly be possible to ask Mr. D.O. to change his pacing, but he would likely not be able to do it for long, even if he were willing to try.

### *Additional Observations of Discourse Pacing*

Of the six other teachers observed, four had pacing styles more similar to Ms. B.I. and Mrs. B.A., which were deliberate and moderately paced and that included pausing and silence. Two of the other teachers were closer to Mr. D.O.'s pacing.

## Explicitness and Redundancy of Discourse

A second characteristic of teaching style that is important for interpreting is redundancy. Redundancy includes both repeated information (such as repeating the answers of students) and the rephrasing or re-formulation of important information throughout the discussions, the tying together of lesson content through discourse structures. These aspects of redundancy are evident in statements like, "This is important and you will see it on a test so make sure you know it—the voltage is. . . ." Redundancy also includes the multiple layers included in any given reference. For example, in referring to a picture, a teacher can simply point toward it. A more explicit or redundant reference might include pointing to it, stating its location (upper left on the board), and naming it ("It's the picture of the liver."). Likewise, when repeating a student's answer, a teacher can simply repeat it or can add explicitness by stating the student's name, for example, "Andrea says that it is true."

TABLE 5 Analysis of Explicit and Redundant Discourse

| Explicit and Redundant Discourse | Ms. B.I. | Mrs. B.A. | Mr. D.O. |
|---|---|---|---|
| Repeats important vocabulary | Usually | Usually | Seldom |
| Repeats or rephrases important info | Usually | Usually | Seldom |
| Adds visual references to spoken English | Yes—models, draws on board, gestures | Yes—poster, book, flashcards | Yes—homework papers, overheads, board |
| **Overall: Modifiable to interpreting?** | Possible | Possible | Difficult given the many implicit references |

In contrast, lack of explicitness and redundancy make interpreting very difficult. An example would be the teacher who stands in the middle of a room, pointing vaguely toward a blackboard and saying, "That shows that finding values is easy if you just follow what we talked about yesterday." Almost every referent in that sentence requires some piece of implied information to be understood. Each time an interpreter must process the implications is a time when misinterpretation might occur and a time when the processing time may be lengthened because of the added levels of processing. The same statement made by the teacher standing at the board after adding explicitness could be "That (formula on the right) shows that finding values (for X and Y) is easy if you just follow what we talked about (the adding and subtracting of each side of the formula) yesterday (in the first period of math while we worked on the workbooks)." Table 5 shows the levels of explicitness and redundancy for each teacher.

## *Ms. B.I.'s Explicitness and Redundancy of Discourse*

Ms. B.I. consistently repeats and rephrases student input. After her previous example, she allows a two-second pause and then repeats both her statement and the question she asked about it (see the underlining in the following example). In addition, she not only names the student she is calling on but also gestures directly toward him, providing both visual and auditory input for the students to make the referent clear. This redundancy makes processing the message by the interpreter less difficult and time consuming and makes an error in interpretation less likely to occur.

Ms. B.I.: *Electricity is invisible, is that a true statement or a false statement*, David?

(*Gestures toward student.*)

Student 1: False.

Ms. B.I.: *It's a false statement*. Why do you say that?

Student 1: Because you can see sparks.

Ms. B.I.: *Because you can see sparks sometimes*. Does everybody agree with that?

The student replies to the question by saying that it is false. Ms. B.I. provides redundancy by expanding the response, making it a complete sentence. She asks for more input from the student, and when he provides it, she again expands his answer. This ongoing redundancy makes interpretation more reliable because the references are clearly stated.

Ms. B.I.'s use of explicit references and redundancy through repetition and rephrasing remains consistent throughout the class. In other examples, she also draws pictures on the board to provide both visual and auditory input for the students, and she gestures to accompany some of her comments. This additional input happened in the example above when she both named and gestured toward the student she called on to respond. She also used gestures to point toward the lights in the room as she talked about them, and she used various gestures to demonstrate actions like electrons circling each other and the pressure of water coming out of a hose.

Although the simultaneous use of speech with gesture can raise a barrier to interpretation, this dual input, when accompanied by her attention to pacing and students' needs for time to process, can accommodate some of the constraints of interpreting. And, if an interpreter is positioned to be able to see Ms. B.I., the interpreter can incorporate the gesture into the interpretation, thus adding redundancy to the interpretation.

### *Mrs. B.A.'s Explicitness and Redundancy of Discourse*

Mrs. B.A. also uses both explicit references and redundant references in her discourse. Like Ms. B.I., she repeats and rephrases her questions, expands comments, and adds visual input to her spoken comments. By using written versions of the readings and by using flash cards to represent specific words, she adds both auditory and visual input for the students.

### *Mr. D.O.'s Explicitness and Redundancy of Discourse*

Mr. D.O.'s discourse frequently lacks explicit reference and redundancy. Although he often stands at the board and talks about things he has written on it, he also often stands in the middle of the classroom and refers to something written on the board without making a clear visual connection. An interpreter may or may not be able to make the connection based on these distant references.

The following example demonstrates another problem for interpreting access. In this example, Mr. D.O. is talking while the students are supposed to be working, filling the "silence" with multiple input, as discussed earlier. He is wandering the room, checking on individual work, talking specifically to different students. He shifts from individual talk to class-directed talk, saying (Tape 11, 1.06 min.),

> Don't forget folks, in a few minutes here you have to convince me that what you are doing is correct! And don't lose sight of what we started with—the log functions, L-O-G function . . .

His comment ("Don't forget folks, in a few minutes here . . .") provides a spoken language strategy for getting attention and clearly indicates that something important is coming up. However, no visual break occurs, and no time is allowed for the shift of focus; hearing students must refocus while listening. In addition to not providing time for students to refocus (calling for their attention and leaving them no time in which to shift their attention to him), his comment lacks explicitness. Although the implicit information may seem obvious, making it explicit, as shown by the underlined text in the following example (Tape 11), would aid interpretation.

> Don't forget (*one purpose of this activity*), folks, in a few minutes here (*as we move on to the next part of the activity*) you have to convince me (*through the use of examples and clear explanations of your processes*) that what you are doing (*while you are figuring out the logical steps to solving these problems*) is correct (*for solving these problems*).

Although none of these expansions are required, the explicitness that any one of them adds would clarify the source for the interpreter and support clearer interpretation. This teacher does not include any of them, making a large part of the information implicit and more difficult to interpret. He does add some repetition and redundancy at the end of this comment, explicitly stating that what they started with was the log function, then spelling it for them. The relative infrequency of this type of explicitness and redundancy, especially when combined with his fast pace and his consistent expectations of multitasking, make his overall discourse much less amenable to interpreting.

This lack of explicit reference and redundancy is consistent throughout his classes. He does use the board for writing formulas and sometimes uses an overhead. However, when he refers to these visual supports, he often uses references like "that" or "this one" while talking from across the room. A more explicit reference might be "that first formula written on the board"; a more redundant statement to add would be that the formula is the one that corresponds to question number X on their homework sheet.

This discussion of Mr. D.O.'s discourse style should not be interpreted as criticism of his teaching. Whether his input is too much, too fast for the group or whether it is just right is not the question here. Likewise, whether Ms. B.I.'s style is too slow or is appropriate for the group is not being analyzed here. The point here is that some of these discourse styles are more amenable to being interpreted and are, therefore, more appropriate in a classroom that will be chosen for interpreting an education.

### *Additional Observations of Explicit and Redundant Features*

As with discourse pacing, of the other six teachers observed, the same four teachers whose pacing was more deliberate tended to have more explicit and redundant features in their speech. The three who used a faster pace with little intervening silence tended to rely more on implicit references and less redundancy.

## Turn-Taking

The third discourse pattern analyzed here is turn-taking management. Both pacing and explicitness are very important to interpreted turn-taking, especially

TABLE 6 Analysis of Turn-Taking

| Turn-Taking | Ms. B.I. | Mrs. B.A. | Mr. D.O. |
|---|---|---|---|
| Each turn is regulated by teacher | Usually | Usually | Seldom |
| One person speaks at a time | Usually | Often | Sometimes |
| Teacher explicitly names each speaker | Usually | Usually | Seldom |
| Teacher repeats student input | Usually | Usually | Seldom |
| **Overall: Modifiable to interpreting?** | Possible | Possible | Difficult given the multiple speakers and spontaneous input |

because of the added lag time required for the identification of speaker shift that adds to the lag time for a deaf student. Table 6 illustrates the styles of turn-taking of each of the three teachers.

### *Ms. B.I.'s Turn-Taking Style*

In the earlier example of Ms. B.I.'s class, she not only explicitly states the need to raise hands to get a turn but also follows through on this instruction by managing the turn-taking consistently throughout the class. In the example, she gestures toward and names the student she is recognizing for response, and when the student has stated, "false," she adds redundancy by saying, "It is a false statement."

Other examples of this type of managed turn-taking occur throughout her class. She almost always names the student recognized as well as repeats or expands the student input.

### *Mrs. B.A.'s Turn-Taking Style*

Like Ms. B.I., Mrs. B.A. manages turn-taking by naming each student before that student responds, and repeats that student's input, often expanding on it. In this younger class, students tended to forget the interaction rules and, thus, spontaneously respond, but Mrs. B.A. consistently recognizes respondents by name and ignores the occasional multiple responses.

### *Mr. D.O.'s Turn-Taking Style*

Mr. D.O. manages turn-taking differently. He seldom calls on a specific student, allowing any student who might want to respond to do so. This practice often results in several responses at the same time. When several responses do occur, he repeats the response that was correct, adding some redundancy to his discourse.

If a single student responds, he rarely states that person's name and even more rarely repeats the response. The speed of the turn-taking in his class, especially when added to the lack of naming and the nonrepetition of the responses, makes this type of turn-taking strategy particularly difficult to access by means of interpreting.

### *Additional Observations of Turn-Taking*

In the classes of the other six teachers observed, turn-taking followed similar patterns to discourse pacing as well as explicitness and redundancy. Although each teacher at times regulated turn-taking to single student responses and sometimes named a student as well as gestured to indicate that student's turn, this management was neither consistent nor frequent.

Although each teacher and academic subject used in the previous discussion focused on a different grade level and although the two classes that are more amenable to interpreting were taught by women teachers whereas the least accessible was taught by a male, this limited set of data shows no indication that grade level, subject, or gender influenced these styles. Mrs. Bayers's elementary level English class, while problematic, has potential for an interpreted education. Another elementary English class taught by a woman did not. That teacher's presentation and discourse styles were more similar to Mr. D.O.'s. History and science classes at the high school level, taught by males, ranged from being fairly interpretable, like Ms. B.I.'s class, to being unamenable to interpreting, like a history class and an English class at the high school level, both taught by women.

## Discussion of Discourse Patterns

In the classes observed, teachers consistently followed the same discourse style throughout a single class and, when observed across classes, also used the same style. All teachers who had a slower pace were also more redundant; teachers with a faster pace were more likely to be less redundant, although some redundancy was found in each teacher. Although teachers might be able to change their style of pacing and redundancy, years of experience and anecdotal input make it clear that this kind of change does not happen very often. Asking a teacher to slow down has a very brief effect, if any. Asking a teacher to add redundancy is somewhat more effective. Teachers are often willing to write terminology on the board more frequently and will try to repeat student responses and names more often. But the changes are not usually consistent.

Pacing and redundancy, unfortunately, can be a two-edged sword in real-life interpreting. The more redundant the input, the less likely a misinterpretation may occur. However, given the skills and knowledge of many educational interpreters, redundancy and pacing are often used by interpreters to mask their lack of skills. For example, interpreters who are unable to keep up with the pace of a teacher look for silences so they can catch up. Consequently, even though the teacher may have a slow and deliberate pace, the deaf student may never benefit from it unless the interpreter is skilled enough to work with it. Likewise, a teacher's redundancy performs different important functions: emphasizes important information, makes sure each student has time to process it, or repeats sounds so students can figure out spelling. Many interpreters, both skilled and less skilled, see redundancy as an opportunity to take a break, without recognizing (and certainly without interpreting) these essential functions of redundancy. Although a teacher may repeat a word three times, an interpretation might present it only once because the interpreter does not want to repeat the fingerspelling. In other instances, an interpretation may present a word more than once, as the teacher does, but may present it once as a fingerspelled word and once or twice as an invented sign. The function of redundancy when introducing these types of nonce signs is very different than the function the teacher has in mind.

It is true that the functions of redundancy in an English classroom discourse may be different from those in a signed classroom; for example, emphasis that is marked by repeating a word in English might be marked by holding the sign in the air for a longer than usual period. The point of this discussion is that the function of the redundancy must be included in the interpretation; too often, interpretations include neither an English discourse marker nor an ASL discourse marker. A repeated sentence is simply a chance to take a break or to catch up. The effect is that the deaf student does not receive the same structuring in formation that the hearing students do. Consequently, the deaf student does not know which words are most important, which points are essential, and which ideas are central to the lesson.

Likewise, the redundancy that is added when a teacher names a student in class must also be interpreted, not left out in an attempt to catch up. The repetition of a student's answer must also be interpreted and not deleted in the interests of interpreting the next question. Thus, slower discourse pacing in combination with redundancy of the teaching are essential to an interpretable classroom, but they must be part of the interpretation, not opportunities for shortcuts.

Thus, the slower pacing can to some extent alleviate the constraints of lag time in an interpreted education. However, slower pacing cannot eliminate lag time, and it should not be used as a time for an interpreter to catch up. Similarly, the inherent redundancy of a teaching style can greatly reduce the opportunities for misinterpretation that occur from misunderstanding of inferences, but it cannot be used as an excuse for eliminating the redundancy to keep up with the message.

Although all teachers and classes had activities that were barriers to an interpreted education, the factors of pacing, redundancy and explicitness, and turn-taking as well as the added visual references can make the same type of presentation more or less accessible. Even the ever present barrier of lag time can be, to some extent, mediated for more effective interpreting. A credible prediction is that classes with teachers who naturally use more features that are compatible with interpreting should more easily adapt to an interpreted education.

## SUMMARY AND CONCLUSIONS

Given that all analyzed activities pose a barrier because of lag time and, at least to some extent, because of visual and linguistic accessibility, no interpreted class in this study provided adequate access for an interpreted education. Most of the class time analyzed consisted of teacher-led discussions with other visual content. Although all these classes presented similar challenges, some seemed more modifiable than others. Although most teachers used discussion in combination with some type of focus on English, they demonstrated differences in their styles of talking, of timing, of redundancy and explicitness, and of turn-taking within their presentations. Some teachers tended to speak quickly, rarely repeating anything, relying on inference, allowing rapid-fire turn-taking and students' spontaneously shouted out answers or questions. Others spoke deliberately, including pausing and silence as important parts of their presentations. Some teachers tended to moderate the turn-taking, calling on one student at a time and discouraging multiple, spontaneous input; their commentary included much explicit information and was fairly redundant at several levels.

The teachers who tended toward the faster pace also tended to rely on multitasking and multiple channels of simultaneous input. For example, they might talk while writing on the board, read out answers while students simultaneously correct papers and take notes, and demonstrate an example while talking about it.

The teachers who tended to maintain a more deliberate pace with explicit references and redundancy also tended toward a more naturally sequential approach to content presentation. They would first explain something, then show it, then leave time for the students to take notes.

Given the previous discussion of the lag time imposed on all interpreted educations, the teacher who teaches at a slower pace, who includes pauses for processing, and who allows silence while students think are the teachers whose classrooms and teaching are more interpretable. Likewise, given the problematic nature of turn-taking for interpreting and deaf students, the teacher who regulates turn-taking carefully and consistently—so only one person speaks at a time and only after being recognized by the teacher—will be much more interpretable than the teacher who encourages overlapping and spontaneous questions, chorale responses, and quick interactions.

Finally, some teachers tended to be more visual than others. Some, when relying on other visual input, used only basic text—papers, written information on the board, books. Others included a wide range of visual input; in addition to written English, they also showed models, drew pictures, used colors for classifying, and gestured. This research has looked at effects of classroom environment and teaching style to analyze the ramifications of interpreting the education being provided in that classroom. Both visual and linguistic accessibility have been discussed, and the teachers own style of presentation has been discussed in relation to these factors.

Classroom activities may be visually inaccessible (e.g., requiring eyes in two places at once); these activities may be alleviated by the teacher's style. The teacher who allows silence and processing time for all students may be more able to adapt the classroom for interpretation than one who prefers a fast-paced, rapid-fire interaction. The teacher who allows all students time to look at visual input, including the text, the homework, and the notes, without talking is already making the simultaneous activity more sequential. The teacher who says a word, then writes it on the board, then spells it for students is already adding redundancy and sequentiality that is missing in a classroom where a teacher talks and writes while expecting students simultaneously to copy into their notes. Teachers who include strategies for students to first learn a word, then see it in written English form are already including some access to the bilingual and bimodal needs of deaf students. Classrooms that have the least number of visually problematic issues—classrooms in which teachers provide additional time and redundancy of the information they are offering—provide the best opportunity for an interpreted education.

Almost anyone can perform an analysis of the visual accessibility in a classroom. Likewise, anyone who can observe the redundancies of a teaching style can assess a classroom for that feature. Analyzing the linguistic issues, however, requires someone with an understanding of bilingual or bimodal language acquisition. An interpreter is one person who can do this analysis. Even more effective is the educator who is deaf; this person is knowledgeable about teaching, has experienced bilingual and bimodal language learning, and has experienced the challenges of accessing education through interpreting. A deaf person is able to point out issues that are important to consider and is usually more adept at suggesting possible modifications based on personal experience of visual educations. For example, an interpreter may suggest adding a note-taker to alleviate the need for a deaf student to look at the interpretation and simultaneously take notes. A deaf person will be quick to point out that note-taking is a learning process that is helpful and that taking it away from a deaf student denies him or her access to that aspect of education. Likewise, a deaf professional will be able to suggest placements of interpreters based on what works visually rather than on what works for the teacher or the interpreter.

## NOTES

1. Although video is essential for initial research, it is possible to conduct classroom assessment using the categories identified through the research without recording. A skilled observer can collect sufficient information about the suitability of a classroom for an interpreted education without use of recording equipment other than paper and pencil.

## REFERENCES

Cazden, C. 1988. *Classroom discourse: The language of teaching and learning.* Portsmouth, N.H.: Heinemann.

———. 2001. *Classroom discourse: The language of teaching and learning.* 2nd ed. Portsmouth, N.H.: Heinemann.

Colonomos, B. 1992. *Processes in interpreting and transliterating: Making them work for you.* Westminster, Colo.: Front Range Community College.

Commission on Education of the Deaf. 1988. *Toward equality: Education of the deaf.* Washington, D.C.: U.S. Government Printing Office.

Grasha, A. 1996. *Teaching with style.* Pittsburgh, Penn.: Alliance Publishers.

———. 2004. "Grasha's 5 teaching styles." http://web.indstate.edu/ctl/styles/5styles.html (accessed January 2004).

Johnson, R. C., and O. P. Cohen. 1994. *Implications and complications for deaf students of the full inclusion movement.* Gallaudet Research Institute Occasional Paper 94-2. Washington, D.C.: Gallaudet University.

Jones, B. E., G. M. Clark, and D. F. Soltz. 1997. Characteristics and practices of sign language interpreters in inclusive education programs. *Exceptional Children* 63(2): 257–68.

La Bue, M. A. 1998. Interpreted education: A study of deaf students' access to the content and form of literacy instruction in a mainstreamed high school English class. Ph.D. dissertation, Harvard University, Cambridge, Mass.

Livingston, S., B. Singer, and T. Abramson. 1994. A study to determine the effectiveness of two different kinds of interpreting. In *Proceedings of the Tenth National Convention of the Conference of Interpreter Trainers: Mapping our course: A collaborative venture,* ed. E. A. Winston, 175–97). N.p.: Conference of Interpreter Trainers.

Marschark, M., P. Sapere, C. Convertino, and R. Seewagen. Forthcoming. Educational interpreting: It's about deaf students. In *Educational interpreting and interpreting education,* eds. M. Marschark, R. Peterson, and E. A. Winston. New York: Oxford University Press.

Marschark, M., P. Sapere, C. Convertino, R. Seewagen, and H. Maltzen. Forthcoming. Comprehension of sign language interpreting: Deciphering a complex task situation. *Sign Language Studies.*

Metzger, M. 1995. *The paradox of neutrality: A comparison of interpreters' goals with the reality of interactive discourse.* Ph.D. dissertation, Georgetown University, Washington, D.C.

Monikowski, C., and E. A. Winston. 2003. Interpreters and interpreter education. In *Oxford handbook of deaf studies, language, and education,* eds. M. Marschark and P. E. Spencer. New York: Oxford University Press.

National Association of the Deaf. 2003. White paper: 2003 reauthorization of the Individuals with Disabilities Education Act. http://www.nad.org/openhouse/action/alerts/idea/whitepaperIDEA.html (accessed January 3, 2004).

Neumann Solow, S. 1981. *Sign language interpreting: A basic resource book.* Silver Spring, Md.: National Association of the Deaf Publications.

National Task Force on Educational Interpreting. 1989. *Report on the National Task Force on Educational Interpreting.* Rochester, N.Y.: National Technical Institute for the Deaf, Rochester Institute for Technology.

Public School in Action Videotapes. 1993. Professional development endorsement system materials (Videotape/DVD series). Available through Northwestern Connecticut Community-Technical College, http://www.nchrtm.okstate.edu/

Ramsey, C. L. 1997. *Deaf children in public schools: Placement, context, and consequences.* Washington, D.C.: Gallaudet University Press.

Roy, C. 2000. *Interpreting as a discourse process.* New York: Oxford University Press.

———. Forthcoming. What educators need to know about language to teach interpreting. In *Educational interpreting and interpreting education,* eds. M. Marschark, R. Peterson, and E. A. Winston. New York: Oxford University Press.

Schick, B. 2003. The development of American Sign Language and manually coded English systems. In *Oxford handbook of deaf studies. language, and education,* eds. M. Marschark and P. E. Spencer, 219–31. Oxford: Oxford University Press.

Schick, B., K. Williams, and L. Bolster. 1999. Skill levels of educational interpreters working in public schools. *Journal of Deaf Studies and Deaf Education* 4(2): 144–55.

Seleskovitch, D. 1978. *Interpreting for international conferences: Problems of language and communication.* Silver Spring, Md.: Registry of Interpreters for the Deaf Publications.

Seleskovitch, D., and M. Lederer. 1989. *A systematic approach to teaching interpretation,* trans. J. Harmer. N.p.: Registry of Interpreters for the Deaf.

Sofinski, B. A. 2002. So, why do I call this English? In *Turn-taking, fingerspelling, and contact in signed languages,* ed. C. Lucas, 27–50. Washington, D.C.: Gallaudet University Press.

Turner, G. H. 2002. *Issues and implications of the deafness research and development project.* Paper presented at the Deafness Research and Development Seminar, University of Central Lancashire, Great Britain.

———. 2004. *Challenging institutional audism.* Paper presented at the Supporting Deaf People, Online Conference. http://208.185.150.197/ (accessed February 12, 2004).

Wadensjo, C. 1998. *Interpreting as interaction.* New York: Longman.

Wilbur, R. B. 2003. Modality and the structure of language: Signed languages versus signed systems. In *Oxford Handbook of deaf studies, language, and education,* eds. M. Marschark and P. E. Spencer, 219–31. New York: Oxford University Press.

Winston, E. A. 1990. Mainstream interpreting: An analysis of the task. In *Proceedings of the Eighth National Convention, Conference of Interpreter Trainers,* ed. L. Swabey. N.p.: Conference of Interpreter Trainers.

———. 1994. An interpreted education: Inclusion or exclusion. In *Implications and complications for deaf students of the full inclusion movement,* eds. R. C. Johnson and O. P. Cohen. Gallaudet Research Institute Occasional Paper 94-2. Washington, D.C.: Gallaudet Research Institute.

———. 2001. Visual inaccessibility: The elephant (blocking the view) in interpreted education. *Odyssey* 2(2): 5–7.

———. 2004. Language myths of an interpreted education. Paper presented at the Supporting Deaf People, Online Conference. http://208.185.150.197/ (accessed February 12, 2004).

Yarger, C. C. 2001. Educational interpreting: Understanding the rural experience. *American Annals of the Deaf* 146(1): 16–30.

## APPENDIX A

| | Science | History/Social Studies | Math | English/Reading |
|---|---|---|---|---|
| Elementary | | | 1 female<br>1 female | 1 female<br>1 female |
| Middle School | 1 female | 1 male | 1 male | 1 female |
| High School | 1 male<br>1 female | 1male<br>1 male | 1 male<br>1 male | |
| | 1 male | | 1 male | |

Part 3

# Improving Interpreted Education

# Educational Interpreting: Developing Standards of Practice

Melanie Metzger and Earl Fleetwood

Although circumstances surrounding the advent of educational signed language interpreting are well documented, the goals and processes defining the practice are not. Since its inception, educational interpreting has taken on a "try everything" approach, resulting in a practice that is highly unstable with respect to the nature and scope of its responsibilities and, consequently, the outcomes it yields for deaf and hard of hearing students (Fleetwood 1995). A variety of communication "methods," an acquiescent and vacillating role, and inconsistency with respect to goals and processes have come to define the practice of educational signed language interpreting (see Stuckless, Avery, and Hurwitz 1989; Rittenhouse, Rahn, and Morreau 1989). Furthermore, efforts to codify educational interpreting are founded in descriptive rather than prescriptive processes. That is, some of the first important attempts to gather data and describe current practices in the field of educational interpreting (compare Stuckless, Avery, and Hurwitz 1989; Seal 1998) have been transformed into curricula and even testing mechanisms, without research with respect to the effectiveness of the practices that have been described. Efforts such as these serve to denote and promulgate a profession without its viability ever having been demonstrated. In fact, evidence suggests that educational signed language interpreting practices are, at best, restrictive with respect to the education of deaf and hard of hearing children (Winston 1992, 1994; Metzger 1992; Patrie 1993; Fleetwood 1995). The findings in Brown Kurz and Caldwell Langer (see chapter 1) serve to reflect this lack of standards from the consumer's perspective.

The need to establish functional standards for individuals who serve as educational signed language interpreters is undeniable. As with any profession, the establishment of these standards is an essential precondition to ensuring the existence of an effective and efficient service. Without a clear understanding of what a profession intends to support, the profession's viability cannot be measured, and consequently, the profession cannot be held accountable. For example, if it is not clear whether an educational interpreter is hired to ensure successful student learning or to foster equal opportunity in mainstream education (including the opportunity to fail and learn from that experience), then it is not clear whether an academically failing student falls short despite competent, well-implemented educational interpreting services or because those services are inadequate .

In light of past and current practices and as participants begin to establish an appropriate professional direction for the field of educational signed language interpreting, educational interpreters would need to identify their raison d'être and, subsequently, identify what professional behaviors support or interfere with it. The following five steps are recommended to accomplish this effort: (a) identify the purpose for which the job exists; (b) define standards of practice that identify job boundaries; (c) identify that corpus of knowledge and skills necessary for an individual to practice; (d) develop programs and materials that teach the identified corpus of knowledge and skills; and (e) develop a formal testing mechanism (Fleetwood 1995). These steps are further described in the following sections.

## IDENTIFY THE PURPOSE FOR WHICH THE JOB EXISTS

The job of "educational interpreter" was not created as a result of, and should not be defined by, the needs of teachers, administrators, or other school personnel. The educational interpreter's job exists because of the needs of deaf and hard of hearing students who find themselves needing to access education in hearing-mainstream classrooms. Nevertheless, many interpreters, teachers, and students do not share an understanding of the interpreter's functional goal (Mertens 1990, Hayes 1992; Taylor and Elliot 1994). Further, many job descriptions highlight "noninterpreting tasks" that actually interfere with an interpreter's time and ability to provide services that support desirable student outcomes (Stuckless, Avery, and Hurwitz 1989; Hayes 1992; Jones 1993; Fleetwood 1995). For example, for an interpreter to effectively interpret the wide variety of subjects that arise in K–12 and postsecondary settings, a tremendous amount of preparation is required. The preparation time an interpreter should have for tasks such as previewing upcoming lessons and educational videos is, instead, often devoted to noninterpreting tasks such as "grading papers, making bulletin boards and disciplining students—tasks much like those of a teacher's aide" (Hayes 1992, 12; see also Brown Kurz and Caldwell Langer in chapter 1).

Paramount to the interpreter's ability to provide services that support desirable deaf and hard of hearing student outcomes is that interpreter's understanding of the purpose for which the job exists. The purpose of the job might be thought of in terms of what outcomes educational interpreting is intended to foster. Research that links interpreter attributes with deaf and hard of hearing student outcomes would seem desirable. For example, Seal (1998) seeks to find relationships between the success of the deaf student who uses interpreting services and certain attributes of the student and the interpreter that might affect that success. However, in terms of deaf student outcomes where educational interpreters are employed, "success" remains undefined. In other words, data collected are often the product of idiosyncratic opinions about what constitutes success without success being qualified or quantified as a clearly articulated benchmark.

Questions about job boundaries also arise daily in the multitude of decisions that confront an interpreter. This is because, in every instance, an interpreter must determine what level of information should be conveyed and how it should be presented. Interpreters navigate the reality that their decisions produce either more literal or more idiomatic renderings that frame any subsequent interaction. For example, an interpreter confronted with the following sentence must first determine whether a teacher is offering the student an option or is expecting immediate compliance: "Would you like to give me your homework now?"

Answers to other questions also serve to define the interpreter's job. For example, should an interpreter attempt to include a speaker's or signer's accent or dialect? What if the interpreter is Euro-American and the student is African American? Interpreters must be knowledgeable about and be able to appropriately function in a multicultural environment (Lewis 1997).

The implications of interpreters' decisions are not always direct or obvious. For example, during classroom discussion, should the interpreter indicate the source of a comment by doing something other than simple pointing? This question goes to the point that students in a Deaf class, like hearing students in a hearing class, have an equal opportunity to evaluate which peers would make good friends or who might be a good study partner.[1] Students make these evaluations, in part, through opportunities to observe who contributes and what they contribute to class discussions. Thus, to provide an inclusive experience that allows for this type of socialization, an interpreter not only must interpret what people say or sign but also must be sure that the identity of the source of every utterance is accessible (see Metzger, Fleetwood, and Collins, forthcoming, for a discussion of source attribution by interpreters). Brown Kurz and Caldwell Langer (see chapter 1) give evidence of students' reactions to interpreter decisions; interestingly, neither the students nor most interpreters have a sense of what "should" be. This unclear purpose reflects the lack of standards and definition in the job. The examples above represent some of the questions and professional decisions that an educational interpreter must face. These kinds of decisions can be made well and consistently only when interpreters work toward a clearly identified goal.

## DEFINE STANDARDS OF PRACTICE THAT IDENTIFY JOB BOUNDARIES

A profession is defined not only in terms of its attention to explicitly identified obligatory behaviors but also by its ability to recognize the significance of exclusive behaviors. In other words, that which lies outside the domain of a profession's obligations is as important to defining the profession as that which lies within.

Teachers and other professionals enjoy job boundaries that have been established through years of experience and exposure. Professionals earn the right to practice by successfully completing degree programs that have been shaped by these boundaries and that prepare them to work in their particular job. Furthermore, a wide audience has come to have expectations of the professional that are consistent with the profession's goals. Even so, teachers, for example, might be asked to take on responsibilities that, although related to the school, still reduce the time they have to devote to the teaching task. Nevertheless, one would rarely expect a teacher to leave a class unattended for three hours to prepare and serve lunch in the cafeteria. No matter how important it is for students to eat and to be healthy so they can learn, the fact is widely known and accepted that asking a teacher to prepare and serve lunch would interfere with his or her ability to perform the job for which he or she was hired. Three-hour lunch preparations during class time are outside the domain of the teaching profession in most schools.

Unfortunately, the domain of an educational interpreter is not as well known. Neither experience nor exposure to educational interpreters is commonplace among hearing students, teachers, or administrators. Furthermore, educational interpreters do not enjoy goal-driven, prescriptive professional standards. Thus, interpreters are commonly asked to perform tasks that interfere with their ability to provide students with services that support specific and desirable student outcomes. For example, an interpreter striving for inclusion of deaf and hard of hearing students in a hearing-mainstream context must articulate the socialization aspects of the educational environment. To omit accessibility to social behavior is clearly an exclusive practice. Yet, the only way to encourage hearing and deaf students to be willing to interact through an interpreter is to ensure that these students can trust the interpreter. Asking an interpreter to discipline students tends to have the opposite effect; it likely ensures that students will *not* trust the interpreter to maintain the confidentiality that they experience when an interpreter is not present (Fleetwood and Metzger 1990). Thus, expecting interpreters to discipline students is counter to the inclusion of deaf and hard of hearing students in mainstream settings. Similarly, asking interpreters to report behavior and study problems in an interpreted environment often runs counter to their efforts to build trust with students.

## IDENTIFY THAT CORPUS OF KNOWLEDGE AND SKILLS NECESSARY FOR AN INDIVIDUAL TO PRACTICE

When the goals of educational interpreting have been explicitly identified and after subsequent functional standards supporting those goals have been delineated, then the next relevant step is to identify the requisite knowledge and skills. To be meaningful, this body of required knowledge and skills must enable those in the profession to realize the profession's identified functional standards. The importance of improving the quality and relevance of educational interpreter knowledge and skills cannot be overemphasized (Jones 1993; Patrie 1993; Winston 1994; Fleetwood 1995).

Winston (1992, 1994) points out that many activities in a predominantly hearing public school require that hearing students use both their ears and eyes to accomplish a given task. These tasks include, but are not limited to, video or film quizzes, assignment instructions, lectures with note-taking, and interactive verbal games in foreign language classes. An interpreter who will be working in educational settings must learn how to identify what activities require special attention and what strategies, if any, can make these activities accessible to someone who is using only his or her eyes to accomplish what hearing classmates approach as both an acoustic and a visual task. The interpreter not only must have the skill to accomplish the aforementioned task but also must recognize the inequity to affect its resolve. In addition, and perhaps more obviously, an educational interpreter must have the linguistic skills and ability to comprehend a wide variety of subjects if he or she is to accurately interpret them.

As Seleskovich (1978) and others have pointed out, interpreters cannot interpret what they do not understand. Thus, an educational interpreter must be able to both comprehend and construct utterances in two languages or modes (English and ASL, speaking and signing) regardless of whether the topic is history, mathematics, science, athletics, or language arts. For example, an interpretation of a volleyball unit requires that the interpreter be familiar with not only the rules for reporting scores in English—in which linear ordering indicates which score goes with which team—but also in ASL—in which spatial ordering serves a similar function. Only with communicative competence in both of the languages and in all of the subjects being interpreted can the interpreter then render a competently crafted interpretation. In this example, the interpreter must reserve the score-keeping conventions of the game in accordance with how those conventions are represented in two languages and modes. Exactly this sort of sociocultural linguistic information, which can arise in each subject and class, allows a student to be either included or excluded from the mainstream and peer interaction as well as from the learning process itself.

Research in this area must focus on determining not only what body of knowledge and skills is required of the job but also whether it exists and can be learned. Ultimately, this research will determine the viability of educational signed language interpreting.

## DEVELOP PROGRAMS AND MATERIALS THAT TEACH THE IDENTIFIED CORPUS OF KNOWLEDGE AND SKILLS

If research determines that knowledge and skills requisite of educational interpreting exist and can be learned, then a meaningful course of study can be established to teach them. Currently, programs that prepare future educational interpreters include the teaching of skills such as materials preparation and how to tutor. Presumably, these tasks are already covered by other members of the educational team. Omitting them from time-constrained educational interpreter preparation programs would allow more time for interpreters to acquire the knowledge and skills needed for the interpreting task itself.

## DEVELOP A FORMAL TESTING MECHANISM

An effective testing mechanism is one that is based on the purpose of the job, the standards of practice that delimit the job, and the corpus of relevant knowledge and skills. Tests that provide a measure for various aspects of knowledge and skills could be beneficial. For example, an interpreter who passes a Language Proficiency Interview (LPI) in any of the languages in which he or she will be interpreting has demonstrated some of the skills and knowledge related to the interpreting job. However, a test measuring competence in spoken language interpreting or in teaching, or for any adjunct area does not measure an individual's ability to work effectively as an educational signed language interpreter. Only a test that measures all aspects of the job, and only tests that measure the skills and knowledge specific to that job, can help determine who is qualified to support desired deaf and hard of hearing student outcomes. Because no clear goals have yet been identified for educational signed language interpreters, no test currently exists that measures an individual's competence at providing students with an inclusive, interpreted education. The Educational Interpreter Performance Assessment (EIPA), discussed in other chapters of this volume, provides an assessment of interpreting skills related to the message itself. The Educational Interpreter Knowledge Assessment (EIKA) is being developed to assess knowledge; there is still no assessment for decision-making skills and other essential skills required of an interpreter.

Signed language interpreting in educational settings is a relatively young field. At this point in its evolution, the profession has yet to identify either the outcomes it strives to support or the functional role that will achieve these ends. Identifying the goal of the practitioner with respect to deaf and hard of hearing student outcomes can allow a meaningful educational interpreting methodology to be constructed. Subsequently, pursuing this goal will ultimately answer questions of viability with respect to educational signed language interpreting as a productive practice.

## NOTE

1. In this chapter, we follow the convention of using *deaf* to refer to audiological status and *Deaf* to refer to cultural membership in a Deaf community.

## REFERENCES

Fleetwood, E. 1995. The paradox of signed language interpreting in mainstream educational settings. Master's thesis, Gallaudet University, Washington, D.C.

Fleetwood, E., and M. Metzger. 1990. *Cued Speech transliteration: Theory and application.* Silver Spring, Md.: Calliope Press.

Hayes, L. 1992. Educational interpreters for deaf students: Their responsibilities, problems, and concerns. *Journal of Interpretation* 5(1): 5–24.

Jones, B. 1993. Responsibilities of educational sign language interpreters in K–12 public schools in Kansas, Missouri, and Nebraska. Ph.D. dissertation, University of Kansas, Lawrence.

Lewis, J. 1997. The issue of cultural competence: An ethical dilemma or bye bye bi-bi. *RID Views* 14(6): 5.

Mertens, D. 1990. Teachers working with interpreters: The deaf student's educational experience. *American Annals of the Deaf* 136:48–52.

Metzger, M. 1992. Cued Speech transliterating: The sign of success in a mainstream classroom. In *The Cued Speech resource book for parents of deaf children,* eds. O. Cornett and M. E. Daisy, 684–91. Raleigh, N.C.: National Cued Speech Association.

Metzger, M., E. Fleetwood, and S. Collins. Forthcoming. Discourse genre and linguistic mode: Interpreter influences in visual and tactile interpreted interaction. *Sign Language Studies* 4(2): 118–37.

Patrie, C. 1993. *A confluence of diverse relationships: Interpreter education and educational interpreting: RID Keynote Address.* Washington, D.C.: Gallaudet University.

Rittenhouse, R., C. Rahn, and L. Morreau 1989. Educational interpreter services for hearing-impaired students: Provider and consumer disagreements. *Journal of the American Deafness and Rehabilitation Association* 22:57–63.

Seal, B. 1998. Best practices in educational interpreting. Boston, Mass.: Allyn and Bacon.

Seleskovitch, D. 1978. *Interpreting for international conferences.* Washington, D.C.: Pen and Booth.

Stuckless, E., J. Avery, and T. Hurwitz. 1989. Educational interpreting for deaf students: Report of the national task force on educational interpreting. Rochester, N.Y.: Rochester Institute of Technology.

Taylor, C., and R. Elliot. 1994. Identifying areas of competence needed by educational interpreters. *Sign Language Studies* 83:179.

Winston, E. A. 1992. Mainstream interpreting: An analysis of the task. In *The challenge of the '90s: New standards in interpreter education. Proceedings of the eighth national convention of the Conference of Interpreter Trainers*, ed. L. Swabey, 51–67. Pomona, Calif: Conference of Interpreter Trainers.

———. 1994. An interpreted education: Inclusion or exclusion. In *Implications and complications for deaf students of the full inclusion movement*, eds. C. Johnson and O. Cohen, 55–62. Gallaudet Research Institute Occasional Paper 94-2. Washington, D.C.: Gallaudet Research Institute, Gallaudet University.

# Assessment and Supervision of Educational Interpreters: What Job? Whose Job? Is This Process Necessary?

Marty M. Taylor

Educational interpreters often work in isolation without the support of other interpreters. They may live and work in rural communities, interpreting in a school or a school district where only one deaf or hard of hearing child attends. Perhaps no other interpreters are in the vicinity. Interpreters may not have the opportunity to participate in professional interpreting organizations either because none exist in their area or because interpreters do not receive support for or time from the school district to attend these events.

Because of their highly specialized area of expertise and their responsibility for all access to aural communication, interpreters rarely have the day-to-day contact with others who share their experiences. This crucial difference distinguishes interpreters from others in the educational setting. Teachers have other teachers with whom to discuss issues; in addition, most administrators or principals have teaching backgrounds and can discuss relevant issues with teachers as well as assist them with problem solving, providing meaningful input on a regular basis. Even counselors have other counselors, if not in the same school, then at least in the district, with whom they can share their learning and from whom they can gain support for their work and their ideas. Usually, interpreters lack this camaraderie, support, and vital input.

Educational interpreters must be placed in appropriate settings with deaf or hard of hearing students. In these arrangements, the deaf or hard of hearing student must be able to work well with the interpreter, and the interpreter must be able to effectively express the communication that occurs in a classroom setting, including communication from the teacher, from the students to the teacher, and from students to other students.

Interpreters need to be assessed before being placed in a classroom with a deaf or hard of hearing child. This assessment includes consideration of their skills, expertise, knowledge of the subject matter, and ability to suit the needs of the situation and the individual child. Interpreters must be competent to provide interpretation for the specific students and teachers for whom they are being hired.

Once interpreters are successfully placed in the classroom, they must be assessed on a regular basis. This ongoing assessment is vital for the success of deaf and hard of hearing students enrolled in mainstream classes. These assessments include on-site observations by qualified individuals who can assess the accuracy of the interpreted messages expressed between English and sign language.

In addition, qualified experts in interpreting must have a clearly defined role in supervising interpreters. Unfortunately, supervision is often the responsibility of the teacher in the classroom, the principal, or at best, the itinerant teacher of the deaf. Consequently, supervision by these people will consist of reviewing interpreter behaviors such as timeliness and appropriateness to the classroom situation rather than the language proficiency and interpreting abilities used in the classroom. Although the type of supervision these professionals provide can be useful and is necessary, it is limited and does not provide supervision for the primary component of the interpreter's job—interpreting. Typically, these staff members have minimal or no signing experience, and they do not have any training or education that qualifies them to supervise the interpreting skills of the interpreter. Thus, expertise must be brought in from external resources to assist in supervising the effectiveness of the communication process and the interpretation as well as to provide evaluations and recommendations for enhancing the interpreter's language and interpretation skills.

## THE NEED FOR ASSESSMENT

Before any discussion begins about the assessment of interpreters, one must first identify the interpreting needs that must be addressed. Addressing the interpreting needs should not be taken lightly or decided only on face value. The process is a complicated one that requires examination and reflection from all involved. Many questions come to the forefront when examining this important issue. For example, is a specific deaf child interested in enrolling in the school? Does this child know sign language or not? If the student does not possess adequate language, then an interpreted education would not be an accessible placement. If he or she does have language, from where did he or she learn it, and how fluent is the child? Is the child's language adequate to enable him or her to benefit from interpreting? Does the child have adequate world and content knowledge to benefit from an interpretation? What communication support does the child require? Is the child hard of hearing? If so, what can he or she pick up aurally, and what, if any, additional assistance is required to make the environment accessible to the hard of hearing child? Often, these questions are overlooked, or if they are asked, they sometimes are not answered fully.

An important point to note is that those needing access to communication include not only the deaf and hard of children but also the rest of the school: nondeaf students, teachers, coaches, secretaries, and principals. Deaf and hard of hearing students should have opportunities to participate in the school as a whole, not just opportunities within their classrooms. They must have opportunities to participate in sports; leadership roles such as editor of the yearbook, officer in the debate club, student-body president; and other activities that are available to the general student population and are essential to a complete education.

Of course, the teachers and administrators must determine whether or not deaf and hard of hearing children can be adequately served in their school. This decision is based on the knowledge of what the student requires to succeed in the mainstream setting after identifying the needs stated earlier. Often, schools do not have the expertise available to them to make this determination. They must locate appropriate resources that can assist in the decision-making process to determine whether or not they have an appropriate situation with the necessary accommodation that will allow deaf and hard of hearing children to excel in their learning at this particular school.

After the teacher (or teachers), the school administrators, the parents, and the deaf or hard of hearing child determine that the child's needs can be effectively accommodated within the mainstream school setting (e.g., classroom, extracurricular activities). When all opportunities for the student are determined, then identification of all the services necessary to properly support the student can continue. Interpreters may be only part of the necessary package; many other support personnel such as language development specialists and aural rehabilitation workers may be required. This chapter focuses on interpreters and not the other personnel who may be required for well-rounded support to individual deaf and hard of hearing children. After the needs of the students and the school staff members have been identified and a decision has been reached requiring interpreters, then the hiring process of interpreters can begin.

## EDUCATIONAL INTERPRETERS: WHO ARE THEY? WHERE DO THEY COME FROM?

Interpreters are not all alike. They come from a wide range of backgrounds and experiences. Those involved in the hiring process must consider three important questions to consider before recruiting and hiring interpreters: (a) What academic credentials do they have? (b) What is their experience in providing interpretation in school settings? (c) How well will they be able to work as team players with the other professionals in this specific educational environment?

### What Academic Credentials Do They Have?

Interpreters who graduate from interpreting programs are more likely to be appropriate for working in educational settings than those who have not had academic preparation in interpretation. Having made this claim, interpreter graduates are not all the same, nor are interpreting programs. Interpreting programs cover a multitude of topics within their course of studies. These may include English and ASL language development; interpretation skill and professional behaviors; and specialized work, including interpreting in educational or medical settings and working with different consumers such as those who are deaf-blind or oral.

Interpreting in educational settings is a very specialized area of study. Interpreting programs may or may not cover this area of expertise. For example, graduates of some interpreting programs may have no exposure to working in the educational setting, especially at the K–12 grade levels. Others will have graduated from programs that specialize in K–12 educational interpreting; these graduates would have learned about the various facets of educational environments and, most likely, would have completed at least one work placement in it.

## What Is Their Experience in Providing Interpretation in a School Setting?

A degree from an interpreting program is quite different from actual experience working in a classroom with deaf and hard of hearing students. Interpreters should have experience in this setting, including interpreting for teachers, administrators, and deaf and nondeaf students. Interpreters should be able to document this experience through recommendations from the stakeholders who have had to rely on them for successful communication in the educational setting. Ideally, the interpreters applying for the position will have knowledge about and experience in the specific grade level involved; interpreting for a second grader is very different from interpreting for a tenth grader.

## How Well Will They Be Able to Work as Team Players With the Other Professionals in This Specific Educational Environment?

When an interpreter has both the education and experience in interpreting in educational settings, then the questions about his or her background and experiences become more specific. Interpreters need to be able to work appropriately as a member of the professional team. They are professionals in the classroom, and they must have the responsibility and authority to act as professionals. They must have access to the teacher (or teachers) to discuss the content of lessons so they can prepare their interpretations in advance. They must be able to articulate their role to others and to participate in IEP meetings as these functions relate to the communication needs of the deaf or hard of hearing child. They must be able to professionally represent the effect of interpreting on the educational process and have the knowledge and skill to perform these tasks.

# THE ASSESSMENT PROCESS BEGINS: WHAT ARE THE ELEMENTS OF AN EFFECTIVE ASSESSMENT PROCESS?

When the school personnel fully understand the needs of the deaf or hard of hearing child (or children) and the qualifications to look for in seeking appropriate interpreters, then recruitment can commence. Assessment of interpreters begins at this stage of the process, during the recruitment and interviewing stages, before actually hiring interpreters.

The placement of an interpreter (or interpreters) in the appropriate class with a deaf or hard of hearing student is crucial to the overall success of the learning experience of the child. All too often, educators assume that someone with little interpreting experience is best suited for younger children. This assumption is false. In fact, the younger deaf and hard of hearing children are the students who need the most experienced and highly qualified interpreters because young children are still developing their language skills (Seal 1998). They do not have the ability to assess the interpretation and figure out what is accurate or inaccurate in it. Young children need exceptional interpreters for all of their classes so they can acquire the foundation for language and learning before being exposed to novice and inexperienced interpreters.

After interpreters are hired, their assessment should be a process, not a one-time event like an annual review. Assessment should be ongoing and should be done at frequent intervals, especially with newly hired interpreters. Often, a probationary period is appropriate during which the interpreter, the deaf or hard of hearing child, and the school personnel can judge whether or not the mediated interpreted situation is working.

Elements of assessment should begin with a clearly stated series of purposes. These purposes should be directly related to the roles, responsibilities, and expectations of the interpreter. The purpose of the assessment is to determine

- the interpreter's strengths and weaknesses in the interpretation process;
- the effectiveness of the interpreter in the classroom as perceived by the
  teacher (or teachers),
  student (or students),
  interpreter (or interpreters); and
- the effectiveness of the interpreted environment as perceived by the
  teacher (or teachers),
  student (or students), and
  interpreter (or interpreters).

Then, the frequency for assessing each of the above elements should be outlined and forms for assessing them should be provided and completed at each stage. For example, assessing the interpreter's strengths and weaknesses in the interpretation process would be crucial shortly after he or she is hired, then again in two to three months, and again before the end of the year to determine what steps, if any, need to be taken during the summer break before the interpreter's contract is renewed. The forms related to the perceptions of the students, teachers, and interpreters could be completed weekly by each party in the beginning, then monthly or quarterly as deemed appropriate by each party.

Another purpose of the assessment process should be to determine which of the assessments are formative and which are summative. The assessment results must be shared directly with the interpreter, and the particular assessments that will be kept in the interpreter's permanent personnel record should be clearly identified.

## Why Should Interpreters Have a Written Professional Development Plan?

In addition to the assessments mentioned above, the interpreter may create a professional development plan to improve her or his own skills and knowledge. The interpreter's priorities should be determined in conjunction with the specified needs of the classroom setting as well as the assessments done to date, and they should be developed in conjunction with and supported by the school administration.

This professional development plan might include working with an interpreter mentor. The association with a mentor would allow a newer interpreter an opportunity to improve his or her skills associated with signing and the interpretation process in an educational environment. At the same time, the opportunity could provide structured time to share experiences, which could lead to helpful advice for problem solving.

## Why Are External Evaluators Required to Assess Interpreters' Skills?

Administrators, teachers, and parents must base their decisions on the expert input of those who know about interpreting. Unfortunately, all too often, schools and school districts do not have the expertise to assess interpretation skills. At these times, during the assessment process, an external evaluator will have to be hired to provide this assessment. The external evaluator can provide input into what should be assessed and how often. One assessment tool used by many states is the Educational Interpreter Knowledge Assessment (EIKA) and the Educational Interpreter Performance Assessment (EIPA). See chapter 10 for more detailed information on this screening tool. Some states use the national interpreting tests offered by the Registry of Interpreters for the Deaf that include assessments for both skill and knowledge of the interpreter who works in a variety of settings. It is not specifically designed for assessing educational interpreters like the EIKA and the EIPA, but it provides a standard for assessing knowledge and skills of interpreters.

After an interpreter is hired, an external evaluator should be used to assess the interpretation process occurring in the classroom. This assessment can be conducted in one or several classes on a particular day. However, to have a complete assessment, the evaluator should optimally observe several times over the course of a month to provide a broader review of the skills used at different times, in different classes, and (if more than one child requires interpretation) with a variety of students.

Keep in mind that an interpretation at one time in one class may be effective and successful, yet at different times and in different classes, the same level of interpreting skill may be ineffective and unsuccessful. For example, interpreting for science may be more difficult for the interpreter than interpreting for an English class. Difficulties may occur because of the content, the teacher's style, the interest level of the student (or students), or the technical nature of the presentation that day. If the interpreter is working with more than one student, the interpretation may be very successful for one while being inadequate and inappropriate for another.

The external evaluator, when viewing interpreters in the classroom, should assess both the interpreter's interpretation skills and the decision-making process that is used when the interpreter chooses to interpret or not to interpret. For example, the interpreter may decide that refraining from interpreting is more helpful when the teacher is writing on the board and simultaneously saying what she or he is writing. Or when another child in the classroom wants to communicate with the deaf child, the interpreter may respect their choice to try to communicate without interpretation. Sometimes, allowing attempts at uninterpreted communication is very appropriate because it supports independent behavior. It allows the deaf child direct communication access to individuals other than the interpreter, communication through which the child can begin to develop independent relationships with others in the classroom. Or, perhaps, the interpreter provides only a partial interpretation, rather than the entire interpretation, because the nondeaf child already has accomplished some of the communication him- or herself. All of these moment-to-moment decisions of when to interpret and how much to interpret are an important part of the assessment process as evaluators look at the interpreter's role in effectively facilitating communication.

Another area where schools and school districts may not have the necessary expertise is the ability to assess the degree to which the classroom environment is accessible to the deaf or hard of hearing child. For example, the interpreter may be providing an effective interpretation, but does the deaf child understand it? If not, why not? And if so, how well? In this situation, the school may need to hire a different evaluator who can assess the child's language skills and ability to comprehend the interpretation. This type of assessment is totally different from that of the interpreter's performance, yet it is integral to the success of the mainstream experience for deaf and hard of hearing children.

## HOW IS SUPERVISION OF INTERPRETERS UNIQUE AND WHY IS IT NECESSARY?

The interpreter's direct supervisor, with the input from the external consultant, is responsible for the probationary period of employment. As mentioned above, the probationary period is crucial to the interpreter and to the educational success of the deaf or hard of hearing student.

Interpreters working in a mainstream setting are in a unique situation. Because their skills are so specialized, the school, the school district, or both often do not have the necessary expertise or personnel to provide supervision for all the various tasks the interpreter performs. Of course, the school personnel can observe the interpreter's interpersonal skills and behaviors as well as his or her timeliness as an employee of the school, just as they observe these factors in teachers. The difficulty arises in assessing the actual interpretation process and the skills necessary to do this work effectively, which calls for ongoing skill assessments that may have to be provided by external consultants.

The on-site supervisor should be responsible to monitor the day-to-day work of the interpreter, with the exception, perhaps, of the interpretation skills themselves. Supervision also needs to involve assisting the interpreter in achieving a manageable workload, and supervisors must have the authority to act immediately when necessary. For example, the interpreter may need a team interpreter for some or all of the classes and extracurricular activities that require interpreting. Overuse syndrome, or repetitive strain injury (RSI) is a serious result of constant interpreting without sufficient rest periods (Premier's Council 1994). Many schools have lost their interpreters because of the serious nature of this work-related injury. And many interpreters have been forced to stop interpreting altogether because of it.

The supervision should entail monitoring the degree of success in achieving the stated goals in the interpreter's professional development plan. The supervisor must be aware that not all professional development activities designed for teachers are useful for interpreters to participate in or to attend. Alternate professional development opportunities need to be offered to the interpreter, not always, but certainly on occasion. Providing this assistance to interpreters includes allowing them to attend regional and national interpreting workshops and conferences where they can hone their skills and network with other interpreters, thus reducing their sense of isolation.

Interpreters can also study on their own during their planning time. Interpreters should not be in the classroom interpreting from 8:00–3:00 every day. A regimen of this kind is not physically possible over the long run unless interpreting work is scheduled so the interpreter has less interpretation required in some of the classes than in others (Seal 1998; Premier's Council 1994).

Retention of qualified interpreters is essential. Reasons that interpreters either are not able to stay on the job or choose to leave are numerous. One reason is that interpreters may be overworked. They may be required or feel obligated to interpret for everything that occurs in the classroom in addition to extracurricular activities and assemblies. Interpreters can perceive either that he or she must interpret for all of these situations or that the deaf or hard of hearing student will be left out of the communication, the event, and the learning and bonding that occur in these various venues. Another reason interpreters may leave a position is because they feel isolated. Often, interpreters are either the only employee or one of a select few with this skill set and this grave responsibility to facilitating communication.

To retain interpreters, the work must be manageable and the interpreter must feel that he or she is a contributing member of the educational team. Ways to retain interpreters are to offer appropriate professional development opportunities, provide guidance in achieving their professional goals, allow opportunities to team interpret, and respect them as professional members of the educational team.

## CONCLUSION

Interpreters are a unique part of the educational team when it comes to working with deaf and hard of hearing children in mainstream settings. They are highly specialized professionals. Before interpreters are hired, educators and parents must identify the needs of the individual deaf or hard of hearing child planning to attend school. In instances when an interpreted education is deemed appropriate for the deaf or hard of hearing child, the process of recruiting, hiring, assessing, supervising, and retaining interpreters begins and continues throughout the term of employment for the interpreter. Usually, external consultants will be required at several of these stages, including when assessing the interpreter's interpretation skills before hiring and when evaluating the interpreter on a regular basis to determine the effectiveness and completeness of his or her work in the classroom or during extracurricular activities. Interpreters often work alone, and many times, no other interpreters are working at the school or even in the district. To help reduce this sense of isolation, interpreters should have the support from their school to seek appropriate professional development opportunities in which they can participate and learn from other interpreters who do the same work.

## REFERENCES

Premier's Council on the Status of Persons with Disabilities. 1994. *Standards for interpreting in educational settings: Early childhood services to grade 12*. Edmonton, Alberta: Government of Alberta.

Seal, B. C. 1998. *Best practices in educational interpreting*. Needham Heights, Mass.: Allyn & Bacon.

# The Educational Interpreter Performance Assessment: Current Structure and Practices

Brenda Schick and Kevin T. Williams

The Educational Interpreter Performance Assessment (EIPA) is a process that is designed to evaluate the interpreting skills of educational interpreters in a classroom setting (Schick and Williams 1992). The EIPA is not limited to any one signed language or sign system, which is essential given the diverse signed languages that are used in the public schools. The tool can be used to evaluate interpreters who use Manually Coded English, or MCE (English-like signing); ASL, typically viewed as the signed language of the adult Deaf[1] community; or PSE, the type of English signing found among those in the adult Deaf community (Bornstein 1990; Lucas and Valli 1989).[2] In addition, different versions of the EIPA are used for interpreters who work in an elementary school and those who work in a secondary setting. In either version of the test, videotaped stimulus materials are used to collect two samples of the interpreter's work. One sample is of the interpreter's voice-to-sign skills, either translating or transliterating spoken English in the classroom environment into sign communication. The second sample is of the interpreter's sign-to-voice skills, either translating or transliterating what a deaf child signs into spoken English. A specially trained evaluation team, using an EIPA rating form, evaluates both samples. The process is described in more detail in the following sections, and a profile of skills at each level of the EIPA is shown in the appendix.

## THE NEED FOR A TOOL THAT SPECIFICALLY EVALUATES EDUCATIONAL INTERPRETERS

For interpreters who work with adults, certification processes have been established that ensure interpreting competency. The Registry of Interpreters for the Deaf, Inc. (RID), a national organization that has a national testing system, administers an evaluation that provides interpreters with a certificate of competency, or RID certification. Previously, the National Association of the Deaf (NAD) also had a certification system.[3] These certifications are often a requirement for employment in certain settings such as universities. For interpreters working with adults, RID or NAD certification ensures a minimal level of competency.

However, RID certification does not assess how well interpreters work with children and within a K-12 setting. Many differences can be found between interpreting for an adult and interpreting for a child. For example, classroom interaction is notably different from either an adult giving a lecture or two adults talking with each other, which are scenarios used by RID and NAD in their certification tests. Classroom interaction involves a variety of register shifts, often within a single speaker's turn. Also unique to educational settings are the narrative styles used by teachers to support and encourage linguistic and cognitive development. Expressing these register shifts and language variations is essential to providing message equivalency, and most likely, register affects aspects of cognitive development (see chapter 4). In sign language, these register shifts are often represented by changes in prosody, the rhythmic and intonational aspects of language, and other nonmanual behaviors. As described in chapter 4, educational interpreters have a great deal of difficulty representing register, particularly those interpreting at the elementary level where a great deal of shifting in register occurs. Current tests designed to assess adults do not provide the kinds of challenges in communicating register that we see in a typical classroom.

In addition, to varying degrees, teachers use an adult-to-child register, especially with young children who are still learning to process language. An interpreter's product needs to represent this adult-to-child register. Sign language has its own linguistic devices for adult-to-child register (Kantor 1982; Masataka 1992; Reilly and Bellugi 1996). Research with hearing children shows that this adult-to-child register, communicated through prosody, is critically important to young language learners (Fernald 1989; Fernald and McRoberts 1996; Kemler-Nelson, Hirsh-Pasek, Jusczyk, and Wright-Cassidy 1989). The enhanced changes in prosody, as compared with adult-to-adult register, may help a child better identify sentence and clause boundaries, key words, types of discourse, and discourse boundaries. Adult-to-child register also may provide a great deal of information about the meaning of our communication, for example, the speaker's intentions such as teasing, warning, or soothing. Children use the enhanced forms of prosodic contours found in adult-to-adult register to help determine the meaning of our communication even when they may not know the meanings of the words or understand the grammar (Moore, Spence, and Katz 1997). We should expect to find a similar relationship between adult-to-child register in signed language and language development. The EIPA uses actual classroom interaction across a range of ages of children that represents a broad variation in adult-to-child register and that must be represented in the interpreting product.

Another issue about classroom interaction is that it often involves a great deal of language in which the form does not match the function, for example, a teacher saying, "I think you should look at that answer again," which really means, "You are wrong." This mismatching does occur in adult-to-adult communication but not very frequently in the exchange of factual information, which is the context used in the RID assessment. In addition to lecturing about facts, classroom teachers also are supporting and encouraging language development, cognitive development, and social development; are teaching appropriate behavior; are bonding with the students, and so forth. Consequently, in the classroom, a great deal of language occurs in which the teacher's intention may be more important than the content of the message. To interpret this kind of communication, an interpreter must have good control over the prosodic aspect of the language to communicate intention and not just form. The EIPA voice-to-sign classroom testing materials contain a great deal of language for which the interpreter needs to process the teacher's communicative intention, and not just the form.

Finally, children sign much differently than adults. For example, children make more articulation errors and often sign less clearly than adults. They also fail to provide background information to help the speaker understand a message, and their discourse may not be well structured. Note, too, that hearing children also produce speech and language that is not as clear or as well structured as that of adults. As with spoken language, individuals differ in their ability to understand children's speech or children's signed language. Adults who have experience working with a variety of children are capable of understanding children even when their speech and language contains numerous errors. Interpreters who work with children also must be able to understand a child's signing despite age-appropriate errors. The ability to understand language that is not well structured is especially important given that many deaf children in public schools have at least some degree of language delay.

The EIPA also assesses how well an interpreter can use MCE. Of note is the fact that, although only a small percentage of educational interpreters request an evaluation in MCE (about 12 percent), it is still used in some public schools. Although many professionals and members of the deaf community do not believe that MCE signing is appropriate or successful with deaf children (Johnson, Liddell, and Erting 1989; Supalla 1992; Woodward and Allen 1988), after the federally legislated Individuals with Disabilities Education Act of 1990 (IDEA), schools and parents retain the right to decide what type of signing is used with a child. RID or NAD certification is designed only for those interpreters using ASL or some form of transliteration. Interpreters who use a form of MCE would not be able to pass the test. Thus, the RID or NAD test would not accurately assess what many educational interpreters are expected to do in the classroom. Because of this reason and others, too, many educational interpreters and school systems do not see RID or NAD certification as appropriate or obtainable.

The EIPA was designed to evaluate and to weigh during assessment those aspects of interpreting that are necessary to support language and cognitive development. As discussed previously, the classroom is using language and discourse in a manner that scaffolds language and cognitive development in the hearing students. It is very important that a tool used to evaluate educational interpreters assesses how well this special adult-to-child register and discourse is represented in the interpreting product. Assessing how well an interpreter can represent adult-to-adult register and discourse will not provide a true picture of how well the interpreter performs in a school classroom.

## STRUCTURE OF THE EIPA

The EIPA consists of formal assessment materials and a process of evaluation. The following sections describe the materials and procedures in an EIPA assessment.

### Structure of the Stimulus Materials

All of the samples of the interpreter's voice-to-sign and sign-to-voice skills are obtained using stimulus videotapes, summarized in Table 1. Two options of the

TABLE 1 Stimulus Tapes Used to Collect Samples for the EIPA

| Level | Sign-To-Voice Stimulus Tapes Options A and B | Voice-To-Sign Stimulus Tapes Options A and B |
|---|---|---|
| Elementary | Child signer using ASL<br>Child signer using PSE<br>Child signer using MCE | Five elementary classrooms, from first to sixth grade |
| Secondary | Teen signer using ASL<br>Teen signer using PSE<br>Teen signer using MCE | Two secondary classrooms |

exam are available (Options A and B) for each grade level and language. An interpreter could take the EIPA once using either A or B and then take the other option another time. Option A and B each contain different child tapes and different classroom tapes. Thus, an interpreter can choose a grade level and a language, using either Option A or Option B assessment tapes. The sign-to-voice stimulus tapes show a child or a teenager using the target signed language or sign system (ASL, PSE, or MCE). The voice-to-sign videotape shows actual classroom lessons, along with questions and comments from other children in the classroom, and each voice-to-sign tape contains examples of multiple classrooms, as shown in Table 1. All tapes were produced using professional quality video, were filmed by a professional videographer, and were edited in a studio.

For these sign-to-voice stimulus tapes, the children were interviewed using a technique that maximizes complex responses and language. In essence, the interviewer used techniques typically used in a language proficiency interview, asking complex questions as well as asking children to expand and give their opinions, techniques that have been found to elicit language from children that is more complex than what occurs when simply chatting (Schick 1997).

Like with all children, the children's language may contain errors in grammar and pronunciation, disorganizations in their communication and discourse cohesion, fingerspelling that is both precise and imprecise, and references to people and places that are not explicitly identified. The interviewer was unknown to the children, so theoretically, the children should have properly introduced referents. However, like many children, they did not always do so, which was especially true for the elementary-aged children. The language produced by these children reflects what educational interpreters encounter daily. Interpreters who are familiar with how children sign and who understand them despite typical language errors are able to understand an unfamiliar child on a videotape. The stimulus videotapes contain the interviewer's questions in spoken English, and the interpreter is asked to interpret the children's responses. Interpreters are given a warm-up period during which they have the opportunity to watch the child sign without having to interpret. Then they are signaled to begin interpreting, and their interpretation is videotaped for later assessment.

As with the sign-to-voice tapes, two sets of voice-to-sign tapes are used, elementary and secondary. The elementary stimulus tapes include five different, authentic classrooms, ranging from first to sixth grade. All classroom content is challenging, containing lessons in science, reading, geography, or other complex subjects. Reflecting typical classrooms, all lessons are interactive, containing teacher narration and teacher-student dialogue, both requiring interpretation. The classrooms have frequent exchanges wherein the student and the teacher co-construct meaning across several turns, so interpreters must represent not only the content but also who is speaking. Similarly, there are many instances in which numerous children are speaking at once and interpreters need to make decisions concerning which aspects of the communication are essential to the goals of the main lesson. The tapes include frequent interchanges that question, discipline, scold, praise, warn, and challenge as well as the traditional exchanges of information.

Before watching and interpreting the stimulus tape, interpreters are given a set of lesson plans for what they will interpret. These plans contain the goals and objectives of each lesson as well as key vocabulary. This exposure to the lesson plan is intended to reflect best practices where all interpreters should know basic information before interpreting. As with the sign-to-voice stimulus tapes, interpreters are provided a warm-up period during which they can simply watch the classroom and listen to the teacher. The classroom tapes were selected to provide opportunities for fingerspelling, use of numbers, spatial mapping, and complex grammar. Teachers in the videotapes often backtrack in their discourse, repair their own statements, self-reflect, and give clues about what may be tested in the future.

## Structure of the Rating Form

The EIPA uses a specially designed rating form that contains four broad areas of evaluation: voice-to-sign interpreting skills, sign-to-voice interpreting, vocabulary, and overall abilities. Table 2 shows an outline of the skills that are assessed. A five-point numerical scale is used to rate the specific skills. The interpretation is rated for use of prosody across several domains such as prosody to stress words and phrases as well as prosody to communicate affect, emotions, sentence boundaries, and register. Specific items rate the use of space (a) for morphological purposes such as verb agreement and (b) for discourse purposes such as those in comparisons and other forms of spatial mapping. The interpreting product is also evaluated on the correctness of grammatical production, articulation of signs, fluency, and fingerspelling. The amount of vocabulary is rated as to whether the interpreter appears to have a broad and complex vocabulary of signs or whether the interpreted message is affected by the lack of vocabulary knowledge. For sign-to-voice interpreting, the interpreting product is rated on how well the interpreter expresses aspects of register, prosody, and linguistic stress. The interpreter is also rated as to how well he or she understands the grammar, morphology, and vocabulary as well as his or her ability to select appropriate English vocabulary to represent signed language concepts. Finally, to ensure that the interpretation has a sense of a whole message, more global factors are evaluated, for example, whether the interpreter demonstrates sufficient processing time to be able to understand what is being communicated or whether the interpreter consistently indicates who is speaking.

Within each area, the interpreter is rated in approximately ten distinct areas, using a Likert Scale ranging from 0 (no skills demonstrated) to 5 (advanced). An average is calculated from the ratings of the individual items across the results of a team of three evaluators. A useful analogy can be made to grading in traditional educational settings where a student earning an "A" has generally mastered the content area being tested or sampled, a student earning an "F" has generally not

TABLE 2 Domains of Skills and Specific Skills Evaluated in the EIPA

| Category | Skill |
|---|---|
| **I. Interpreter Product—Voice-to-Sign** | |
| Prosodic Information | A. Stresses or emphasizes important words or phrases |
| | B. Appropriately uses face and body to express affect or emotions |
| | C. Expresses register |
| | D. Marks sentence boundaries (not run-on) |
| Nonmanual Information | E. Indicates sentence types or clausal boundaries |
| | F. Produces and uses nonmanual adverbial or adjectival markers |
| Use of Signing Space | G. Uses verb directionality and pronominal system |
| | H. Indicates comparison and contrast as well as sequence and cause-effect |
| | I. Uses ASL classifier system to show location or relationship |
| Interpreter Performance | J. Follows grammar of ASL or PSE (if appropriate) |
| | K. Uses English morphological markers (if appropriate) |
| | L. Clearly mouths speaker's English (if appropriate) |
| **II. Interpreter Product—Sign-to-Voice** (e.g., fluency, pacing, clarity of speech, volume of speech) | |
| Can Read and Express Signer's— | A. Signs |
| | B. Fingerspelling and numbers |
| | C. Register |
| | D. Nonmanual behaviors and ASL morphology |
| Vocal-Intonational Features | E. Demonstrates appropriate speech production (rate, rhythm, fluency, volume) |
| | F. Indicates sentence or clausal boundaries (not "run-on" speech) |
| | G. Indicates sentence types |
| | H. Emphasizes important words, phrases, affect-emotions |
| | I. Selects correct English words |
| Interpreter Performance | J. Adds no extraneous words or sounds to message |

TABLE 2 (*Continued*)

| Category | Skill |
|---|---|
| **III. Vocabulary** | |
| Signs | A. Demonstrates appropriate amount of sign vocabulary |
| | B. Forms signs correctly |
| | C. Demonstrates fluency (rhythm and rate) |
| | D. Uses vocabulary consistent with the sign language or system |
| | E. Represents key vocabulary |
| Fingerspelling | F. Correctly produces fingerspelling |
| | G. Produces correct spelling |
| | H. Uses fingerspelling appropriately |
| | I. Correctly produces numbers |
| **IV. Overall Factors** | |
| Message Processing | A. Demonstrates appropriate eye contact or movement |
| | B. Produces a developed sense of the whole message V-S |
| | C. Produces a developed sense of the whole message S-V |
| | D. Demonstrates appropriate process lag time V-S |
| | E. Demonstrates appropriate process lag time S-V |
| Message Clarity | F. Follows principles of discourse mapping |
| Environment | G. Indicates who is speaking |

mastered the content, and a student earning a "C" has demonstrated "islands" of abilities but still has holes or gaps in his or her learning. In like manner, this description of grading applies to EIPA ratings: An "A" would be like the EIPA level 5; the "F," like an EIPA level 0/1; and the "C," like an EIPA level 3. Thus, an interpreter receiving a state's standard of 3.5 demonstrates a C+ in interpreting skills. An interpreter who receives a level 3.5 is still making numerous errors, omissions, and distortions in his or her interpretation. Typically, these errors occur throughout the interpretation; the interpreter does not simply represent the most important information, omitting only what is less important. Basically, a child who has an interpreter at this level is not receiving the same information as his or her hearing peers.

## Structure and Expertise of the Rating Team

Three raters work simultaneously as a team to evaluate the videotape; one member of the team must be deaf. All hearing raters are RID certified and most possess graduate-level educational degrees. Deaf raters all have postsecondary education, and many are native signers. In addition, they must be proficient in the signed language or sign system being rated. All raters undergo more than forty hours of direct instruction related to the EIPA assessment tool, stimuli materials, curricular design, and English discourse styles used in educational settings. All evaluators undergo training in the role of pragmatics and prosody related to the interpreting process. A specially designed training and rating manual has been authored by the EIPA developers. Videotape materials used during training are professionally captioned. At the completion of this training, all raters work as observers for an additional mentoring period until their judgments are accurate and their observations can be articulated in an appropriate manner. The manual used during training is the same manual raters actually use each and every time they rate a candidate's performance.

## Feedback to the Interpreter

Each interpreter receives extensive feedback from the evaluation. He or she receives a copy of the rating form, with the averaged score for each rated item, and an average overall score. In addition, he or she receives written feedback concerning strengths and areas of need. Finally, the interpreter receives suggestions about which overall areas are in need of development, in particular, those areas that would help the interpreter most improve his or her abilities. For example, many interpreters do not effectively use spatial mapping. Improving this one area would improve several domains of interpreting.

This detailed feedback helps interpreters and interpreter educators know exactly where strengths and weaknesses are so they can better plan professional development. The EIPA report can serve as the basis for an interpreter's professional development plan, focusing on areas of skill development for either working with a mentor or planning in-service training. One common problem that educational interpreters face when they receive their EIPA reports is that they may not understand some of the technical language used to describe strengths and areas in need of skill development. A glossary is provided, but some concepts require more than a definition of a term. For example, recipients often do not understand the terminology used to describe how ASL uses space for discourse purposes, or they do not know what prosody is nor how it is communicated in sign language. Working with a skilled mentor would help an interpreter translate the EIPA evaluation into a professional development plan to build skills that would improve the interpreting product and process across many domains.

Schools could also use the EIPA to plan in-service training for a group of interpreters. A skilled professional can use the results of the EIPA for a group of interpreters to determine whether the entire group has in common domains of skills that could benefit from instruction. Or a skilled mentor could help establish mentoring relationships among the interpreters in the schools by pairing an interpreter who has scored high in a particular domain with an interpreter who needs to develop skills in that particular area.

## Assessing Content Knowledge Related to Interpreting

The EIPA is a performance test in that it evaluates the interpreting performance of an individual. However, the content knowledge essential to working with children or to working in the K-12 setting is broad. Educational interpreters, in addition to demonstrating excellent performance skills, must know basic information about their role and responsibility not only as an interpreter but also as a member of a child's educational team and as a professional working in a public school. They should also know information about language development, reading, child development, the IEP process, hearing loss and hearing aids, Deaf culture, signed language, professional ethics, linguistics, and interpreting. Many interpreters also must know information about tutoring because they are often required to fulfill this role. Although educational interpreters cannot know this content to the same degree as the classroom educator, the deaf educator, or the speech pathologist, they still must understand how to work with these professionals to carry out a child's educational program. They must also be able to communicate with the educational team about their perceptions of how the child is doing.

To assess an interpreter's understanding of basic content knowledge related to working with children, a written test is currently being developed (the EIPA: Written Test, or EIPA:WT) that will assess interpreters' knowledge of a variety of domains. The process of test development will ensure that the EIPA:WT will have good psychometric validity. One intent of content validity is to ensure that the range of information being tested reflects what experts in the field agree is essential for an educational interpreter to know. To this end, a large set of facts were written, representing a basic, standards-based curriculum. These facts were rated by a large number of content experts. Questions were written based on these facts. The advantage of this test development model is that the content standards can be widely disseminated so interpreters will know generally what is on the test, but the exact questions will remain confidential. When this test is completed, states agencies and schools will have the option of requiring this test as part of the EIPA evaluation process.

## Results from Research Using the EIPA

Research has been conducted on a large group of educational interpreters in the state of Colorado (Schick, Williams, and Bolster 2000), using an older form of the EIPA in which interpreters were videotaped in their own classrooms with students for whom they interpreted regularly. The school districts that participated volunteered for the project. The data show that the majority of interpreters would not meet minimal Colorado performance standards, which require an overall EIPA score of 3.5 or greater. Nearly two-thirds of the group scored below a level 3.5 overall, which means that these interpreters are still making a significant number of errors, particularly with more complex language and discourse (see appendix). An interpreter at this level needs continued supervision and should be required to participate in continuing education in interpreting. Teachers and parents of a child whose interpreter scores in this range should be aware that a child's misunderstandings of concepts presented in a lesson may be the result of a poor interpretation rather than problems with the child. However, an interpreter who scores at least at a 3.5 does demonstrate broad areas of competency that should be able to serve as a foundation for further learning.

A psychometric evaluation showed very good test-retest reliability on the use of this older form of the EIPA (Schick, Williams, and Bolster 2000). Specifically, no significant difference was found between scores on an initial EIPA assessment and a subsequent assessment, even though the interpreting samples were different ($t$ (17) = – 2.051, $p$ = .056). This finding indicates that two different assessments on the same interpreter resulted in essentially the same score, even when a different sample was collected. Inter-rater reliability was also very good, with a point-by-point agreement of .78; in other words, when an interpreting sample was evaluated by a different rating team that was blind to the original rating, the interpreter's score was essentially the same.

Although the original EIPA, which used interpreting samples from the actual classroom, showed good reliability, states wanted an assessment that was more standardized in terms of the classroom teaching. Also, because each interpreting sample was different, the deaf evaluator was at a significant disadvantage because captioning all of the incoming assessment tapes was not economically feasible. Because of these factors, the stimulus tape version of the EIPA was created.

A pilot study was conducted to compare the current version of the EIPA, which uses stimulus tapes to collect the interpreting samples, with the older version, which used the interpreter's actual classroom lessons. Data were collected for ten interpreters on both versions. The data show that the "live" version correlated highly with the stimulus tape version, with a correlation coefficient of .94. This finding means that interpreters who did well on the "live" evaluation also did well on the stimulus tape versions and that the stimulus tape assessment predicted to a very high degree how well the interpreter would perform in the actual classroom. However, in general, the interpreters scored one level lower on the stimulus tape version. This finding is not surprising because the "live" assessment involved interpreters providing interpretation for the classrooms and children with whom they worked on a daily basis. It is commonly accepted that interpreters work best with extensive knowledge of the situation, knowledge of the people involved, and general knowledge of the content. The finding also shows that the stimulus videotapes represent challenging material that requires the interpreter to frequently and consistently demonstrate skills measured by the EIPA.

Currently, with funding from the Office of Education[4] (OSEP), the authors of this chapter are conducting additional research on the new stimulus tape version of the EIPA. This research will include the collection of new psychometric data and the completion of EIPA evaluations with interpreters who have received RID certification.

## HOW THE EIPA FITS INTO A MODEL OF ASSESSMENT

The EIPA uses a model of interpreting in which text must be evaluated at a discourse level. It evaluates more than grammatical structures and clarity of signing and more than breadth of vocabulary. To obtain a rating that meets many states' minimum standards, interpreters must demonstrate that they have a sense of the entire message, including the function, not just the form. This comprehensive competence includes broad control over the production of prosody, the use of space for discourse purposes, and facial expression. This competence is required for all versions of the assessment (MCE, PSE, and ASL) because all invented sign systems claim to borrow these aspects of ASL.

### What the EIPA Does Not Evaluate

Although intended as a comprehensive evaluation of the product of interpretation, the EIPA does not assess all of the areas of expertise that are essential to being a well-qualified educational interpreter. For example, the EIPA does not assess an interpreter's performance as a member of a professional team. As they do for all professionals who work in the public school, the staff members at the school best evaluate this performance. Although most schools do not have an individual who is capable of evaluating interpreting skills, the evaluation of professional skills is different. Schools should be responsible for evaluating how well the interpreter performs as a professional, following the guidelines for other professionals in the school. For example, ethical guidelines for interpreters who work in public schools should follow, to a large extent, the same ethical guidelines for teachers. This expectation is especially true in terms of communicating with members of the child's educational team and members of the child's family. It also applies to decisions made with respect to interpreting, which should be made in the context of the educational team. The interpreter's knowledge of professional roles and responsibilities will be assessed in the EIPA:WT.

In addition, many educational interpreters fulfill duties other than interpreting, for example, tutoring and aiding. The EIPA does not evaluate an interpreter's capability to conduct these roles, although the written test that is in development will have some additional roles represented in its content domains. Again, this kind of performance is best evaluated by the local school, which often has many other individuals also fulfilling these roles.

## HOW THE EIPA IS BEING USED AROUND THE COUNTRY

The EIPA is being used in various ways throughout the United States and Canada, ranging from being a legal requirement to a tool used in mentoring. What is clear is that the EIPA is a national assessment system, in that it is used extensively in numerous states, universities, and school districts.

### Certification to Meet Minimal Standards

Many states require a certificate of competency for educational interpreters. Some of these states such as Colorado, Wisconsin, and Louisiana have identified the EIPA as the only form of assessment recognized for state certification-licensure, and some states such as Kansas include the EIPA as one form of evaluation that is acceptable. Table 3 summarizes state requirements or recommendations, including Canada, that involve the EIPA. The Regional Assessment System, which manages EIPA evaluatons for states, will be discussed in the next subsection.

TABLE 3 States and Canadian Provinces Using the EIPA and How It Is Being Used

| State | Date Engaged | How Used |
|---|---|---|
| Alabama | 2004 | EIPA (≥ 3.5) required for interpreting permit |
| Alaska | 2002 | RAS member state; Used for state competency screening |
| Arkansas | 2004 | EIPA (≥ 3.5) required for interpreting permit |
| Arizona | 2001 | RAS member state; Used for state competency screening; used as an exit proficiency exam for the ITP at University of Arizona (four-year program) |
| Bureau of Indian Affairs | 2002 | RAS member organization: Used for state competency screening |
| California | 2003 | EIPA (≥ 4.0) required by 2006 |
| Colorado | 1992 | RAS member state; EIPA (≥ 3.5) required; requires EIPA Written Test |
| Hawaii | 2004 | EIPA to be used in state's educational interpreter training program as exit criterion, EIPA (≥ 3.5) required; under state consideration for licensure tool |
| Idaho | 2003 | EIPA used in a statewide pilot |
| Iowa | 1993 | RAS member state; Used for state competency screening |
| Illinois | 2002 | EIPA used in a statewide pilot |
| Kansas | 1995 | RAS member state; EIPA (≥ 3.0) required |
| Louisiana | 1997 | EIPA (≥ 3.5) required |
| Massachusetts | 2003 | EIPA used in a statewide pilot |
| Missouri | 2003 | EIPA used as option for state licensure; passing score is their own calculation |
| Minnesota | 2003 | Pilot/field test |
| Montana | 2002 | RAS member state; Used for state competency screening |
| New Hampshire | 2003 | EIPA used in a pilot form; under consideration for adoption as state licensure tool |
| North Carolina | 2003 | EIPA (≥ 3.5) required |
| North Dakota | 2002 | Used for state competency screening |

TABLE 3 (*Continued*)

| State | Date Engaged | How Used |
|---|---|---|
| Nebraska | 1993 | RAS member state; EIPA (≥ 3.5) required |
| New Jersey | 2002 | EIPA in Educational Licensure Code, EIPA (≥ 3.5) required |
| New Mexico | 2004 | EIPA (≥ 3.5) required for educational interpreters |
| Nevada | 2002 | EIPA (≥ 4.0) required |
| New York | 2002 | EIPA (live version) used for interpreter mentoring |
| Ohio | 2004 | Used at exit performance exam for the Educational Interpeter Training Program at Kent Sate University (four-year program) |
| Oklahoma | 2004 | RAS Member State: Used for state competency screening |
| Pennsylvania | 1994 | System (videotape-stimuli version) used for interpreter mentoring |
| South Carolina | 2003 | Used for evaluation |
| South Dakota | 2002 | Used for state competency screening |
| Tennessee | 1997 | EIPA (live version) used for interpreter mentoring |
| Utah | 2002 | RAS member state; Used for state competency screening |
| Wisconsin | 1996 | EIPA (≥ 3.5) required |
| West Virginia | 2002 | EIPA (videotape-stimuli version) used for interpreter mentoring |
| Wyoming | 2002 | RAS member state; Used for state competency screening; EIPA (≥ 3.5) required |
| Nova Scotia | 2002 | EIPA piloted and under consideration for adoption |

## Statewide Evaluation

In some states, the EIPA is being used for statewide evaluation, without minimum standards being required, often as a precursor to establishing a certification system. A good example of this approach is the state of New York (Mitchell 2002), which has been conducting an assessment program for three years, using the EIPA but with its own video stimulus materials After the samples were rated, prescriptive plans were designed for each interpreter. With this information, the interpreter knew what training he or she would need and, thus, was able to take appropriate workshops, ASL classes, or both. In addition, the interpreter could receive mentoring, if so needed and desired. The New York State Education Department is now preparing to propose certification requirements for educational interpreters in K–12 settings. Colorado also moved to establish standards in this manner; the state began offering EIPA evaluations in 1992 and, later, began requiring minimum EIPA scores to work as an educational interpreter.

Recently, a large regional effort to use the EIPA for state assessment, training, certification, and reciprocity has been initiated. This system, begun by state directors of special education in the Mountain Plains Special Education region, decided to support the use of the EIPA for their member states (Table 3 indicates which states are members). This consortium pooled funding to pilot a Regional Assessment System, with a director, so any interpreter in the consortium can access the EIPA. Currently, the Regional Assessment System includes eleven states and the Bureau of Indian Affairs.[5] One of their goals is to reduce the duplication that would occur if each state established its own system, each requiring oversight, materials, and information dissemination. Each state will decide on its own how to use the EIPA, as evaluation or as certification, and what proficiency level the state will encourage or require. This model is appealing because it allows coordination across a number of states as well as the pooling of financial resources, and it reduces the duplication of work and materials. This approach may significantly affect how other states integrate the EIPA into their assessment and credentialing systems.

## Measurement of Pre-Training and Post-Training for Interpreter Training Programs

Several interpreter training programs are using the EIPA to quantify the results of their training programs. For example, the Educational Interpreter Certificate Program (EICP), directed by Dr. Leilani Johnson in Denver, Colorado, uses the EIPA to determine whether candidates have sufficient skills to enter the program. The program also uses the EIPA as a post-training exit assessment to quantify the achievements of the students after the two-year program. Preliminary results, using a modified EIPA, showed that, on average, interpreters increased their EIPA scores about one level after completing the training program (Schick, Johnson, and Williams 2004). The EICP's data underscore how much work is needed for an interpreter to advance a full EIPA level in interpreting skills. For example, an interpreter who is scoring at an EIPA level 2 has only basic sign vocabulary and makes numerous grammatical errors that significantly interfere with communication. Although an interpreter scoring at a level 3 is still making many errors and continues to require supervision, the interpreted message is generally intelligible with many major concepts present. Those in the field of interpreter training need data such as these to help document and analyze the effectiveness of different training models. In addition, the interpreter training programs at the University of Arizona and at Front Range Community College in Colorado are also using the EIPA as exit assessments.

Another creative pre-post training effort is under way in the state of Iowa. The Iowa Department of Education has provided funding to conduct a two-year study involving forty interpreters. All subjects in the study were evaluated using the EIPA (during June-July 2002). Using a professional interpreter training agency (SLICES, Minneapolis, Minn.), twenty interpreters will receive training over the next year that is specific to the weaknesses identified on each candidate's EIPA. The remaining twenty interpreters will receive no additional training. All forty interpreters will be reevaluated at the end of the second year of the study. The intent of the study is to determine whether improvements in skills occur in those interpreters receiving specific feedback and training compared with those who do not receive this support.

## A Way to Ensure Interpreting Skills during the Hiring Process

Because many school districts lack the ability to screen applicants for educational interpreting positions, the EIPA Diagnostic Center, located at Boys Town National Research Hospital, has created the Pre-Hire Screening version of the EIPA. This screening is just that; it is not a full EIPA assessment. Many school districts must have information about the skill level of the interpreter more quickly than the typical EIPA assessment procedure takes, which is about two months. Most schools can hire without any assessment information, and even in the states that require certification, schools can receive permission to hire an individual who does not meet standards, using an emergency credential, similar to all other certified professional categories. However, many school districts would prefer to have some information about the interpreter's skills before hiring. The Pre-Hire Screening version of the EIPA can provide schools some feedback about the interpreter's skills within seventy-two hours, with the understanding that it neither constitutes a thorough evaluation nor is an alternative to a full EIPA for those states requiring a minimum score.

Districts using the Pre-Hire Screening are advised of the overall competency of an applicant in a manner that is more general than diagnostic. The Pre-Hire Screening rates three broad categories of skills rather than determines specific numeric scores. Interpreters may receive a rating that indicates skills at the level of at least a minimum standard, indicating that the school can hire with assurance that the interpreter has skills at or above the minimum standards. The interpreter may be in a hire-with-caution zone, indicating (a) that, although the interpreter has some good skills, a full EIPA is needed to determine whether minimum standards are met and (b) that the interpreter requires a skilled mentor or supervisor. Finally, the interpreter may receive a rating indicating that hiring is not recommended because the interpreter could not meet minimum standards using a full EIPA assessment.

Like the full EIPA, the EIPA Pre-Hire Screening is designed for candidates applying for elementary or secondary positions. It features child and teen signing models using ASL-PSE and MCE (SEE II). Schools can contact the EIPA diagnostic center to request testing materials. Materials are sent overnight, and after receipt of the candidate's screening tape, the EIPA Diagnostic Center will provide candidate results in a twenty-four-hour time frame. The Pre-Hire screening review is completed by one trained EIPA Diagnostic Center staff member, who will provide the potential employer with a cursory overview of the candidate's performance. This service is meant to provide only additional guidance to potential employers. The EIPA Pre-Hire Screening is intended to give employers additional information with which to make a more sound hiring decision.

## An Indicator of Minimal Skill Level

To date, the vast majority of states using the EIPA for credentialing purposes have adopted a level of 3.5 or above as their minimal standard. Why? To earn a level 3.5, the interpreter must score significantly above a level 3 across the majority of the thirty-seven measurements on the EIPA. Interpreters who achieve an overall level of 3.5 have broad competencies in grammar, vocabulary, and textual processing. Many states believe that an individual at this level will continue to develop skills.

Many states have adopted the approach that basically asks, What level can we expect from a graduate of an interpreter education program? Of course, it should be noted that the field of interpreter training cannot really answer this question because the field does not have a standards-based approach to curriculum similar to what you see in fields such as speech pathology. In addition, graduates of interpreter training programs do not necessarily graduate with thorough and broad interpreting skills. But again, we really do not know the skill levels of graduates because the field has developed neither standard exit criteria nor the expectation that programs will have a standardized exit evaluation. Nevertheless, for any graduate of a professional training program, we do not expect mastery skills at graduation. No one expects a recent graduate of a teacher-training program to be a master teacher, and schools expect these recent graduates to continue learning. States have tried to apply a similar concept with respect to minimum standards for educational interpreters.

A minimum standard responds to the question, What foundation of skills adequately enables the professional to reasonably function and ensures that the individual has competencies that are sufficiently broad to allow for further development? This concept may be difficult for many of us who believe that the standard should be the highest possible because we understand the ramifications that the interpreter's inability to express classroom content has on a child's development. Many states have articulated the hope that these established EIPA standards are the initial step.

Because the profession of educational interpreting is relatively new, the low supply of educational interpreters is nearly at a crisis level. This situation is exacerbated by the fact that there is also a lack of interpreter education programs specifically geared toward working with children in educational settings. A minimum standard of 3.5 on the EIPA seems to many states to be a realistic compromise between requiring no skills and requiring what those of us who understand child development and education would actually like to see. A reality in most states is that school districts can get emergency certification for a less-than-skilled interpreter. It is possible within many state systems to continue a revolving door in using interpreters who are not certified, especially if schools within those states quite legitimately cannot find an interpreter who meets minimum standards. In addition, school districts have been found to rename an interpreter's position to avoid meeting minimum standards. Realistic standards for schools quite possibly allow the standards to be more consistently met.

However, with the passage of federal legislation in 2002 called the No Child Left Behind Act of 2001, states may have to address the real issue in educational interpreting, that is, whether the student is making adequate progress. NCLB requires that states show that all children are achieving, with no exemptions for children with special needs. Schools are being held accountable for student achievement. The focus may soon change from determining what minimum standards we can expect for an educational interpreter to determining whether the child is able to learn and achieve with an educational interpreter who meets a state's minimum standards. However, what is currently frustrating for the field is that, although NCLB specifies criteria to determine whether teachers and paraeducators are qualified (highly qualified in the case of teachers), the legislation does not describe what determines whether a educational interpreter is qualified.

In addition to specifying minimum standards in interpreting performance, some states have established means by which skill training and general education are designed and provided for educational interpreters. For example, Colorado requires that a minimum of sixty contact hours of continuing education be completed every five years, which must be a combination of skills and knowledge education. In Nebraska, for example, interpreters must annually accrue seventy-five clock hours in CEUs within five years to maintain state interpreting credentials.

## SUMMARY

The EIPA and soon-to-be completed EIPA:WT provide an excellent resource to states, schools, and parents to help determine whether an educational interpreter is qualified. The performance-based evaluation is ecologically valid in that it uses authentic classroom teaching and children signers to elicit an interpreting sample. Interpreters can be assessed at either the elementary or the secondary level, using ASL, PSE, or MCE. A previous version of the EIPA had good psychometric validity, and the current instrument is undergoing a psychometric evaluation. States and school districts can use the EIPA to ensure that a child has access to the majority of classroom content. Although providing a qualified educational interpreter does not mean that the child receives an education equivalent to what his or her hearing peers receive, it does mean that the child has access to much of the classroom interaction.

For parents, even in states that do not require minimum standards, the EIPA provides a means of an independent assurance that their child's interpreter is capable in representing classroom content. In many cases, specifying an EIPA evaluation of the interpreter on the child's IEP may be one means of determining qualifications when the state or school district has no minimum qualifications. For interpreter training programs, the EIPA can be an important aspect of program evaluation. For other types of training programs, it can provide information about the effectiveness of the training.

More states are requiring minimum standards, and the hope is that, in the next decade, all will. The No Child Left Behind Act may be the impetus for states to make sure that basic communication access is provided. However, even more than a decade ago in their report to Congress, the Commission on Education of the Deaf (1988) stated that the IDEA requires that "deaf students be integrated into regular classroom settings to the maximum extent possible, but if quality interpreting services are not provided, that goal becomes a mockery" (Commission on Education of the Deaf 1988, 103). We would add to this concept that without an independent, psychometrically valid assessment that is designed to assess what educational interpreters do, it is impossible for a school to say that a deaf child has access.

# APPENDIX

## Profile of Skills at Each Rating Level of the EIPA

### LEVEL 1: BEGINNER

Demonstrates very limited sign vocabulary with frequent errors in production. At times, production may be incomprehensible. Grammatical structure tends to be nonexistent. Individual is able to communicate only very simple ideas and demonstrates great difficulty comprehending signed communication. Sign production lacks prosody and use of space for the vast majority of the interpreted message. An individual at this level is not recommended for classroom interpreting.

### LEVEL 2: ADVANCED BEGINNER

Demonstrates only basic sign vocabulary, and these limitations interfere with communication. Lack of fluency and sign production errors are typical and often interfere with communication. The interpreter often hesitates in signing, as if searching for vocabulary. Frequent errors in grammar are apparent, although basic signed sentences appear intact. More complex grammatical structures are typically difficult. Individual is able to read signs at the word level and simple sentence level, but complete or complex sentences often require repetitions and repairs. Some use of prosody and space is evident, but use is inconsistent and often incorrect. An individual at this level is not recommended for classroom interpreting.

### LEVEL 3: INTERMEDIATE

Demonstrates knowledge of basic vocabulary but may lack vocabulary for more technical, complex, or academic topics. Individual is able to sign in a fairly fluent manner using some consistent prosody, but pacing is still slow with infrequent pauses for vocabulary or complex structures. Sign production may show some errors but generally will not interfere with communication. Grammatical production may still be incorrect, especially for complex structures, but is, in general, intact for routine and simple language. Individual comprehends signed messages but may need repetition and assistance. Voiced translation often lacks depth and subtleties of the original message. An individual at this level would be able to communicate very basic classroom content but may incorrectly interpret complex information, resulting in a message that is not always clear. An interpreter at this level needs continued supervision and should be required to participate in continuing education in interpreting.

### LEVEL 4: ADVANCED INTERMEDIATE

Demonstrates broad use of vocabulary with sign production generally correct. Demonstrates good strategies for expressing information when a specific sign is not in his or her vocabulary. Grammatical constructions are generally clear and consistent, but complex information may still pose occasional problems. Prosody is good, with appropriate facial expression most of the time. Individual may still have difficulty with the use of facial expression in complex sentences and adverbial nonmanual markers. Fluency may deteriorate when rate or complexity of communication increases. Individual uses space consistently most of the time, but complex constructions or extended use of discourse cohesion may still pose problems. Comprehension of most signed messages at a normal rate is good, but translation may lack some complexity of the original message. An individual at this level would be able to express much of the classroom content but may have difficulty with complex topics or rapid turn-taking.

## LEVEL 5: ADVANCED

Demonstrates broad and fluent use of vocabulary, with a broad range of strategies for communicating new words and concepts. Sign production errors are minimal and never interfere with comprehension. Prosody is correct for grammatical, nonmanual markers and for affective purposes. Complex grammatical constructions are typically not a problem. Comprehension of signed messages is very good, communicating all details of the original message. An individual at this level is capable of clearly and accurately expressing the majority of interactions within the classroom.

## NOTES

1. Common usage capitalizes the word *Deaf* to refer to a cultural identity rather than an audiological measure.
2. PSE is often referred to as Contact Signing (Lucas and Valli 1989).
3. Currently, the RID and NAD are working collaboratively to develop a new certification test. NAD is no longer supporting its evaluation system.
4. Office of Special Education, Programs of National Significance grant (H325 N010013), awarded to Brenda Schick and Kevin Williams.
5. See http://web.jcc.net/academic/ras for more information about the Regional Assessment System.

## REFERENCES

Bornstein, H., ed. 1990. *Manual communication: Implications for education*. Washington D.C.: Gallaudet University Press.

Commission on the Education of the Deaf. 1988. *Toward equality: Education of the Deaf*. Washington, D.C.: U.S. Government Printing Office.

Fernald, A. 1989. Intonation and communicative intent in mothers' speech to infants: Is the melody the message? *Child Development* 60(6):1497–1510.

Fernald, A., and G. McRoberts. 1996. Prosodic bootstrapping: A critical analysis of the argument and the evidence. In *Signal to syntax: Bootstrapping from speech to grammar in early acquisition*, ed. J. L. Morgan and K. Demuth, 365–88. Hillsdale, N.J.: Erlbaum.

Individuals with Disabilities Education Act of 1990, 20 U.S. Code, Ch. 33, Secs. 1400–1491, Pub. L. 10517, 1997.

Johnson, R. E., S. K. Liddell, and C. J. Erting. 1989. *Unlocking the curriculum: Principles for achieving access in deaf education*. Gallaudet Research Institute Working Paper 89-3. Washington, D.C.: Gallaudet Research Institute, Gallaudet University.

Kantor, R. 1982. Communicative interaction: Mother modification and child acquisition of American Sign Language. *Sign Language Studies* 36:233–82.

Kemler-Nelson, D. G., K. Hirsh-Pasek, P. W. Jusczyk, and K. Wright-Cassidy. 1989. How the prosodic cues in motherese might assist language learning. *Journal of Child Language* 16(1):55–68.

Lucas, C., and C. Valli. 1989. Language contact in the American deaf community. In *The sociolinguistics of the deaf community,* ed. C. Lucas, 11–40. San Diego: Academic Press.

Masataka, N. 1992. Motherese in a signed language. *Infant Behavior and Development* 15(4):453–60.

Mitchell, M. K. 2002. Statewide training of educational interpreters: How is this possible? In *Proceedings of the Seventeenth National Conference of the Registry of Interpreters for the Deaf,* 83–117. Alexandria, Va.: RID Publications.

Moore, D. S., M. J. Spence, and G. S. Katz. 1997. Six-month-olds' categorization of natural infant-directed utterances. *Developmental Psychology* 33:980–89.

No Child Left Behind Act of 2001, Pub. L. 107–110, 115 Stat. 1425 (2002).

Reilly, J. S., and U. Bellugi. 1996. Competition on the face: Affect and language in ASL motherese. *Journal of Child Language* 23:219–36.

Schick, B. 1997. The effects of discourse genre on language complexity in school-aged deaf students. *Journal of Deaf Studies and Deaf Education* 2:234–51.

Schick, B., L. Johnson, and K. Williams. 2004. Look who's being left behind: Deaf children with interpreters in the public schools. Paper presented at the Office of Education Personnel Preparation Conference, 24 April, Washington, D.C.

Schick, B., and K. T. Williams. 1992. The educational interpreter performance assessment: A tool to evaluate classroom performance. Paper presented at the conference on Issues in Language and Deafness: The Use of Sign Language in Educational Settings: Current Concepts and Controversies, Omaha, Nebraska.

Schick, B., K. Williams, and L. Bolster. 2000. Skill levels of educational interpreters working in the public schools. *Journal of Deaf Studies and Deaf Education* 4:144–55.

Supalla, S. 1992. Equality in educational opportunities: The deaf version. In *A free hand: Enfranchising the education of deaf children,* eds. M. Walworth, D. F. Moores, and T. J. O'Rourke, 170–81. Silver Spring, Md.: T.J. Publishers.

Woodward, J., and T. Allen. 1988. Classroom use of artificial Manual English sign systems by teachers. *Sign Language Studies* 55:60.

# Theoretical Tools for Educational Interpreters, or "The True Confessions of an Ex-Educational Interpreter"

Claire Ramsey

When I became a sign language interpreter in the 1970s, I was deeply inspired by the politics of access and inclusion. In addition, because I was studying linguistics, I was attracted to the possibility of using my abilities in manipulating symbols to work with languages, in particular, with their meanings and structures. The unique and perhaps odd set of skills that prompts some of us to move from being everyday language users to people who analyze language forms and functions is one that also makes an excellent foundation for interpreting and translating.

However, another set of strengths is needed to work as an interpreter. Without people to use them, languages can easily become abstractions, constructs that barely exist. The best interpreters not only must be able to participate in and correctly render all of the complexities of human interactions into two languages but also must be able to reflect on the effects of interpreting. I spent much of my short career as an interpreter in educational settings from elementary to college level. As an educational interpreter, my analytic skills improved and my short-term memory got a real workout, but my ability to reflect on human interaction seemed to stagnate. Interpreting situations between hearing teachers and deaf children seemed to fall apart—through my hands—for reasons I did not understand.

Trying to assign blame—to myself, to the children, to the teachers—is by its nature unproductive. It did not help me account for the everyday problems I experienced. Worse, one day, I came face-to-face with the fact that some of the school activities that I was interpreting did not make sense to me. Why is it better for profoundly deaf children to attend music class instead of having another reading

An earlier version of this chapter was delivered as a plenary session at the National Educational Interpreting Conference in Kansas City, Missouri, on August 5, 2000. Portions of this chapter appear in Ramsey (2001).

period? Why did educational opportunity mean seating the deaf child and interpreter at a table in the back of the room with a workbook while the teacher taught addition facts to the hearing children? When these two observations came together, that I rarely felt that I was doing a good job and that some of the school activities I was interpreting for deaf students did not make sense, I had to stop interpreting. Although I was fascinated with the role of language in the social, cultural, and psychological puzzles I observed, I did not have the tools to genuinely understand it. The situations were so complex and the stakes so high, that I could no longer tolerate the fragmentation and my inability to figure it out.

A common assumption is that a critical discussion of educational interpreting is "anti public schools," a stance I have been accused of taking more than once. Well-grounded reflection, however, does not necessarily grow from opposition. I am not opposed to public school programs for deaf and hard of hearing children. Opposition would be a pointless stance because these programs are widespread, well populated, and in many cases the only available option. Some programs are excellent, others are not, and it is only fair to assume that all are doing their best. In my view, the circumstances of deaf education are so serious that they merit discussion beyond the dualistic possibilities of being either for or against it.

My professional experience, my knowledge of the schooling outcomes of deaf children, and my reading of theory have led me to a cautious, somewhat skeptical perspective on elementary deaf education provided in public schools through educational interpreters. Despite the resources and knowledge available to us, too many deaf students are still not reaching their intellectual and linguistic potential during their school years. For this reason, I have formed a critical, but I hope well-grounded, view of the ideological reorganization that placed interpreters in educational settings with deaf children. Briefly, I have come to see that, for all the resources devoted to offering education in the least restrictive environment, the primary motivation for integrating children who are deaf with those who are hearing rests on a desire to ensure equal educational opportunity and to protect deaf children's right of access to public education. These desires are not unimportant goals. Indeed, this effort is an extremely unusual step for a society to take, and no other nation in the history of the world has ever made a commitment of this magnitude to children with disabilities. However, the commitment does not guarantee that learning will take place; it is not a commitment about learning or teaching. It is a narrow but sincere commitment to opportunity.

Unfortunately, strategies for providing access for deaf children in public schools are unwieldy, showy, and expensive. Accordingly, the strategies themselves—for example, locating, evaluating, hiring, and integrating interpreters into settings that previously held only hearing children and hearing teachers—have absorbed much attention. Instead of looking to the result of learning and development, the result has become the demonstration of accessibility. Instead of seeing interpreters as a means for providing equal access, interpreters are naively seen as the end in itself. We should not be surprised that deaf children do not learn under these circumstances.

Providing interpreters is not a self-evident strategy for fostering learning. It merely demonstrates that an effort has been made to provide access to educational opportunity. Nonetheless, interpreting is widespread, and it is often very helpful for creating access for deaf children. However, interpreting is often not helpful. Sometimes, having an interpreter is worse than providing no access at all. Many problems are created by thinking that learning can be mediated by an interpreter, and no improvements can occur unless those of us who have experienced these problems ask challenging questions. Because interpreting is sometimes helpful and, sometimes, because it disintegrates and is not helpful, educational interpreting merits critical, respectful, well-grounded attention.

Over the years since I left interpreting, I have studied education and the social and cultural relationships among schooling, deaf students, hearing students, teachers, parents, society, and interpreters. I have also tried to shed the light of theory on my observations of deaf students in public schools (Ramsey 1997). Although many people find the concept of theory to be intimidating, its meaning is quite straightforward. A theory is simply a coherent way to interpret a set of facts and to help predict the possible outcomes of actions or strategies (Cole and Cole 1996). Although few simple or obvious answers have been provided for questions about educational interpreting, theories of language in social context and theories of human development offer models that are potentially helpful tools for those who want to understand and perhaps improve the schooling and learning of deaf students. Theoretical frameworks in sociolinguistics offer analytical categories and accounts of their relationships that clarify some features of interpreted education. Cultural-historical psychology locates human learning and development, especially linguistic and cognitive development, in social settings, and it highlights the fact that individual development cannot take place without participation in social and cultural activities. This chapter briefly outlines these helpful theoretical frameworks, uses them to discuss observations of educational interpreting, and suggests areas that merit further examination.

## SOCIOLINGUISTICS

Sociolinguistics emerged from a crucible of anthropology, linguistics, sociology, and philosophy (e.g., Gumperz and Hymes 1972; Labov 1972). Linguists working in this specialty study the many features of language as it is used in social and cultural groups for a variety of purposes, including education (Cazden, John, and Hymes 1972). The field has adopted research tools from anthropology (Hymes 1964) and has developed other tools for theorizing about and analyzing language in its social context (e.g., Schiffrin 1994). Sociolinguists have also examined ASL, the community of ASL signers, and the social and cultural contexts where ASL comes into contact with English (see Lucas 1989; Lucas and Valli 1992; Ramsey 1997).

Adding to Chomsky's (1957) theoretical constructs of language "competence" (our grammatical knowledge) and language "performance" (the realization of our knowledge), Hymes (1964) introduced the term *communicative competence*. This term captures the rule-governed knowledge we depend on to use language appropriately in the range of communication situations that arise in everyday life. Additionally, Hymes (1972) suggested a framework for analysis of language in social settings, which he presented graphically using the mnemonic SPEAKING (see Figure 1).

Using this framework, researchers can extract and examine key features of communication, including the setting and participants, the goals, and the content of the communication as well as the tone, the form and genre of language selected, and the norms observed by speakers within a speech community. These categories function as a starting place from which complex instances of communication can be closely examined.

| | | |
|---|---|---|
| S | Setting, Scene | Physical circumstances |
| P | Participants | Speaker/hearer; sender/receiver |
| E | Ends | Purpose and goal, outcomes |
| A | Act sequence | Message form and content |
| K | Key | Tone, manner |
| I | Instrumentalities | Channel (spoken, nonverbal, physical) |
| N | Norms of interaction and interpretation | Interpretation of norms within cultural belief systems |
| G | Genre | Textual categories |

FIGURE 1. SPEAKING Matrix for Analysis of Language in Social Settings.

*Source:* Reprinted from D. Schiffrin, *Approaches to Discourse,* (Malden, Mass.: Blackwell), 142.

Two features of the communication situations identified by Hymes's SPEAKING matrix deserve a closer look in educational interpreting: setting and participants. The term *setting* does not refer only to the location where communication is taking place. Rather, it indicates all of the physical, social, and cultural features of the scene that tell us where we are and what should take place there. Some analysts use the term *context* to describe this feature. For example, Cazden (1988) uses "mental context" to describe all of the knowledge and experience that preschoolers apply to novel school activities like understanding stories in print. While they read or listen to a story, for example, they not only attend to the language and structure of the narrative but also use what they know about people and animals; what they have experienced in their families; and what they like, fear, look forward to, and wish for. All of this knowledge and experience creates the mental context in which the story is embedded and through which these preschoolers construct its meaning. Cazden also views context as a multilevel set of relationships. Although language use can create or redefine a context, contexts, especially those in schools, are not completely created by local participants. Rather, any context is nested within several others. Cazden (1988) applies a hierarchy of contexts that begin in the classroom and extend to the community.[1]

Just as the term *setting* is more complex than it appears, the term *participant* also requires finer definition. Several kinds of participant can be identified. Careful observation of language interactions reveals what constitutes a participant and the ways that participation can be fostered or discouraged. Goffman's (1981) analysis of the audience or listener role in discourse contrasts "ratified participants" and "bystanders." The former are the "addressed ones," those for whom the speaker's message is intended. The speaker turns his or her visual attention to the addressed one (or ones) and will relinquish the speaker role to an addressed one. In the context of a classroom, the teacher may call on a student, who becomes the "addressed one" while the other students, still ratified participants, are the "unaddressed ones." Bystanders, in contrast, are not the intended receivers of the message. They are merely close enough to overhear the message and are not addressed by the speaker. For example, when one is being scolded by a teacher or lunchroom monitor, even though one is surrounded by classmates and peers, one hopes that the other children will voluntarily adopt the bystander role. The other children may hear the scolding and even take it as a lesson, but they do not have to endure the scolding. Bystanders have to occupy only a politely inattentive, unaddressed role, then rapidly pretend to forget the classmate's embarrassing moment.

The notion of "footing" (Goffman 1974) is also helpful for understanding the ways that language supplies information about participation. Footing is relayed by discourse cues that tell participants what to do in response to a message. When footing changes, the speaker's relationship with the audience also shifts. An example is a teacher's use of "Now" at the beginning of a turn. "Now" is a discourse marker that calls attention to "an upcoming idea unit, orientation, and/or participation framework" (Schiffrin 1987, 230). Teachers use "Now" at the beginning of an utterance as a management device to inform students that the activity or the topic is about to change. It tells students that their stance should be attentiveness and preparation to participate.

Although I have presented the field of sociolinguistics only sketchily here, the ideas provide a theoretical and analytical starting place for understanding educational interpreting. Interpreting in classrooms is difficult. It requires maneuvering among several kinds of participants—ratified participants, powerful teachers who hold the floor, and bystanders who politely do not pay attention to conversation to which they have complete access. In this cast, the interpreter, too, must adopt a role—a strange kind of bystanding participant. Interpreters must also understand the setting because the participants, the distribution of turns, and the adoption of roles are determined by settings. Last, the interpreter must understand and express to deaf students the delicate strategies by which a teacher covertly directs the stance of his or her audience.

## CULTURAL-HISTORICAL PSYCHOLOGY

Classrooms are complicated settings with a shifting, sometimes ambiguous set of participant roles and many covert but necessary messages that must be decoded by students. These facts in themselves make interpreting a difficult job. Interpreting in classrooms is also critically important because the primary function of communication in classrooms is to foster and to construct learning. Accordingly, another key to understanding the challenges that interpreted education might present for deaf children is to move away from the "input-output" model on which interpreted education rests (content is emitted by the teacher, passes into and out of the interpreter, and enters the student's mind) and move toward understanding the role that language plays in learning and development.

One can think about learning and development in several ways. The most commonly discussed sources of development are "nature and nurture," or biological factors and environmental factors, and their respective influences. Cole and Cole (1996) structure an excellent discussion of developmental theory around the possible relationships between nature and nurture. In some domains, "nature," that is, genetic inheritance and biological maturation, appear to drive development. In other domains, "nurture" appears dominant, and development consists of the shaped and adapted behavior that constitutes learning. A third possible relationship is exemplified in Piaget's (Piaget 1973; Piaget and Inhelder 1969) constructivist view of development in which nature and nurture play complementary roles and in which individual children are seen as active "constructors" of development through their interactions with the people and world around them.

Cultural-historical psychologists propose a fourth view: that biological factors and "universal features of the environment" (Cole and Cole 1996, 34) each influence development in "the way they combine in a specific cultural-historical context" (38). This view provides a powerful perspective from which to consider educational interpreting. Deaf people confront both biological factors (their physical lack of hearing) and environmental features (a world where most people have intact hearing and use spoken language). For deaf education, nature and nurture combine in a specific cultural-historical context, that is, the school. Despite the widespread "inclusion" of deaf students, the organization of schooling in the United States rests on several critical assumptions: (a) that spoken language acquisition begins at birth, (b) that transmission of culture proceeds from parent to child, and (c) that students will enter schooling with language and cultural knowledge sufficient to participate in the activities that are organized to promote development of basic literacy and numeracy skills.

Of the constructs of cultural-historical psychology, the "Zone of Proximal Development" (Vygotsky 1978) is the best known. Vygotsky held the view that higher cognitive functions such as language and thinking have social origins.[2] He made the strong claim, based on this view, that learning drives development and that we can learn only through our access to interactions with others. The Zone of Proximal Development (ZPD) is a metaphorical space where interactions that promote learning take place, where the learner, who cannot yet do everything that the teacher is trying to teach, and the teacher meet. Through interaction, which is mostly carried out through specific kinds of language (e.g., conversation, questioning, coaching, or language play), the teacher leads the learner toward development.

The characteristics of the "teacher," or more experienced person, in the ZPD are important. Specifically, to exploit the ZPD, teachers act on several kinds of knowledge. Teachers must have an idea of the way the task unfolds. They must identify what the student does and does not know and must predict what the student will be able to do next. Most important, teachers must ensure that the forms of language that they use are accessible and comprehensible to the learner as they monitor the learner's engagement with the language and the task. This last characteristic constitutes intersubjectivity, or joint shared attention, which occurs in the "space" between a teacher and a learner. Metaphorically, we can think of intersubjectivity as a meeting of minds, the basis for shared experience between people. When a mother and infant play with a ball, the mother uses language, gesture, eye gaze, and the ball itself to establish intersubjectivity with the baby, to keep the baby's attention on the game. Although the baby cannot use adult-like language to confirm his or her shared attention, the baby's participation (looking at the ball, reaching for it, laughing) does so. Only when intersubjectivity is established can participants in interactions share understanding.

The language processes that establish intersubjectivity are not random or invented on the spot. Rather, they have evolved over time as cultural strategies. In teaching, key processes are establishing and maintaining joint attention. Without intersubjectivity, the teacher's language will be broadcast through the ZPD, but the receiver will not be tuned in. Thus, without intersubjectivity, this language, though real to the teacher, will not serve the developmental and instructional purposes that he or she intends. A common and straightforward example is a deaf, second grader at a rural school, with an interpreter who is adequately skilled. Like many deaf children, this child's language development has been delayed, as has his more general knowledge of the world. He can neither sign well nor hear. The interpreter believes that this second grader needs some communication support. Because he looks like a typical second grade boy to the teacher and because his teacher does not know enough about deaf children's developmental issues, the teacher cannot engage his Zone of Proximal Development and fine-tune instruction. The interpreter's presence and moving hands have convinced the teacher that the lessons have been well translated for the child (and they have been). But the child's development is not that of a hearing second grader. Language support by means of an interpreter is not what he needs. What he needs is a teacher who can observe him, directly perceive that the lesson is out of his reach, and adjust instruction so he can meet the teacher part way in his ZPD. The teacher is broadcasting instruction, but the deaf student is in another zone and cannot receive it. In this situation, the most skilled interpreter will assist neither the teacher nor the student, and this child's schooling will continue to be derailed, as will any future contacts the naive teacher has with deaf children. This brief review does not do justice to the richness of cultural-historical psychology nor to the contemporary psychologists who work in this theory, but it is enough for a beginning examination of educational interpreting and deaf education.

## APPLYING THEORETICAL CONSTRUCTS TO THE "FACTS"

During my years as an educational interpreter and researcher in deaf education, I have been well positioned to observe the joint activities of teachers and students. People are prone to explain things to the newcomer, and as an interpreter, I sometimes occupied a type of "novice" status in a public school, especially when deaf students were a novelty and the members of the general education faculty and staff had little knowledge about them. In addition, my later identity as a researcher in a school immediately established a "telling" frame of reference in others. General education faculty and staff members always acknowledged my specialty (deaf education or sign language) but treated me as an initiate to the ways of their particular school. What I report here was either observed by me (some instances are discussed in Ramsey 1997) or related to me by helpful school staff members during my periods of work as an interpreter or fieldwork as a researcher. Other educational interpreters have confirmed that my experience was not unique.

It is important to note that, although this discussion touches on educational interpreters' language fluency and interpreting skill, as noted above, the work of even the most skilled interpreters can be compromised by the sociolinguistic context of deaf education. The skills issue is both timely and critical but, by itself, provides an incomplete account of educational interpreting. Thus, I take a more systemic view of assumptions about education, interpreting, and deaf children's learning in the following section.

## THE NESTED PERSPECTIVES OF DEAF EDUCATION

A range of perspectives on education of deaf students, access to school, and equal opportunity influences the everyday lives of interpreters and deaf children in schools. Community perspectives reflect the hopes and misconceptions embodied in legislation and public policy. Participants hold perspectives from the very naive to the pragmatic, and views of deaf children's language needs and abilities reflect categories that have little grounding in reality or in theory. Nonetheless, the perspectives must be examined so their assumptions can be detected.

## Community Perspectives

The first set of observations reflect an understanding that the school does not exist by itself. Schools are embedded in communities, some local (a neighborhood, town, or school district) and some regional or national (a state, or the entire United States). Most school personnel hold a good-hearted, optimistic view of the goal of providing education for children with disabilities, which they know is supported by a commitment from their school administrators, their state department of education, and the federal government. These contexts are nested, like Russian dolls. Schools are small relative to districts in which they are embedded. Districts are small relative to states. States are smaller than the federal government, which ironically, sets the policy without necessarily providing the funds to carry out the commitment (for equal educational opportunity for all children or, currently, for "leaving no child behind"). The following syntheses of comments addressed to me in schools indicate that a much larger set of forces frame educational interpreters' work:

1. "The public school is the "least restrictive environment" for deaf children."
2. "Deaf children have a right to be in the classes with hearing children."
3. "It is so good for the normal children, to be around the handicapped."
4. "When these abled-bodied, hearing kids grow up, they will be more accepting of differences."
5. "Deaf children are required by law to have an interpreter go with them to the bathroom."

All of these comments, though not directly about interpreting, were generated by general education personnel who worked in elementary schools with programs for deaf and hard of hearing students. My informants had little direct experience with deaf children, although many had attended in-service presentations about Public Law 94-142 or about the Individuals with Disabilities Education Act (IDEA). On the surface, their comments reflect knowledge about society's obligation to provide students with disabilities access to instruction and learning (however poorly understood) within the educational environment. There is nothing wrong with these observations. Indeed, with the exception of the fifth observation, all may be accurate. Nonetheless, most interpreters know that the purpose of schooling goes beyond offering equal rights to deaf students, beyond providing a beneficial experience for hearing students, and beyond creating a more understanding future world.

Daily, I saw that placing deaf and hearing children in the same classroom with an interpreter did not remove all restrictions to learning and peer friendship. Hearing children who do not sign cannot communicate well enough with deaf children to develop relationships. Indeed, since Public Law 94-142 became law in 1975, the most confusing and contentious issue in deaf education has been defining "least restrictive environment" (Commission on Education of the Deaf 1988). For Americans, the discourse of rights is powerful. Even the somewhat abstract goal of protecting or ensuring the rights of a group to move toward a better society is very appealing, as it should be. I have been accused of cynicism when I report my attempts to look beneath the surface of the rhetoric that has been so disturbing in the education of deaf students. Still, those of us who care about deaf children and their learning must do so.

Staff members may express general beliefs about rights and the least restrictive environment; meanwhile, for teachers, tension builds between compliance with the abstractions that define deaf students' rights and those students' specific developmental and educational needs. This tension is difficult to resolve (see Ramsey 1997 for a more in-depth description of this tension). In many schools, the participant who is most aware of the tension is the diligent, caring, general education teacher who receives deaf students into his or her classroom for academic subjects. (Teachers of the deaf must also find a way to resolve the tension, but they are usually better prepared to do so.)

The most serious problem is that general comments about the benefits of mainstreaming, especially those that focus on the benefits to hearing students, offer no information about deaf children and the reasons why most of them need fine-tuned, "special" education. At best, these general comments lead to benevolent neglect in that teachers acknowledge the presence of deaf students but do little to engage them. These teachers take limited responsibility for deaf students' learning because they assume that the interpreter's presence guarantees that learning occurs. At worst, this neglect creates situations where deaf students are scolded for and evaluated on behavior that is rational (e.g., watching the interpreter instead of looking down at the textbook as the hearing children do) and situations where they are viewed as less-than-competent students when they achieve at levels below those of their hearing peers (see discussion in following sections).

Interestingly, specialists in deaf education who have in-depth knowledge about the kinds of educational support that their deaf students need are less likely to use the vocabulary of "rights" to describe a school setting. The legal organization of school settings is not their prime interest. Rather, they are more inclined to assess a setting according to its comprehensibility to deaf children and according to the likelihood that the children will be able to learn there. This different focus does not mean that deaf children's rights to access are not also important to the specialist. It simply emphasizes that members of the deaf education staff are more likely to focus their energy on organizing settings where instruction is comprehensible, developmentally appropriate, and engaging rather than focus their energy on achieving integration at any cost.

In the education of deaf children, placement of deaf students in classes with hearing students and the addition of interpreters were intended to be means to an end. In fact, one can identify several ends to schooling, and realizing deaf students' right to educational access is only one of them. Once access is granted, another objective should certainly be to provide to deaf students vital opportunities to learn and develop, which is what school offers to most hearing children. Unfortunately, since the mid-1970s, mainstreaming and the use of interpreters have become the ends in themselves. Worse, they are sometimes exploited as a demonstration of the benevolence of the school and the general education personnel, even while the deaf students struggle to learn. In the final analysis, then, using protection of rights as the basis for the education of deaf children creates a seductive image that offers general education teachers almost no information about how to help deaf children learn and directs attention away from the learning and developmental goals of education that all students and their parents have a right to expect.

The observations discussed here are generated by the outermost of the nested contexts of schooling—that of the community and, in this case, its legal organization. While this community context is quite powerful in its requirements about the structure of schooling for deaf students, it is also very distant from the students and their needs. The next set of observations brings us closer to students by discussing the notion of participant.

## Participants' Perspectives

At some point in their work, most educational interpreters have made observations such as the following about the behavior of deaf students with interpreters as participants in schooling:

1. The students I interpreted for did not always look at me during instruction.
2. They sometimes looked at me but did not participate with hearing classmates.
3. Some of the deaf students told me they did not like to go to the "hearing class."

In my interpreter education program in the 1970s, we discussed the fact that deaf people may not watch interpreters. At that time, no one in my cohort was planning a career exclusively in public schools, although many of us interpreted for postsecondary students. We felt that deaf people, like hearing people, could make choices about paying attention to communication, although, of course, it is much more obvious when deaf people fail to attend since a common expectation is that they must watch the interpreter at all times. The reasons for inattentiveness were not our business; interpreters felt no obligation to offer instant replay. (An ASL metaphor, TRAIN ZOOM, encodes a caution about inattention to signers, that if you do not see a signed utterance, it is gone.) Correctly, I think, interpreters considered it disrespectful and bad practice to treat inattentive deaf people like children, to demand their attention—or worse, to make a fuss or report their inattentiveness to the hearing participants.

Yet, when the deaf person is a child and the interpreter is viewed as a member of the team responsible for the child's learning, then inattentiveness is a more serious matter. No one who is provided with an interpreter, deaf children included, naturally understands how to learn through interaction mediated with an interpreter; every participant needs to be taught the conventions of learning (and teaching) through interpreting. For deaf children who use interpreters, this instruction occurs early and often. Still, even a student who seems to understand his or her own role with respect to interpreters sometimes fails to watch. And even those who watch are often reluctant to use the interpreter to participate with hearing peers and teachers.[3] For hardworking interpreters and for teachers who depend on student participation to evaluate learning, it is puzzling and disturbing when deaf students do not fulfill their role in the process. And, again, to hearing teachers and fellow students, the deaf students look less than competent.

Foster's (1989) research suggests that deaf students provided with interpreting services can easily become marginalized participants in a classroom. Often, they sit together, physically apart from hearing students, to better view the interpreter. In addition, deaf students cannot keep pace with the rapid give and take of spoken English discourse, especially during discussions, because of the necessary interpreting processing time. Last, language itself, the academic variety of English, is not always accessible to them. In this context, deaf students must struggle to find their own identities as genuine peers of the hearing students who have the advantage of direct and immediate access to the teacher. For some, this identity remains out of reach, discouraging participation in class and making integrated settings uncomfortable.

La Bue's (1998) research is especially revealing here. She analyzed interpreted discourse in a ninth-grade English class within a large (fifty-four deaf and hard of hearing students, twenty-five staff members) middle through high school mainstream program in the public school system, where half of the students attended integrated English courses with interpreters. Her research was designed to examine the extent of deaf students' access to literacy instruction in the interpreted classes. Although she compared the teacher's utterances with the interpreter's rendition, she went beyond looking for equivalence at the level of vocabulary and meaning and carefully examined the teacher's discourse markers, the functions of those markers, and the ways they were interpreted.

Recall the earlier discussion of footing, the features of discourse that help the audience know their position and responsibilities. Changes in footing are rapid and frequent. Student access to and comprehension of footing shifts are especially critical in classrooms because they are key to understanding the structure of instructional activities and their content. Of particular importance are footing shifts that tell students (the ratified participants) that the teacher has shifted responsibility for discourse to them. When these subtle shifts are expressed, the ratified participants (students, in this case) are obligated to carry out the interaction. When a teacher invites participation, students must bid for turns and answer according to teacher expectations or run the risk of being judged inattentive or, worse, incompetent.

La Bue's (1998) analysis of the ninth-grade teacher's discourse identified his routine footing markers. Those that engaged student participation referred to shared knowledge ("y'know") and linked propositions ("I mean" and "so"). Next, La Bue analyzed the interpreter's signed rendition, looking for equivalent markers. What she found, among other problems, was that the interpreter did not express these markers to the deaf students. The teacher's footing shift was not interpreted, the deaf students did not receive the invitation to participate, and they did not participate because they had no access to the language markers that shifted responsibility from teacher to student. La Bue suggests that deaf students with interpreters can unintentionally be reduced to a different participant category, the "modified bystander" (220). They are, indeed, ratified participants in school. But interpreting limits their access to participation in such a way that they can "tune in" to some content without participating. Although the incomplete interpretation was not intended, in fact, the discourse conventions that invite participation have not been directed to them at all, so despite their true ratified participant status, they are never the addressed ones.

La Bue's work accounts for educational interpreters' observations that deaf students fail to participate, even when directly called on by the teacher. Language interaction, especially language interaction in classrooms, is dense and rich, and in accordance with our cultural expectations, is intended for groups of participants who have full access to the complete message. Most hearing students either enter the classroom already communicatively competent or have the access they need to rapidly gain the competence necessary to successfully take on the student role. In contrast, many deaf students do not enter school with the specialized communicative competence needed for taking on the student role, and they likely do not have access to complete language interactions from which they could acquire the competence. Unfortunately, training a deaf child in the conventions of an interpreted education will not eliminate his or her developmental linguistic needs.

Three additional issues must be considered here. The first is the lack of preparation and the resulting limited skill of most educational interpreters. Few training opportunities exist for those who want to specialize in educational interpreting (Dahl and Wilcox 1990). More disturbing, a high proportion of classroom interpreters likely have skills that are so basic and undeveloped that they can express only some information, which contains errors at the levels of vocabulary, grammar, and discourse (Schick, Williams, and Bolster 1999).[4] La Bue's work suggests the serious consequences of discourse errors and omissions and makes clear that unqualified interpreters cannot serve either as those who relate information or as those who provide language models.

The preparation of educational interpreters has not kept pace with the enthusiastic inclusion of deaf students in public schools. Many school districts, especially those in rural areas, feel fortunate to locate anyone who can sign. Few administrators have the personnel to evaluate interpreting ability; worse, most do not understand the critical difference between signing and interpretation.[5] Interpreters are rarely evaluated before hiring, few hold any kind of interpreting certification (Jones, Clark, and Soltz 1997), and many are never evaluated. American parents expect their children's teachers to have academic and practical training as well as to hold at least a bachelor's degree. Only in emergency circumstances would they allow an unqualified person to teach their children. Yet, educational interpreters, who are arguably at least as important as teachers, are routinely accepted without any kind of professional preparation.

The second intervening issue is the preparation of general education teachers to work with deaf children. Most teachers have no experience working with deaf children and have almost no knowledge about their complex and varied developmental histories and their resulting highly individualized special educational needs (see Scruggs and Mastropieri [1996] for a telling report of general education teacher attitudes toward inclusion). Like the general public, they tend to believe that having an interpreter in the classroom is all that is necessary to "include" the deaf students. Few hearing people know sign language, and even fewer can evaluate the fidelity of interpreted messages. In my experience, general education teachers are surprised when they learn that their deaf students are weak readers, that their English vocabularies are small and concrete (Marschark 1997), and that their written English is basic and sometimes error ridden.

On an intellectual level, it is not difficult to provide information to help teachers understand the classroom challenges that they and their deaf students face. The task takes time (which no teacher has enough of), and planning, and willingness on the part of school personnel at all levels. Yet, even assuming that the information is provided and that teachers comprehend it, hearing speakers of English in teaching roles have difficulty altering their patterns of communication so interpreters can do their work and so deaf students can be part of the classroom speech community. The most obvious pattern is the pacing of teacher discourse and the rapid give and take of turns. Every competent educational interpreter has asked teachers to slow down and has explained processing time, including the fact that the interpretation may be three to five sentences behind the speaker. Again, intellectually, this delay makes sense. In practice, however, control of habitual patterns of speaking is rarely possible or long lasting because these patterns are almost completely unconscious.[6] Similarly, when several children call out answers simultaneously, interpreters remind teachers that they can interpret for only one person at a time. Again, though this limitation makes perfect sense, in practice, simultaneous responses are difficult to control.

La Bue's (1998) research describes a teacher who is more than willing to have deaf students in his class. However, this teacher does not know that his engagement strategies and invitations to participate are not being interpreted to them, and he does not realize that the deaf students have almost no opportunities to display their knowledge or to ask questions during class. Rather, like other general education teachers (e.g., Ramsey's 1997 informant, "Mrs. Rogers"), he accounts for their classroom behavior by resorting to his underlying knowledge about high school students, believing them to be unsophisticated and, in the case of one deaf student, more immature than the hearing students. His judgments are not only incorrect but also potentially damaging in the high-stakes context of high school education.

The third issue, as Winston (1992) points out, is that a certain amount of classroom interaction is not interpretable. Winston's research focus is the organization of instruction and the way it determines the tasks that deaf students must undertake to have access and to participate. Her primary comment on instructional organization is that it assumes that students can both hear the teacher and see what is going on. Profoundly deaf students, obviously, have access only to that which is visual, which creates "a basic difference in accessibility to information" (60), even with an interpreter. Winston found that lectures are interpretable, but she notes that they are relatively uncommon in elementary grades. Instead, question-and-answer formats dominate. In Winston's analysis, the interpretability of this discourse form depends on the teacher's style and pacing as well as on the topic of discussion. If it is built around print texts where the student must search for information to answer, a task designed to take advantage of both hearing and sight, then even the best interpreter cannot eliminate the disadvantage that deaf students face.

Other language routines are common among teachers—speaking while writing on the board, speaking while asking students to read along in a book or to correct a paper, speaking from the back of a darkened room while showing slides, placing students in small groups for work, speaking to the class while they are doing seat work to bring an important point to their attention, leading the flag salute from the front of the room while students turn to recite the pledge to a flag hanging in the back of the room. In all of these routine speech situations, the deaf student is at a disadvantage; even with a highly skilled interpreter, he or she will not have the "same" learning experience as hearing children.

## Perspectives about Deaf Children's Language Development

Finally, teachers and interpreters describe deaf students themselves and their observations of those students' schooling outcomes. My general education teacher informant, "Mrs. Rogers" (Ramsey 1997) offered versions of the first two comments below. The third observation is my own, from my work as an educational interpreter in elementary through postsecondary settings. An analysis, which follows, based on cultural-historical psychology helps to account for these observations.

1. They did not seem to learn much from their time in mainstreaming.
2. The deaf children do not seem to know English very well. Why aren't they better readers?
3. Some of the deaf students could not sign very well. Even so, they were expected to follow what the teacher of the deaf and the interpreters signed.

Even the most naive observer knows that children who are born deaf have infancies that are quite different from those of hearing children. Whether you take an audiological, medical, psycholinguistic, or cultural approach, the underlying fact is that deaf infants do not have sufficient hearing to acquire spoken English in the typical way. Although age of diagnosis is likely to drop as universal newborn screening spreads, diagnosis of hearing loss and the age when language interventions begin are disturbingly late. Padden and Ramsey (1996) found that the average age of detection of hearing loss was one year in a sample of eighty-three fifth- and seventh-grade residential deaf students; average age at first educational contact was 2.34 years. In a sample of fifty-two fourth- and seventh-grade public school deaf students, average age of detection was 2.2 years, and first educational contact was 3.1 years.

Lack of hearing coupled with late diagnosis creates a developmental linguistic emergency. In our species, acquisition of language begins at birth; indeed, late first-language acquisition is so atypical that it is virtually impossible to find except in the case of deaf children (Mayberry 1993). In all cultural contexts, development unfolds to ensure that most of that language is mastered within five or six years. But the circumstances of deaf children's development (with some exceptions) do not match the broader design. The unavoidable fact is that, through no fault of their own, most deaf children have a late start at language acquisition. This late start has consequences for all areas of their lives, but it especially threatens their schooling. In our industrialized, information-steeped society, schooling is organized on the assumption that children enter their years of formal education with native command of their first language, "ready to learn."

Cultural-historical psychology, as noted, locates developing individuals in the larger context of culture. Theory does not specify which culture (e.g., Deaf culture, Mexican culture, hearing culture). Rather, the definition of *culture* from this point of view is quite broad. Culture is what defines us as human beings, "the unique environment of human life" (Cole 1996, 327). Cole further reminds us that "culture comes into being wherever people engage in joint activity over time" (301). This unique environment has evolved over the histories of groups to foster the development of the individual and to create and maintain his or her connection to his or her social group. An individual can neither invent culture nor develop or survive in isolation from others. We develop through participation in the activities of those around us, usually parents or caregivers, older siblings, and others who have been around for a longer than we have. Language not only is a component of the environment of human life but also encodes culture in words and serves as the primary vehicle for transmitting culture from one generation to the next.

The notion of culture has become clouded in deaf education. Because the term is so heavily contested, one could easily assume that all discussions of culture in the context of deaf education are discussions about Deaf culture.[7] This assumption is not correct. Cole's (1996) "garden metaphor" offers a general way to think about culture and its role in human development and, I hope, an objective way to consider the developmental difficulties that underscore deaf children's struggles in school. Cole describes what many of us remember as a kindergarten project, planting a seed in damp soil, keeping it in the dark until it sprouts, then placing it in the light to grow. If you leave the jar in the dark, the seed will stop developing and die; it cannot grow without sunlight. "Like a seed in soil, the human child must be provided with sufficient support to maintain life; it must be kept warm enough and fed, or it will die" (200).

Unlike nasturtiums, babies come pre-specified, not to sprout leaves, but to acquire language. Babies born deaf also have this inborn capacity, but in most deaf babies, language does not "sprout and flower." In cultural-historical terms, deaf babies cannot hear spoken language—that cultural medium that nourishes spoken language and that works perfectly for hearing babies—and thus, spoken language contains nutrients that are not helpful for deaf babies. Babies who cannot hear spoken language require a somewhat different growing medium to acquire human language, for example, a culturally designed medium that fosters acquisition of a signed language. In a "signed language medium," culturally designed support rests on several centuries of problem-solving adaptations undertaken by people who could not make use of spoken language. To our knowledge, only cultures of Deaf people provide this kind of support. Indeed, this support is the truly unique feature of Deaf culture and is the one most worth educational consideration.

It is a mistake to think that deaf babies do not get culturally designed support in the "spoken language" medium. They do. But they simply cannot take advantage of it to use their inborn language capacity. Cole (1996) uses cultural-historical terms to describe the situation of deaf babies born to hearing families with no access to a culture of Deaf people. The deaf child is included in numerous culturally mediated social interactions in the spoken language medium: families eat together, babies go with others on errands or to church, they are toilet trained. "They live in a world that is suffused with meaning, although they lack access to the specifically linguistic behavior that fills the gaps between actions" (202). Even so, like all children, deaf children have active minds that develop ways to represent the world. This capacity is enough to allow a kind of participation with others in many activities; it is a myth that deaf children begin their educations with no communication ability and no knowledge of the world. But this capacity is not enough for typical language acquisition to occur. For typical language acquisition to unfold, babies need unrestricted and undistorted access to that language as it is used in everyday life.

Goldin-Meadow's (1985) work demonstrates that individual deaf children without access to signing are able to invent very rudimentary systems of home sign, uttered in one- to three-sign sequences. However, their home sign does not develop beyond this level. Although it is communicative, it does not constitute a complete human language. Rather, home signs are a response to a developmental emergency, indicating development that is atypical. To return to the garden metaphor, the growing medium of a child in this situation is not nourishing enough. Language acquisition requires full access and participation. Unfortunately, children who do not have full access to their family's language, used in culturally organized contexts, will not develop it, even if they can communicate and participate in some of the actions that occur in these contexts.[8]

To complicate matters, in many cases we cannot predict with any confidence that exposure to one or more of the languages and modes of communication possible in deaf education (spoken English, a manual code for English, American Sign Language) will lead to a native-like language outcome for the child. A proportion of the deaf children who use interpreters in elementary school do not have the language ability necessary to understand the interpreter's signing.[9] In my work, I was usually told what each child's language preference and strength was supposed to be. Often, I was told that the child used Pidgin Signed English (or PSE), the teacher's term. (Teachers continue to use this label, although a more linguistically descriptive and accurate term exists: *contact signing*. I use the informants' terms here rather than put words in their mouths.)[10]

*PSE* is an especially problematic term when applied to deaf children. First, it is technically inaccurate. Although PSE is signed, it is not a true pidgin (Lucas and Valli 1992). Although it has an assumed relationship with English, that relationship is unclear. PSE is not a form of English that is recognized or understood by typical native speakers. More seriously, in educational settings, the use of the term *PSE* is not helpful because it often describes, not the existence of language ability, but its absence. Unfortunately, in everyday language, it has become a default category for students who do not sign ASL and do not exhibit complete grasp of one of the forms of manually coded English (or MCE).[11] Nonetheless, interpreters, teachers, and parents continue to use this term as if it were the name of a language variety. As with all languages, a great deal of variation exists in ASL (Lucas, Bayley, and Valli 2001; Lucas and Valli 1992). Among adults, a signed variety best called "contact signing" (Lucas and Valli 1992) arises when ASL and English come into contact. It emerges as a result of specific social contexts (not always the result of "contact" between Deaf and hearing people) and is generated by people who usually are fluent in both ASL and English. "Contact signing" labels only one of the linguistic and social sources of language variation among adult signers. Still, it is not a satisfactory educational term, at least for deaf children, because most students called PSE signers do not likely have mastery of both ASL and English.

Given the developmental circumstances of deaf children, several possible sources of signing that are neither ASL nor MCE are evident. In some cases, PSE is actually "learner signing with ASL as the target." In other cases, PSE might better be called "learner signing with MCE as the target." Among other possibilities, PSE can also be (a) the signing of a late learner with either target, (b) the highly idiosyncratic signing of a child who has received degraded signed input, or (c) signing generated by an ASL native in an effort to accommodate to an educational context where print English is the dominant variety and the signing ability of the children is unknown. The relevance of these varying sources for education and an interpreted education is not a trivial matter. These varying sources of so-called "PSE" indicate extreme differences in language development. An ASL native who is accommodating will have very different educational needs from a child who has had such degraded sign input that he or she has mastered no conventional language. The continued use of the term *PSE* camouflages a very real educational problem.

An additional problem with PSE as a descriptor of child signing is the focus on language forms (e.g., "word order"[12]) rather than language use in context. In my experience with young deaf signers, I have observed that their signing is idiosyncratic in form and suffers pragmatically. Their discourse abilities vary greatly. As discussed above, these disadvantages will affect their ability to participate in school, to engage with learning, and to demonstrate their areas of competence as students. Given deaf students' developmentally strained histories, their limited real-life opportunities for developing as users of either English or ASL, and the possible ideologies that guide parental and teacher language choices, no one term can unambiguously categorize the signing of most deaf students in public school programs. Accordingly, even the most skilled interpreter has difficulty fashioning a target language for his or her work with the child that can serve as a medium for information transmission (a medium—not a language model, which interpreting should never be viewed as providing).

To return to the observations, deaf children struggle to learn English, in part, because they have limited or distorted access to it and, in most cases, because they get a very late start. The fact that languages are the primary media by which teaching and learning occur also partly explains deaf students' struggles to learn the content of schooling. Even if exceptionally skilled interpreting is available to the deaf child, the child will likely not be able to take full advantage of it. Recall that Cole (1996), while recognizing the culturally organized activities that surround the deaf child, also notes the developing child's need for access to these activities. Although educational interpreters appear to provide access (and, in some cases, they do), in many cases, this "access" does not prove sufficient to support development and learning (e.g., La Bue 1998; Winston 1992, 1994).

## BELOW THE SURFACE OF EDUCATIONAL INTERPRETING

The theoretical tools discussed in this chapter suggest new questions about educational interpreting. Deaf children's needs are serious, and because educational interpreting now plays a substantial role in their education, it merits well-grounded research. Several urgent topics lend themselves to examination by sociolinguists. First, the context (or contexts) of educational interpreting need to be carefully defined. By itself, this topic is of interest. However, it will also help participants in educational interpreting understand the distinction between the means of providing educational access and its ends (i.e., learning and development). We also need grounded descriptions and analyses of the interactions of interpreting and interpreters with other sociolinguistic features of educational settings, in particular, the effects of interpreting on student participation. Last, although interpreters and teachers understand that processing time is necessary, we know very little about the extents to which English-speaking teachers and students can tolerate the delays necessitated by interpreter processing time during instructional discourse. This tolerance must be examined in light of knowledge about the pacing of instructional discourse in noninterpreted settings, where the pause between a teacher's question and subsequent student response averages less than one second (Rowe 1987).

Cultural-historical psychology provides theoretical and analytical tools that are helpful in two ways. First, it provides a broad and very basic definition of culture that is stripped of the ideologies, discussions of "learning styles," and lists of traits that routinely appear in discussions of bicultural and multicultural education. Second, it offers foundational constructs for examining development and learning, for example, the Zone of Proximal Development and joint shared attention. Again, since educational interpreting has become the medium of instruction for so many deaf students, we must look beyond the accuracy and fidelity of interpreted renditions to its functions. In our current state of knowledge, we know nothing about the ways an interpreter affects the establishment and maintenance of joint shared attention in teaching interactions. The teacher-interpreter-deaf student triad must be examined carefully to determine whether intersubjectivity between teacher and student is possible when an interpreter is in the middle, whether establishing intersubjectivity among three people is possible, and if so, how participants manage it. The real issue is the potential obstacle of the interpreter, which makes the teacher-student connection indirect. Last, it is urgent that cultural descriptions of Deaf people (which make perfect sense) not be extended to deaf students without careful reflection. Most of the current population of deaf students had atypical early language development. Very likely, their ability to engage with the language and possibly the content of schooling, especially through interpreting, has been compromised to some degree by delayed first-language acquisition. Making unwarranted assumptions about their communicative competence (e.g., applying "PSE" as a default) and placing an interpreter in their classrooms will not compensate for their language learning needs.

In Nebraska where I lived for several years, high standards for educational interpreter skill and knowledge were written into law. As we work to improve the interpreting services offered to deaf students, we have a parallel obligation. We must continue to question the effectiveness of even the most competent interpreting as a medium of instruction. Although judiciously providing highly skilled educational interpreters can contribute to civil rights and educational goals, interpreting should never be seen as a perfect conduit for education or a complete replacement for teaching. Deaf students deserve access to genuine opportunities for learning, and it is not yet clear that these opportunities can be brought about through educational interpreters.

## NOTES

1. Other metaphors are possible. For example, Cole (1996) portrays context as a set of concentric circles, with the child representing the most central circle and the community, the outermost.

2. This view contrasts slightly with American educational psychology tradition, which is to locate and examine thinking, language, and problem-solving abilities primarily in individual students' abilities. For this reason, in deaf education, we have a great deal of knowledge and many hypotheses derived from experimental research about deaf children's abilities to manipulate language and solve problems, for example, the "reader-based" variables that contribute to their problems learning to read (Paul [1998] provides a clear and complete discussion). We have less knowledge about deaf children's social worlds and the quality, content, and outcomes of their interactions with others.

3. A University of Nebraska, Lincoln (UNL), student reported observing deaf students dash away from the interpreter to join other deaf children in hiding during recess (L. Orta, UNL graduate student in deaf education, personal communication, September 13, 2000).

4. When I worked in elementary school mainstream programs, I was unusually highly trained. I had graduated from a community college interpreter training program, which I attended after I completed a bachelor's in linguistics, and I also held a master's degree in linguistics. Even if I had wanted to continue working as an educational interpreter,

however, I could not have afforded to do so because the pay was so low that I could not support myself.

5. As an analogy, a hearing person who takes one or two semesters of French may be able to speak basic French. However, this person does not have the ability to simultaneously interpret from English into French or vice versa. Nevertheless, a task similar to this one is what educational interpreters are called on to carry out.

6. I hold one degree in sign language interpreting and another in sign language linguistics, yet I am almost unable to control the pacing of my instructional speech so deaf students are equal participants. When possible, I prefer to teach using only one language in a class, ASL.

7. The term *deaf* indicates having the condition of limited, nonexistent, or impaired hearing, which can be measured by an audiologist. The term *Deaf* indicates the culture of Deaf people, not the condition of having impaired hearing.

8. Interestingly, Cole notes that the opposite it also true. Children who have access to language but do not have access to culturally organized interactions with other people also fail to develop full language (e.g., children who are left alone in front of a TV that is broadcasting a foreign language do not acquire that language).

9. It is important here to distinguish this problem—that the child does not have sufficient language fluency of any kind to understand the interpreter's signing of the teacher's message—from an issue that sometimes arises in interpreting for Deaf adults. When the interpreter's language fluency and that of the Deaf audience might be mismatched or when the interpreter has selected the wrong variety of a signed language for the Deaf audience, then understanding may also be compromised. The reasons are quite different, though, and the issue in those situations is not the Deaf person's language competencies but the interpreter's choice of language.

10. Woodward (1973) provides an early description of PSE.

11. The prominent MCE is Signing Exact English (Gustason, Pfetzing, and Zawolkow 1972).

12. Word order arguments are often based on the incorrect belief that ASL does not share a basic subject-verb-object syntactic structure with many of the world's languages, including English.

## REFERENCES

Cazden, C. 1988. *Classroom discourse*. Portsmouth N.H.: Heinemann.

Cazden, C., V. John, and D. Hymes, eds. 1972. *Functions of language in the classroom*. New York: Teachers College Press.

Chomsky, N. 1957. *Syntactic structures*. The Hague: Mouton Press.

Cole, M. 1996. *Cultural psychology: A once and future discipline*. Cambridge, Mass.: Harvard University Press.

Cole, M., and S. Cole. 1996. *The development of children*. New York: W. H. Freeman.

Commission on Education of the Deaf. 1988. *Toward equality: Education of the deaf*. Washington D.C.: U.S. Government Printing Office.

Dahl, C., and S. Wilcox. 1990. Preparing the educational interpreter: A survey of sign language interpreter training programs. *American Annals of the Deaf* 135(October):275–79.

Foster, S. 1989. Life in the mainstream: Reflections of deaf college freshmen on their experiences in the mainstreamed high school. *Journal of Rehabilitation of the Deaf* 125(2):27–35.

Goffman. E. 1974. *Frame analysis*. New York: Harper and Row.

———. 1981. *Forms of talk*. Philadelphia: University of Pennsylvania Press.

Goldin-Meadow, S. 1985. Language development under atypical learning conditions. In *Children's language*. Vol. 5, ed. K. E. Nelson, 197–245. Hillsdale N.J.: Erlbaum.

Gumperz, J., and D. Hymes, eds. 1972. *Directions in sociolinguistics: The ethnography of communication*. New York: Holt, Rinehart, and Winston.

Gustason, G., D. Pfetzing, and E. Zawolkow. 1972. *Signing Exact English*. Silver Spring, Md.: Modern Signs Press.

Hymes, D. 1972. Models of the interaction of language and social life. In *Directions in sociolinguistics: The ethnography of communication,* eds. J. Gumperz and D. Hymes, 35–71. New York: Holt, Rinehart, and Winston.

———. 1964. Introduction: Towards ethnographies of communication. *American Anthropologist* 66(2):12–25.

Jones, B., G. Clark, and D. Soltz. 1997. Characteristics and practices of sign language interpreters in inclusive educational programs. *Exceptional Children* 63(2):257–68.

Labov, W. 1972. *Sociolinguistic patterns*. Philadelphia: University of Pennsylvania Press.

La Bue, M. 1998. Interpreted education: A study of deaf students' access to the content and form of literacy instruction in a mainstreamed high school English class. Ph.D. dissertation, Harvard University Graduate School of Education, Cambridge, Massachusetts.

Lucas, C., ed. 1989. *The sociolinguistics of the deaf community*. New York: Academic Press.

Lucas, C., R. Bayley, and C. Valli. 2001. *Sociolinguistic variation in American Sign Language*. Sociolinguistics of deaf communities series, vol. 7. Washington D.C.: Gallaudet University Press.

Lucas, C., and C. Valli. 1992. *Language contact in the American deaf community*. San Diego, Calif.: Academic Press.

Marschark, M. 1997. *Raising and educating a deaf child*. New York: Oxford University Press.

Mayberry, R. 1993. First-language acquisition after childhood differs from second-language acquisition: The case of American Sign Language. *Journal of Speech and Hearing Research* 36(6):1258–70.

Padden, C., and C. Ramsey. 1996. *Deaf students as readers and writers*. Final Report, Grant no. H023T30006, to the U.S. Department of Education. Washington, D.C.: U.S. Department of Education.

Piaget, J. 1973. *The psychology of intelligence*. Totowa, N.J.: Littlefield & Adams.

Piaget, J., and B. Inhelder. 1969. *The psychology of the child*. New York: Basic Books.

Paul, P. 1998. *Literacy and deafness*. Boston: Allyn & Bacon.

Ramsey, C. 1997. *Deaf children in public schools*. Washington, D.C.: Gallaudet University Press.

———. 2001. Beneath the surface. *Odyssey* 2(2):18–24.

Rowe, M. 1987. Wait time: Slowing down may be a way of speeding up! *American Educator* 11(1): 38–43, 47.

Schick, B., K. Williams, and L. Bolster. 1999. Skill levels of educational interpreters working in public schools. *Journal of Deaf Studies and Deaf Education* 4(2):144–55.

Schiffrin, D. 1987. *Discourse markers*. Cambridge: Cambridge University Press.

———. 1994. *Approaches to discourse*. Cambridge, Mass.: Blackwell.

Scruggs, T., and M. Mastropieri. 1996. Teacher perceptions of mainstreaming/inclusion, 1958–1995. *Exceptional Children* 61(1):59–74.

Singleton, J. 1989. Restructuring of language from impoverished input: Evidence for linguistic compensation. Ph.D. dissertation, University of Illinois at Urbana-Champaign.

Vygotsky, L. 1978. *Mind in society*. Cambridge Mass.: Harvard University Press.

Winston, E. 1992. Mainstream interpreting: An analysis of the task. In *Proceedings of the Eighth National Convention of Conference of Interpreter Trainers,* ed. L. Swabey. N.p.: Conference of Interpreter Trainers.

———. 1994. An interpreted education: Inclusion or exclusion. In *Implications and complications for deaf students of the full inclusion movement,* eds. R. C. Johnson and O. Cohen, 55–62. Gallaudet Research Institute Occasional Paper 94-2. Washington, D.C.: Gallaudet Research Institute, Gallaudet University.

Woodward, J. 1973. Some characteristics of pidgin sign English. *Sign Language Studies* 2(3): 39–46.

# Contributors

Earl Fleetwood
Washington, D.C.

Bernhardt E. Jones
Special Education, Rehabilitation, and School Psychology
University of Arizona
Tucson, Arizona

Kim Brown Kurz
Interpreter Training Program
Johnson County Community College
Overland Park, Kansas

Elizabeth Caldwell Langer
Speech, Language, and Hearing Sciences Department
University of Colorado
Boulder, Colorado

Melanie Metzger
Department of Interpretation
Gallaudet University
Washington, D.C.

Christine Monikowski
Department of ASL and Interpreting Education
National Technical Institute for the Deaf
Rochester Institute of Technology
Rochester, New York

Claire Ramsey
Teacher Education Program
University of California, San Diego
La Jolla, California

Brenda Schick
Speech, Language, and Hearing Sciences Department

University of Colorado
Boulder, Colorado

Kelly Stack
Corporation for Education Network Initiatives in California
Cypress, California

Marty M. Taylor
Interpreting Consolidated
Edmonton, Alberta, Canada

Kevin T. Williams
EIPA Diagnostic Center
Boys Town National Research Hospital
Lied Learning and Technology Center for Childhood Deafness and Vision Disorders
Omaha, Nebraska

Elizabeth A. Winston
Project TIEM.Online
Northeastern University
Boston, Massachusetts

# Index

Page numbers in italics denote tables or figures.